BENDING THE ARC

BENDING THE ARC

Striving for Peace and Justice
in the Age of Endless War

Edited by

Steve Breyman, John W. Amidon,
and Maureen Baillargeon Aumand

SUNY
PRESS

Cover photo credit: Jeanne Finley

Published by State University of New York Press, Albany

© 2020 State University of New York

All rights reserved

For information, contact State University of New York Press, Albany, NY
www.sunypress.edu

Library of Congress Cataloging-in-Publication Data

Names: Breyman, Steve, editor. | Amidon, John W., 1948– editor. | Aumand,
  Maureen Baillargeon, 1946– editor.
Title: Bending the arc : striving for peace and justice in the age of endless war /
edited
  by Steve Breyman, John Amidon, and Maureen Baillargeon Aumand.
Description: Albany : State University of New York, [2020] | Includes
  bibliographical references and index.
Identifiers: LCCN 2020000059 (print) | LCCN 2020000060 (ebook) | ISBN
  9781438478753 (hardcover : alk. paper) | ISBN 9781438478746 (pbk. : alk. paper) |
  ISBN 9781438478760 (ebook)
Subjects: LCSH: Tekakwitha, Kateri, Saint, 1656–1680—Influence. | Kateri

  Tekakwitha Interfaith Peace Conference—History. | Peace movements—New
  York (State)—History. | Pacifists—United States—Biography. | Peace—Congresses.
Classification: LCC JZ5584.U6 B46 2020 (print) | LCC JZ5584.U6 (ebook) |
  DDC 327.1/720922—dc23
LC record available at https://lccn.loc.gov/2020000059
LC ebook record available at https://lccn.loc.gov/2020000060

10 9 8 7 6 5 4 3 2 1

This volume is dedicated to Blase Bonpane

(April 24, 1929–April 8, 2019)

A gentle soul with a fierce heart and mind deeply committed to peace and justice.

Presente!

Contents

Introduction

STEVE BREYMAN

Peace and justice are ancient and (nearly) universal goals. They are values for a large majority of people in most places, across time and space—excepting a nontrivial number of sociopaths in positions of power. Politicians pay regular lip service. Clergy dutifully include the values in their sermons. A few committed teachers instruct their students in the history of nonviolent campaigns against war. A small number of Americans, however, actively engage in civic struggles to realize these enduring human values. A yet smaller subset of these people gathered the past eighteen summers in Upstate New York for the Kateri Tekakwitha Peace Conference organized by John W. Amidon and Maureen Baillargeon Aumand. This book relays the personal and political voyages of seventeen of those courageous few, all of whom were keynote presenters at one or more Kateri Peace Conferences over the years.

They are courageous for a variety of reasons. To protest war or preparations for it automatically sets one up for harassment as "unpatriotic" and "un-American," even if a combat veteran. Activists risk personal and professional relations, and can be isolated in their communities. Peace advocates have found their jobs at stake, and direct action protestors may end up in federal prison. Peace and justice campaigners can feel like strangers in their own countries once they decide to oppose dangerous weapons systems or Endless War.

Our activists share a few features in common. Given their backgrounds, these are not people one would normally expect to become professional or even part-time dissidents. They are, unsurprisingly, given the profile of most contemporary American peace campaigners, Baby Boomers from white middle-class families. They are now middle-aged or older. They are well educated, cosmopolitan, open-minded. They came to manifest antiracist, feminist, pro-immigrant and -environment stances; most have radical politics.

This requires an explanation. What caused these otherwise "normal" citizens—seemingly destined for conventional careers and existences—to develop lives of opposition and resistance? Understand, again, that their chosen lives often subjected them to derogatory abuse, and in some cases even prison. For most, one or more catalytic events triggered critical questions and growing skepticism about the actions and priorities of their government and society. These events were in each instance eye-opening, often traumatic. For many activists, raised on myths about the beneficence of their country's role in the world, the experience is often akin to a religious conversion in its far-reaching force and impact on their lives. The shift in outlook and attitude generally leads to deep study and discernment that confirms suspicions about the nature of Washington's foreign and defense policy.

While from similar backgrounds, our activists came to their peace work on various paths. Some are veterans like this editor, who, raised on war movies and comic books, went into military service as teenagers with naive hopes and expectations for adventure. We believed American military superiority was the path to world peace, before learning the hard way that militarism was the problem. Others are clergy. They found that their faith traditions often fail to advance peace and justice, and modify their ministries to advance their work for peace. Some were already activists who, busy with global-justice organizing around so-called trade agreements, international financial institutions, and the World Trade Organization, returned to peace work following September 11, 2001. Others are academics who were able to transform their teaching and research into forces for peace and justice.

Most of our contributors have decades of experience on the frontlines of the struggle for a peaceful, livable planet. Their personal qualities shine through their work: resilience, bravery, persistence, creativity. They are by no means superheroes, with powers fundamentally different from the rest of us. They are, rather, hard-working, dedicated people who use their talents for diverse noble causes. Their sustained action is not dependent on its varying effectiveness or impact. It depends instead on firm belief in the righteousness of the struggle itself.

Our contributors' causes evolved over time. Some number got their start opposing the war in Vietnam. Many were active in the Nuclear Freeze and Central American Solidarity Movements of the 1980s. They resisted the bel-

ligerence and arms racing of the Reagan administration, as well as its support
for political Islamists fighting against the Soviet occupation of Afghanistan
(with whom Reagan met in the Oval Office). The years-long campaign to close
the U.S. Army's School of the Americas—known by opponents as the School
of Assassins—was especially important for a number of our contributors who
worked in Latin America. Many of our activists rallied against the Gulf War
in 1991. Resistance and alternatives to corporate-led globalization animated
several of our authors during the nineties. Then came 9/11.

Our authors were familiar with the Project for a New American Century's
plans for regime change years before al-Qaeda's attack on the Twin Towers.
They knew the dangers posed by the worldviews and policies of George
W. Bush's stable of neoconservatives: Dick Cheney, Donald Rumsfeld, Paul
Wolfowitz, John Bolton. Contributors to this volume immediately sensed
the wrongheadedness of the U.S. invasion of Afghanistan, and were among
the few Americans able to resist the widespread demands for revenge. They
were organizers of and participants in the legendary February 15, 2003,
worldwide demonstrations against the imminent U.S. invasion of Iraq. They
disbelieved the lies—relayed by Colin Powell and endlessly repeated by the
lapdog news media—regarding Saddam Hussein, weapons of mass destruction, and al-Qaeda, and predicted the horrors that followed.

Some of our activists hoped to prevent the invasion by directly embed-
ding with Iraqi civilians before the war. Failing that, they worked consistently
to bring public attention to Islamophobia, mass surveillance, torture, extraordinary rendition, Abu Ghraib, CIA black sites, assaults on civil liberties,
and all the rest. Our contributors opposed the Surge, and labored to close
Guantanamo Bay. They understand the essential role played for American
defense policy by the "Empire of Bases," seek to close as many as possible,
and to prevent the construction of new ones.

Today, our activists resist the use of armed drones as prosecutor, judge,
jury, and executioner. They are strong proponents for a just resolution to the
Israeli occupation of Palestine. They oppose U.S. intervention in Venezuela.
Were it up to them, the U.S. defense budget would shrink considerably. They
see international law and unwavering respect for human rights as founda-
tions for U.S. foreign policy against anachronistic calls for "America First."
They are stolid opponents of U.S. rogue state behavior, and lament Trump's
withdrawal from the Paris climate accord, the Iran nuclear deal, the INF
Treaty, and the move of its embassy to Jerusalem.

Persistent tactics and targets accompanied the shifting threats to peace
and justice. Our contributors' action repertoire includes frequent visits to war

zones, conflict witnessing, and solidarity with refugees and the displaced. They remain focused on the evils of militarism, poverty, jingoism, American exceptionalism. They oppose renewed Cold War with Russia, and warn against the dangers of conflict between a United States in decline and a China on the rise. Fear of nuclear war grew with the development of North Korean bombs and ballistic missiles; our contributors strongly support sincere efforts for denuclearization and peace on the Korean peninsula. Activists mobilized against U.S. complicity in Saudi Arabia's war on Yemen. They oppose U.S. eagerness under Trump to sell weapons to human rights abusers. Some avoid paying federal income taxes through voluntary simplicity to protest the vast sums wasted on war and preparations for it. Above all, they understand that war is not the answer.

We editors provided some guidelines for chapter authors. We asked each of them to reflect on:

1. their own lives as activists, to examine the roots of their personal commitment to peace and justice; to examine the place faith, spiritual traditions, education, and experience played in their commitments; to share the inspiration provided by specific individuals, moments, and events in history, or on a specific illuminating moment in their lives.

2. the features of their peace work: the details over time plus particular anecdotes that illuminate it; on the challenges and imperatives that drive their work for peace, the challenges that mark it, and what it taught them.

3. the dynamics that give rise to war as well as peace and justice; on the deepest needs of humanity; on the greatest obstacles to peace and justice, and on the contours and opportunities of the current historical moment.

4. their personal visions: on how political and spiritual engagement affect their belief in a "world beyond war"; on what people need to know to enable them to engage in protracted struggle; on what core beliefs sustain their work.

The *Bulletin of Atomic Scientists'* Doomsday Clock now stands at two minutes to midnight. This dangerous state of affairs is neither inevitable nor irreversible. The answers to the problems—the roots and causes of conflicts and how to avoid and resolve them peacefully—that have long bedeviled the planet are in the following pages. Our authors show the way forward. We hope that more will join with us to put an end to the scourge of war and to build a world upon the principles of justice. The moral arc of the universe does not bend of its own accord.

Chapter 1

The Kateri Tekakwitha Interfaith Peace Conference

The Early Years: An Intimate History, 1998–2006

JOHN W. AMIDON

The Beginnings

During my forty-first year, she began appearing in my dreams. She was dressed modestly, wore glasses, and was pretty. Looking directly at me, I could hear her say, "I am doing everything I can to get this man to learn some Spanish, but he just won't learn." Why was my fourth-grade Spanish teacher still insisting I learn Spanish?

After several of her appearances, I thought: if someone wants me to learn some Spanish, why not? Soon afterward I began traveling to Central America, and my political/spiritual awakening commenced. I didn't know it then, but this dream was likely the original impulse for the Kateri Peace Conference.

In 1989, *60 Minutes* aired a report on Belize showing the cayes and the beauty of the Belize Barrier Reef. With little forethought or planning, I booked a flight to Belize. A side trip to Guatemala's Tikal National Park—a UNESCO World Heritage Site, ancient Mayan city, and ceremonial center—made me feel immediately at home, and for the next several years I spent winters in Guatemala, with two to three weeks dedicated to learning Spanish in Quetzaltenango.

Guatemala's thirty-six-year-old civil war had finally wound down, and while the peace accords would not be signed until December 29, 1996, rarely did I feel threatened. The extreme violence of the early and mid-eighties had passed, and there was an informal agreement between the government and revolutionary forces to leave tourists alone, since the economy desperately needed the money we brought. Still, there was tension, and a dangerous shadow seemed to always be present. I did not understand how a country as poor as Guatemala could financially support the level of violence and horror at the scale it had experienced.

December 20, 1991, brought the Quincentennial Interfaith Pilgrimage for Peace and Life, its starting date commemorating the 1989 U.S. invasion of Panama. The pilgrimage would end on October 12, 1992, marking the five hundredth anniversary of the arrival of Columbus. It was billed as an interfaith pilgrimage, yet it was also clearly a Buddhist peace walk. Buddhist monks and nuns were the largest and most visible single group, dressed in their yellow and white robes, drumming and chanting as they walked. Here was my first in-depth experience of the poor in Latin America. We walked in the spirit of atonement, working to foster both healing and understanding.

Elizabeth Pearson, an elderly Quaker from Albany Friends Meeting, was planning to walk the entire distance. Before she left, I casually remarked that I would join her in Managua, Nicaragua, later that winter. Surprisingly, over time my casual interest evolved to become what seemed like a sacred obligation; in February, I flew to Managua to join the pilgrimage. Like few other pilgrimages in modern times, I understood this as the current incarnation of the "League," an imaginary religious order detailed in *Journey to the East* by Herman Hesse. I was excited and delighted to join as a novice disciple.

Leaving Managua, we walked with hundreds of excited Nicaraguans, then headed north on the Pan American highway, stopping at many small towns. Seeing the full moon rising in La Trinidad between twin mountain peaks was a vivid and lovely sight. And there was the argument about what time we would arrive: Would it be Sandinista time or UNO time, the National Opposition Union? The time of day was often changed by an hour when a new political party came to power and the UNO was recently victorious. So engrossed in this argument were the two factions, our actual arrival was a surprise for both groups. And the deep sadness from viewing the portraits of the dead (from what is now called the Contra War, an effort to overthrow the Sandinista government) at the Hall of Martyrs in Gondola, Nicaragua, has stayed with me.

Subsisting on rations similar to a peasant's diet, walking fifteen to twenty miles a day in the hot sun, I lost about thirty pounds in two weeks.

This experience brought home to me how truly crushing poverty could be and how brutally insensitive we remain to each other allowing such conditions to exist.

I also realized then, that no matter how much money might be raised for humanitarian work, it would always remain a drop in the bucket. I saw that systemic political change was necessary. Our national resources needed to be utilized for life-affirming work rather than war.

I learned that American citizens were willing to give money for building tangible infrastructure, such as a community center, a water system, or a road or school, but seemed unwilling to challenge or change questionable and destructive policies of our government.

After building a community center in El Madrono, Nicaragua, this brief foray into humanitarian work left me firmly committed to working for political change so that we might truly have the required resources needed to care for our neighbors. I left the "League's" pilgrimage but continued the walk for peace, justice, and nonviolence, sometimes alone and sometimes with others.

The Kateri Tekakwitha Interfaith Pilgrimages

There was little antiwar activism in Albany in the early and mid-nineties. It wasn't until 1996 that I learned of the School of the Americas Watch and traveled to Fort Benning, Georgia, to protest the U.S. Army School of the Americas. Two years later, in September 1998, I began the Kateri Peace Interfaith Pilgrimages as part of my continuing efforts to close the School of the Americas (SOA), a training school for Latin American military that has subverted democracy and is directly responsible for the deaths of hundreds of thousands of Latin American citizens. So vile was this institution it was dubbed the "School of Assassins" and kicked out of Panama. U.S. foreign policy, specifically crafted to undermine democratic reform and empower the ruling class in Latin America, had become extremely violent. By exposing its wrongdoings to the American public, I reasoned (naively) that our representatives would implement the necessary changes to end its criminal wrongdoing. However, there were many steps that preceded this understanding.

In Guatemala, Mayan people were the primary victims of governmental oppression. Locally, I saw the National Kateri Tekakwitha shrine as an intersection of both the Indigenous peoples and Catholics, the two major groups subjected to the extreme violence of SOA graduates. Kateri Tekakwitha was a Mohawk woman who converted to Roman Catholicism in the late 1600s and was known for her devotion to Jesus. She lived in what is now Fonda, New York, and in 2012 was recognized as a saint.

I thought that here might be a place where I could find support to close the SOA—and I was correct, but for unexpected reasons. Father Kevin Kenny, the shrine's director, had lived in Guatemala in the mid-eighties at the height of the violence and very much understood my reasoning. He was very supportive of the pilgrimage and an early and important source of encouragement for the Kateri Peace Conference.

The Truth Cannot Be Silenced, a School of the Americas Watch pamphlet, recounts the trial of the SOA 13, activists who were intent on closing down the SOA, who walked onto the base and were charged with trespass. A segment of Father Bill Bichsel's testimony addressed to the trial judge is particularly compelling:

> The other day, as I was walking down to the jail to visit a Native American who is in jail constantly, I was stopped by a man that had been on the streets for a long time. He said, "Bill, you still living in the same place up at Guadeloupe House?" I said, "Yeah." He said, "Are you still involved in that SOA kind of thing?" "Yeah." "That's about killing Indians, isn't it?" he said. Well, I was a bit taken aback by the starkness of it, but I said, "Yeah, that's right."
>
> I know that in the history of our country, our armies, our military, our cavalry have crossed our country. American people in certain ways have been complicit with the genocide that has happened to our own Native American population. We export to Central and South America that same kind of violence now that we have completed, rather successfully, the genocide in our own country. We add atrocity upon atrocity directly though institutions such as the School of the Americas.
>
> Your Honor, Judge, I think there comes a time as a people when we're called upon to admit guilt. We're called to reparation, to repentance, to profess our sins and do penance and to amend our lives. I think this is such a time.

I believed then that the spiritual influence of the Kateri Tekakwitha shrine was lending support for our work to close the School of the Americas. However, U.S. oppression in Latin America was not well understood and was not a concern of most Catholics, nor of the local Mohawk and Indigenous population. Regardless, the first pilgrimage, starting from the Kateri shrine in Fonda, New York, was named "Prisoners of Conscience Interfaith Pilgrimage" and was inspired by Father Roy Bourgeois, Sister Megan Rice, Ed Kinane, Ann Tiffany, Carol Richardson, and so many others who served prison time for civil disobedience to raise consciousness to close the SOA.

That first pilgrimage began in August 1998, with seven people: Father Kevin Kenny, Brother Ken Lucas, June Gurnett, Antonia Walsh, two representatives of the media, and myself. Addressing the small group and attempting to put the best face on this very low turnout, I said it was an auspicious beginning. My mood lightened. The work had begun. My faith and belief in the unseen spiritual forces that permeate our world was strong, and I was undaunted that for most of the way I would be walking by myself. June Gurnett and Antonia Walsh walked the first six miles to the Shrine of the North American Martyrs in Auriesville, New York. Four days later I was met by a handful of friends at the Leo O'Brien Federal Building in Albany.

The second Kateri Tekakwitha Interfaith Pilgrimage took place in September 1999. About two hundred people turned out to support our efforts. The Interfaith Alliance of New York State joined the walk, as well as the Albany Catholic Workers, members of the Grafton Peace Pagoda and the Nipponzan Myohoji Buddhist order. In retrospect, the pilgrimage and preceding rally in West Capitol Park were notable for the scope of interfaith participation and the willingness of mainstream clergy to join. Bishop Howard Hubbard, Rabbi Paul Silton, Imam Djafer Sebkhaoui, and others spoke to close the SOA. Wolf Clan Chief Jake Swamp addressed indigenous lands claims in New York and spoke of the Tree of Peace society. Charlie Liteky, the only Congressional Medal of Honor winner ever to renounce his medal and its considerable benefits, also spoke to the necessity of closing the SOA, as did Felipe and Elena Ixcot of the International Mayan League. Sadly, almost all local media chose not to cover the story; the one exception was a picture of Bishop Hubbard in the *Troy Record*. Clearly the Fourth Estate was failing the American people.

A Question of Effectiveness and Underlying Beliefs

After the second pilgrimage, I realized I would not reach the number of people needed to close the School of the Americas by walking pilgrimages. I thought a peace conference, ideally held in the summer, would help raise consciousness and effectively reach more people. Unaware at the time of

Howard Zinn's *A People's History of the United States*, our fledgling conference intuitively adopted the people's perspective. My own early experiences as a United States Marine (1965–69), and an antiwar protester after leaving the Marine Corps taught me to question our government. Then my subsequent travels in Central America and knowledge of the SOA, clearly illustrated the brutal and oppressive designs of U.S. foreign policy. The need to help the marginalized and the poor was clear also. I firmly believed then, as I do now, that peace is not only possible, but that it is up to us to choose and act for peace.

The Kateri Peace Conference would strive to tell the truth about war and peace. The shrine and its grounds, with the tall pines gracing the picnic area, a thousand-year-old oak tree, the archaeological remains of Kateri's ancestral village, and the lush green summer lawns provided a peaceful and relaxing setting for conference attendees. The Mohawk River, a ribbon running through the valley, brought life and mystery and a cooling presence to the summer heat. Even the shrine's conflicted history, with the past lingering so close and a traditional Mohawk Center nearby, was still felt strongly. The generosity of the Franciscan Friars who have hosted us certainly has added a helpful and welcoming dimension, as did local farmers who offered the sweetest of sweet corn, which for many years was a staple for lunch. Our conference would attempt to be a "voice for the voiceless," and we would work to dispel the great lie—that war is noble and heroic—because until this lie is dispelled, we will sleepwalk through a perpetual nightmare of violence and death.

First Conference

"Preparing Fertile Fields," which was held on August 26, 2000, was a qualified success. Chief Jake Teharonianeken Swamp of the Wolf Clan of the Mohawk Nation, the keynote speaker, was unable to attend, pulled away by an emergency. The Iroquois who did attend seemed disconcerted when I criticized the military. I had yet to learn of the powerful need for societal recognition and acceptance that was strongly desired by the Indigenous community. Nor did I understand the warrior ethos and that the U.S. military was seen as a way of achieving at least limited acceptance.

Frankly, I still do not understand how the U.S. Army could be reasonably well thought of by American Indians after committing genocide against them. The day was an awkward affair with those attending viewing me as someone who was both naive and ignorant.

My knowledge of Iroquois history, especially of their complex and troubling relationship with the Black Robes (the early Catholic missionaries), was lacking. The traditional Indian held the Black Robes responsible for destroying their culture, which was not part of my public school history where European settler aggression was almost always presented as self-defense. In addition, that Catholics and Christians had little use for nonviolence and for the most part fully supported war had also escaped my awareness but was brought home deeply by this first conference. The deep-seated and strongly held animosities between the traditional Indian, the Christian Indian, and the Catholic Church, as well as recognition of this contemporary ongoing oppression, were a startling discovery. It was also disconcerting to me that few believed in peace or trusted the concept of peace, regardless of their background.

In 1996, I led a Quaker group to Guatemala as part of an Albany Friends Meeting social concerns project. In the Central Highlands of Guatemala are the remains of a small village, Chantala. The mountains, a branch of the Sierra Mountains were covered with pines, steep, rugged in beauty and the roads little more than carved gashes and cattle trails in a series of switchbacks which slowly climbed in precipitous ascent and left one dizzy in dangerous descent. We were riding in an old pickup. It was an unlikely group, cobbled together, Quakers and lesbians, dreamers and Presbyterians, the young and old who were in love with hope and in love with the belief that knowledge and compassion would somehow transform us and the many injustices suffered in the highlands of Guatemala. This morning we would meet with the women of Chantala, listen to their stories and buy their weavings.

Juan Diego, a Methodist minister and a Ladino, had arranged our visit. He spoke Spanish and Quiche, the local Mayan dialect. The blue Nissan stopped and we all jumped down from the back of the pickup except for Judith, whose ankle had been run over the day before in a freak accident. A Mayan woman motioned to us and we followed her down a steep mountain trail, single file and pleasantly silent, to the village's small cooperative building. The women had been waiting for our arrival and passing the time by sewing. Finding a space to sit each member of our group slowly eased their way down to the floor and within a few moments when everyone had settled Francesca began quietly telling the village's story.

One day the army came. They gathered up all of the people from the village, all they could find and brought them to the church. The people were herded inside. After a period of waiting, three to four hours, suddenly the army began shooting into the church

and then fire bombed the building. Everyone was killed. Our
village of three hundred and twenty at the beginning of the day
was reduced to eighty people by night's end. I lost my husband
and son.

Tears streamed down her cheeks as well as those of the other women, and
soon most of us were crying softly as the women remembered their loss and
we shared in their grief.

The 2001 and 2002 Kateri Peace conferences, both titled "Indigenous
Peoples Under Siege," were strongly centered on closing the School of the
Americas. The conferences questioned whether the SOA was a terrorist
training camp and examined its role in the attempted genocide of the Mayan
and other Indigenous groups in Latin America. Luis Yat, a Mayan born in
Quiche, Guatemala, spoke to the Mayan struggle and the long civil war in
Guatemala. Compelling evidence supported the charge that the SOA was a
terrorist training camp; U.S. documents revealed that graduates were trained
in torture, involved in the murder of Archbishop Oscar Romero of El Salvador, the El Mozote massacre, and many others.

In 2001, the grassroots education campaign conducted by the School of
the Americas Watch gained strength. The energizing civil resistance, coupled
with the imprisonment of Father Roy Bourgeois and, locally, Ed Kinane,
Ann Tiffany, and Rae Kramer, led to the closure of the U.S. Army School
of the Americas. Unfortunately, it was soon reopened with a disingenuous
name change and cosmetic changes to its curriculum. It was rebranded as
the Western Hemisphere Institute for Security Cooperation (WHINSEC).

We also critically examined Plan Colombia. Part of the plan was the aerial
spraying of an herbicide (glyphosate) throughout large regions of Colombia
to kill coca plants. The results included displacing the *campesinos,* forcing
their relocation, and poisoning both the land and water with no significant
reduction of the cocaine supply. Few at the conference had any idea of the
hardship and misery inflicted on the Colombian people.

September 11, 2001

Nine-eleven forced a shift in focus of the Kateri Peace Conference. October
7, 2001, marked the beginning of Operation Enduring Freedom: the U.S.
invasion of Afghanistan. The invasion of Iraq would follow, but not before
there was a massive worldwide demonstration against it. On February

15, 2003, between six and eleven million people protested the impending invasion; approximately one million turned out in New York City alone. A substantial portion of Manhattan was thrown into peaceful chaos as demonstrators flooded into the streets. Ignoring the will of its citizens (and the rest of the world), Operation Iraqi Freedom was launched by the United States government on March 20, 2003.

On May 1, President George W. Bush gave his famous "Mission Accomplished" speech aboard the USS *Abraham Lincoln*. "Because of you, our nation is more secure. Because of you, the tyrant has fallen, and Iraq is free." While world events unfolded at a rapid pace and the U.S. war machine marched through the Middle East, the peace movement began work on the formidable task of ending both wars and altering the course of U.S. foreign policy.

"Ethics, Truth and Terrorism: A Closer Look at America's Role" was the subject of the 2003 conference beginning a comprehensive discussion of U.S. foreign policy. The war and subsequent occupations of Iraq and Afghanistan clearly illustrated U.S. imperialism and an extension of the U.S. empire. The erosion of civil liberties and the suppression of opposition to the war became normal occurrences in the United States. New York City police prevented citizens from assembling to protest the invasion of Iraq by barricading streets in Manhattan and the government's interference with the First Amendment right of free assembly was the beginning of a rapid descent into the extreme incompetence and criminality of both local and federal governments. Given the subsequent revelations and documentation offered by Chelsea Manning, Edward Snowden, Wikileaks, and a host of others, our conference was an honest attempt to create some understanding of U.S. policy.

Cynthia Banas, a former librarian from Vernon, New York, spoke about witnessing "Shock and Awe" in Iraq. She, along with Kathy Kelly, Ed Kinane, Father Jerry Zawada, and others greeted the arrival of U.S. troops into Baghdad. This group hoped their presence might in some way mitigate against the impending invasion and also report on events taking place in Baghdad.

Antiwar activists in Albany were now energized. On November 15, 2003, an all-day symposium, "Confronting the Politics of Fear: A People's Assembly," was held at Albany High School. Its goals were to envision world peace and to confront "the lies, the manipulation, the failures, the regime—its premises and polices," and to "create convergence and connection for peaceful change." These goals also spoke to the heart of the Kateri Peace Conference. Maureen Baillargeon Aumand and Cathy Callan, two of the symposium's main organizers, would soon become friends and co-facilitators of the Kateri Peace Conference.

Creating Peace in a World at War

Bishop Thomas Gumbleton and Kathy Kelly, two of the most dynamic and active peacemakers in the United States, joined our 2004 conference and exemplified what might be accomplished "when the heart and mind are unified, when actions taken are for the common good." The Kateri Shrine newsletter, *Tekakwitha News* (Fall 2004), offered the following summation of Bishop Gumbleton's address: "Bishop Gumbleton inspired us all by his direct appeal to everyone to resist war in EVERY form. Christians should not support the policies of government leaders who are committed to continuous military exploits. . . . Christians must work toward turning the tide, to urge our political representatives to be peace-makers rather than passive supporters of evil and destructive wars. The church needs to speak out on this. It is presently far too silent when it comes to putting an end to war."

Kathy Kelly, a frequent Nobel Peace Prize nominee, who greeted the U.S. Marines with dates and water as they came into Baghdad during "Shock and Awe," was also mentioned in the *Tekakwitha News*. "Kathy Kelly . . . spoke from experience about the unjust savagery of the war and the shameful way in which our young people are being trained to kill."

Perhaps more than any other conference, "Creating Peace in A World at War" was filled with hope, joy, and the belief that we might transform our world in the not-too-distant future. With more than 250 people in attendance, there was a palpable sense of creative energy and love. Collectively, we challenged the inevitability of war and suggested paths to peace, gained from our experience and vowed to continue the work of restoring sanity to our culture.

Conscience is "the internal recognition of right and wrong as regards one's actions and motives." In 2005, our conference, "Call to Conscience," directed us to look deeply both within and without at our nation's conduct. Considering our spiritual traditions, the Constitution and Bill of Rights, we asked, "Are we as a nation doing the right thing?"

Blase Bonpane, Bill Quigley, and Colleen Kelly (presenters for this conference) each had profoundly troubling experiences. They looked deeply within, found ways forward to choose life-affirming responses to the violence, death, and tragedy they had experienced. Colleen Kelly lost her younger brother during the September 11 attacks on the World Trade Center. Asked why she chose peace, she replied, "It was a question I struggled to sort out—what this meant in my life, in my family's life, for our country, and for the world. I struggled with forgiveness, death, meaning: how to respond as a Christian." Colleen chose peace and co-founded September 11th Families for Peaceful Tomorrows.

As part of his presentation, Bill Quigley, a professor of law at Loyola University and advisor to the St. Patrick's Four, invited those activists to join our conference. On St. Patrick's Day, March 17, 2003, Daniel Burns, Clare and Teresa Grady, and Peter De Mott, extremely troubled by the impending invasion of Iraq, had gone to the military recruiting center in Ithaca, New York, and poured their own blood on the walls of the center and also on the flag. In doing so, they followed a time-honored tradition of American antiwar protest. The four were arrested and charged with trespass and criminal mischief.

Their first trial ended with a hung jury; the federal government then moved the trial from Ithaca to Binghamton and brought new charges of conspiracy—the first conspiracy charges since Vietnam for antiwar protestors. Facing six to eight years and a $250,000 fine, the four and their community staged daily courthouse protests. They were acquitted of the conspiracy charge, but found guilty of "damage to government property and entering a military station for an unlawful purpose," and each served four to six months in prison.

Hurricane Katrina

Bill Quigley lived in New Orleans. Bill's wife Debbie was an oncology nurse at Baptist Hospital in New Orleans when Katrina hit. In a later email Bill stated, "I joined her there before it was surrounded by 8 feet of water and lost all power. Many died. We remained there several days before being evacuated by boat." The government's response was slow and inept and callous. Imperialism and racism combined to abandon the poor, black, and marginalized in New Orleans and along the Gulf Coast.

In September 2005, shortly after Katrina, joining with Academics For Peace, I traveled to Iran and Syria, meeting with many governmental officials including President Bashar Assad in Syria. Our delegation was led by Dr. Jim Jennings, president of Conscience International. His friendly and gracious manner along with his extensive knowledge of the Middle East and his ability to speak fluent Arabic made him an excellent leader. Other members included Stephen Eric Bronner, a distinguished professor of political science from Rutgers University, Lawrence Davidson, a professor of Middle East history, and Janet Amighi, a professor of anthropology who speaks fluent Farsi and had lived in Iran. In upcoming years, all would speak at the Kateri Peace Conference.

In March 2006, Veterans for Peace, Iraq Veterans Against the War, and others sponsored "Walkin' to New Orleans," a march that highlighted "the connections between the economic and human cost of war in the Middle East and the failure of our government to respond to human needs at home. Many of us were shocked into wakefulness concerning climate change. Hence our 2006 conference, "The Convergence of Hope and History: Sustainable Solutions for a Peaceful World," seriously attempted to address climate change as well as our peacemaking efforts. Our conference flyer read, "The capacity for hope is one of the most sustaining and helpful qualities of the human spirit. Even when the world looks bleakest, history is replete with ordinary men and women who still find cause for hope."

Looking back, it truly was ordinary men and women who gave cause in New Orleans for hope, who seized the initiative and began the work of rescue and reconstruction, while the federal government and FEMA wallowed in ineptitude and disgracefully failed its citizens.

Attempting to find sustainable solutions, we called upon Jim Merkel, then the sustainability coordinator at Dartmouth College. Previously, he had been an engineer for a military contractor; however, Jim changed his life after the Exxon Valdez disaster and had recently authored the book *Radical Simplicity*. The conference also featured Dr. Jennings and his hands-on experience with Academics for Peace and Conscience International. This conference highlighted the need for peace activists to integrate environmental concerns directly into our work, while suggesting that environmentalists more fully consider the impact of militarism on the environment.

Chapter 2

History of The Kateri Peace Conference, Part 2

Leaving the Comfort of Home

MAUREEN BAILLARGEON AUMAND

Since 2004, I have had the privilege of acting as co-coordinator of the Kateri Peace Conference (KPC). If you had told me—wife, mother, teacher, librarian, quiescent citizen, grandmother—that this would be the case a few years prior to that, I would have been quite puzzled.

On September 11, 2001, buoyed by the crisp, blue-skied beauty of the morning and the high spirits of a new school year, I was working to settle the energies of the high school students who had just found their second period way to my library. The first plane hit and then the next and then, as for so many, everything changed.

I remember my ensuing thoughts and reactions as those early few minutes of national chaos played across our screens. A sinking surety that this was not an accident; a fear for the psychological well-being of the teens who surrounded me; a shared sense, adult and child, of disbelief and horror at seeing the strangely silent procession of dust-shrouded survivors; a longing to embrace my husband, my own kids, my family and friends; and, finally, a strong and startling visual hologram-like illusion that in the image, repeated over and over, of the towers falling in real time, resided images and screams which already deeply haunted my psyche: the horrors of Dresden, Hiroshima, Nagasaki, accompanied by a voice deep inside: "If you live by the sword, you will die by the sword."

Perhaps, most acutely, in those early hours, especially as they were followed by a manic call to fear and arms, came a realization: I did not truly understand the current historical moment. I had much to learn, much to do. To that point, I was a concerned citizen, in fact, a committed peacemaker. I was a conscientious teen in the early sixties, after all. Hadn't I deeply recoiled at searing images of violence inflicted on civil rights activists, of the unspeakable depravity of the Holocaust, the untenable horrors of Hiroshima? As a devotee of folk lyrics celebrating peace, love, and brotherhood, didn't I chose to sing Peter, Paul and Mary and Pete Seeger songs in a high school talent show? Wasn't I on the Catholic Worker mailing list?

Though my years as a cloistered novice in a religious community precluded direct participation during the late-sixties antiwar movement, I deeply felt the pain of the Vietnam War, was seared by its imagery. I wept for my age mates who were caught in its churning maw, and wrote an outline for a play about conscientious objection. Hadn't I made a "singing nun" album with colleagues celebrating the necessity of love in the world, and thrilled to the activism encountered at many a monument the summer of '68 when I taught in D.C.? Hadn't I been a welfare rights "streetwalker" in religious garb in Albany, New York, for two summers, and used contemporary music and parlance to teach theology?

As a public school English teacher and then librarian, hadn't I made sure that even as our students studied history—so often taught through the lens of war and jingoistic pride—they also had access to literature and film, research projects that underscored the horrors of war? They encountered performing artists whose work explored the costs of violence and war, and the reality of a shared humanity across the planet. Hadn't I thrilled to travel with students to Moscow to stay with Russian families and work on common classroom projects in a bid to cut through the "Iron Curtain"?

I had, at the same time, however, ignored the pain and suffering of our Latin American brothers and sisters and understood little of America's complicity in the Central American civil wars of the eighties. I sensed the complexity of the Iranian Revolution and hostage crisis but made little effort to understand their roots. I paid minimal attention to the war in Lebanon or the Iran/Iraq war. I felt a vague unease, an unfocused anger, at American readiness for war against an already ravaged Iraq in the early nineties.

Popular news magazines' skinny on foreign wars and foreign policy sufficed as information sources. Like the vast majority of my fellow citizens, I assumed that the United States is a white hat nation at root and that the world was much closer to peace following the end of the Cold War. In truth, I also said I would eventually, when I had time, get around to better understanding the forces at play in the world but "not now"! I was too busy. I did not have time. I had three kids. I was a working mom. I had bills to pay, housework to do. I was going to grad school, planning lessons, cooking meals, dealing with my own problems. I was an English major, for goodness sakes, not a historian or political scientist.

I cursorily read those superficial news articles and analysis but paid only passing attention to root causes and kept at bay any imperative to act beyond the confines of my little world. What did I know; what could I do anyway? Take to the streets? I stayed home! Perhaps the fact that my own sons were at a soldiering age was a goad but in the aftermath of 9/11, I could see the naiveté and laziness of my shallow commitment to peace. A quest began.

My husband and I invited those we knew who seemed to deeply care and know more than we did to our home to plumb their knowledge. We invited a local imam to one of our meetings. As Islam became a sudden focus of concern, media attention, national animus, I realized that even with two advanced degrees I knew relatively nothing about this ancient faith tradition and culture. As the drums of war pounded, I began to read everything I could to understand the driving forces behind fear and violence. And I felt great angst at the unbridled militarism that shaped the discourse of our "peace-loving" nation.

A writer/artist friend, who had spent many hours with my husband and me trying to understand the moment, decided to go to Iraq on a delegation organized by Voices in the Wilderness, founded by peace and human rights activist Kathy Kelly. The hope was for everyday citizens to see and know the people of Iraq firsthand so that upon return home they could detail the human face of this nation caught in our crosshairs and thus prevent the looming invasion. My job was to make contacts for him so that there would be a wide audience for what he would learn. This clarified and focused my efforts. In addition to online research acquiring background, perspective, and understanding, I worked to discover every local organization, individual, and media outlet that might help strengthen the will to peace. And so a new world opened for me and laid the foundation for my now long-term connection to the Kateri Peace Conference.

Hiding in Plain Sight

As I began to emerge from the safety of my middle-class cocoon to actively seek out avenues of connection, what I discovered was that we were, even here in the Capital Region of New York, surrounded by a small army of activist mentors as well as fellow citizens who were filled with a common desire to avert yet another war. I found notices of relevant talks. We attended, and were thrilled to hear questions and commentary that reflected our own concerns about the threatened war. Letters to the editors and op-ed pieces began to appear in our local papers. These writers became points of contact. Local peace groups—Women Against War, Veterans for Peace, the Solidarity Committee, Bethlehem Neighbors for Peace—provided arguments and avenues. These groups also provided the most profound sense of shared angst: others, strangers, fellow citizens were speaking my mind's greatest fears, my heart's deepest desires.

I remember quite clearly walking up to the first peace rally and march I ever attended. I was carrying the most recent message from our friend in Baghdad looking for someone who might read it aloud and I found myself weeping for joy as my husband and I saw arrayed signs that expressed our anger as well as hopes, watched a young man climb a war memorial in order to put a flower in the barrel of the iron soldier's gun, heard the chants, the folk songs made real by the context in which they were now sung and felt the common palpable passion for peace. Stepping into the street with others became empowering and transformative.

Empowering and *transformative* might also best describe the many individuals who began to emerge from these crowds and experiences in all their three-dimensional histories, talents and commitment to the national good, the well-being of others, the sustainability of the planet, the possibility of peace. There were many who had been walking, talking, rallying, marching, advocating, writing, working for peace for decades; some, like us, new to the work.

They were Quakers and atheists, Buddhists and Marxists, Catholic nuns, war vets and Peace Corps Vets, college professors, street organizers, long-time movement organizers, writers, musicians, moms and dads, other grandmothers and grandfathers, all, in truth, our neighbors. Some stood on the shoulders, the past activism, of their parents and other childhood mentors, some were new to activism, some had crossed lines, which led to imprisonment. Many embraced voluntary poverty, many worked for other causes and saw a commitment to peace and justice as clearly intertwined: antipoverty, antiracism, pro–gender equality, union building, voters rights, feminism, international human rights, environmental justice, prison reform. Others were searching as we were; it became clear that the regional peace movement was diverse, inclusive, and welcoming.

For those like me who had stayed home for much too long, the door was open and the message was clear: you can do this too. You can write letters to the editor and op=ed essays, speak on camera, do radio interviews. You can organize meetings with the media, build conferences and rallies, invite speakers, give speeches. You can join us as we meet with legislators and provide them information that contradicts what the vested interests want them to hear. You can fast with us in community, my Women Against War sisters said, and stand with us on the steps of the Capitol as we proclaim our reasons for doing so. You can record public service announcements, join us in the streets, help organize buses to Washington, D.C., and New York City, and shout in united chorus. You can do quiet peace walks through familiar suburban neighborhoods beating out a heartbeat with ancient drums. You can stand on the corner at the mall, invade the mall, invade the recruiting office at the mall, get thrown out of the mall. You can risk arrest. You can do clergy outreach, media outreach, political outreach. You can pray with us, sing with us, perform with us, protest with us, proclaim poetry with us. This is your birthright as a citizen and the door is always open and, if you look, we are always here, a community united in common concern, imperative, and commitment.

Why Kateri?

This is the personal context which brings me to the task of writing the following overview, providing some sense of the tenor, for the past ten years, of the KPC initiative which is the ground for the compilation of essays to follow.

If the annual Kateri Peace Conference is marked by anything, it is a deep commitment to peace and community. This is what has moved me to involve myself with it for the past fourteen years. Clearly, the antiwar efforts in the Capital Region of New York State (aligned, even as they were, with global antiwar efforts) were not successful in stemming the national tropism to war. We are, at this very moment, still sadly experiencing the predicted dissolution and destruction as they play out in Iraq, Afghanistan, Syria, and Yemen.

However, many lessons resounded clearly to me from the effort: We must be in it for the long haul; issues of peace and justice are intertwined; it is essential, if one is to act wisely and strategically, to study and read without end, to seek out learned wisdom, to listen to those on the front lines, to be inspired by those who risk all in speaking out. To sustain it, one must ground one's activism in deep spirit and one's holy rage in a deep love of planet and people. One must believe always that peace is both possible and imperative. Finally, I learned that it is important to surround oneself with music and creative energy, nature and friendship, seeking out the "beloved community" for sustenance on the journey.

For these reasons, I have been fortunate to assist John W. Amidon in envisioning and organizing this annual initiative, because these are the values that he holds dear and which have consistently infused the Kateri Peace Conference effort from the beginning. Myriad challenges to peace and justice, to the creation of a global society that is viable and sustainable, proliferated during the past decade. The focus of the Kateri Peace Conference thus morphed with the challenges while adhering always to these central visions and values.

To see how we walked this tightrope over the past decade of conference history, I turn to a few of the annual introductory statements, to highlight themes and provide a sense of the richness and diversity of the speakers and workshops. I highlight the connections to other efforts and entities locally, nationally, and internationally, which were made and mined over the past decade of conferences, and note any innovations we found valuable as organizing strategies.

This conference history is shared as background to the profound and personal reflections of the authors included in this volume who, over the years, were some of the many who brought their experiences, motivations, strategies, and passion for peace to the KPC. It is our hope that this book might add in some way to the historical record of early-twenty-first century peace activism and that through this record of the Kateri Peace Conference and through the shared voices of many of its key presenters, we can provide inspiration and pathways for other enduring efforts for peace.

Before the brief review, however, I must digress once more. I suspect that many wondered over the years why we continued to hold this non-denominational conference at a shrine dedicated to an Iroquois Catholic saint. As I sat, year after year, in the Iroquois Peace Grove with a large sign, emblazoned with the call to peace issued centuries ago by the Iroquois activist Handsome Lake, as backdrop, I came to the conclusion that tied the place with its ancient history to our present efforts and which connects all efforts at creating peaceful human societies across time. Within this context, I would like to share this reflection, which I wrote in August 2012:

> The site of the annual Kateri Peace Conference lies in close proximity to the ancient village of, Caughnawaga, where Mohawk families and their leaders sought to live their lives in harmony and peace with one another and with the natural world, even as

they struggled to understand, confront, integrate into a meaningful framework the geopolitical forces of imperialism, colonialism, capitalism, materialism and racism which were surrounding them with the arrival of Europeans warring among themselves for resources and domination.

One can imagine, that in the spirit of the Longhouse, the Iroquois Confederacy, which had come to bind peoples of many tribes into a network grounded in the Great Peacemakers vision of negotiated understanding, elimination of war as solution to conflict, and commitment to reconciliation and peace, the very woods surrounding the site of the Kateri Conference resounded with the speeches of many bringing words of considered council as the Mohawk people who lived here then tried to make sense of and build a future in the face of such daunting forces. "What are we to do?"

As we meet once again to explore the realities which confront us in our own 21st century time, we do so mindful of the truth of this place and in the same spirit of questing for understanding and guidelines for action, desiring, as the first people's did, to live in peace and harmony and with assurance of a viable future. We gather to hear the wisdom of our guest speakers who all come to us with a deep commitment to peace and to share insights born of our mutual deep desire for finding a way forward.

Kateri: 2007–2017

To garner a sense of how these energies, values, and an overriding desire for meetings that would "find a way forward" created the framing for the last decade of the Kateri Peace Conference, it is valuable to turn to some of the conference calls that appear for this period in full on the online archives kateripeaceconference.org.

We invited participants in 2007 for a conference entitled "Hope and Resistance" to reflect that "while the powerful attempt to narrate our lives and convince us that the course of history" is determined by them, "we refute that idea" believing instead that "the ordinary man and woman can transform history and build a better society" by working for "peace and justice tempered with compassion and understanding," by working together "to know what is right and then acting in accordance."

The 2009 invitation for "Harnessing The Winds of Change," the first Obama-era conference, read, "We recognize that many of the problems we confront are deep seated and will require careful discernment, patience and systemic change," and that to bring about such change we had to learn how "to move past fear and ignorance" in order to work "constructively for our children's future."

Reflecting on the challenge raised for activists by "A Question of Balance," we argued in 2010 that in the face of economic troubles, environmental degradation, the persistence of war and its handmaiden militarism, it was difficult to see how our early-twenty-first-century society was moving in an "effective, sustainable" direction even as "many of us yearn for peace, security and a sense of well-being." In the hope of addressing this frustration and the need to find a balanced way forward, the conference promised to "turn to a left brain/right brain synthesis wherein traditional lectures on current political issues would be paired with workshops on inner exploration and self-growth" in the hope that this pairing would bring about a "new heartfelt understanding of the world and our place in it."

The 2013 gathering—"The Moral Imperative of Activism"—brought a roster of speakers who lived out this imperative in a day "designed to encourage nonviolent standing up and speaking out" by inviting presenters to provide suggestions for "some of what we need to learn and know" as well as suggestions needed for "the important steps to take to address such untenable choices as torture, drone assassination and the paradigm of endless war" in order to "ensure that peace and justice form the bedrock of all national policy."

A call for creativity preceded 2014's "Rise Up! Resist! Transform Now!" conference. Using the visionary architect Buckminster Fuller's frameworks for transformative change, presenters were invited to "grapple with the serious core issues and major obstacles" in ways that would lead to "synergistic engagement . . . a quantitative leap in inspiration and creativity" as we envisioned alternative approaches to peace and justice building.

A call for action grounded in mind and heart for the 2016 conference "Confronting The Politics of Fear" challenged attendees to become "citizens prepared to think rationally and deeply about root causes" for war and injustice "in order to support life affirming solutions for the numerous and seemingly overwhelming obstacles." Solutions should be "based on a commitment to global interconnectedness and a belief that another world is possible . . . [in order] to develop an analysis and a praxis forged in love . . . that can transform the seemingly intractable forces confronting us today." (See Appendix A for a complete list of conference titles.)

This brief sampling from the KPC archives highlights the undercurrents that run through year after year: the primacy of love and compassion; the bedrock of peace and justice; the disavowal of war; the quest to understand root causes for very real obstacles to peace and justice; the need to feed a deep belief in the possibility of historical transformation through systemic change; the power of the people; the need to confront one's own fears in order to confront the untenable realities of the time; the need to do this in community and with discernment; and the moral imperative in all of this, finally, to act.

The evolving historical moment was reflected in the changing themes over the last decade. Even as Iraq and Afghanistan remained in focus, Yemen, Syria, Iran, Somalia, and Palestine, among others, rose to attention. Refugee numbers exploded and millions across the planet suffered. The effect of war on soldiers impacted by the most recent incursions became increasingly evident. Military budgets and bases soared. Drones and new technologies of war proliferated. A trillion-dollar nuclear weapons "modernization" got underway. Guantanamo Bay and torture continued to haunt the national psyche. Income inequality became more and more pronounced. Health care became a political football. Civil liberties remained under siege. The FBI's entrapment of Muslims in structured stings was felt locally as well as nationally. The effects of the Anthropocene proclaimed themselves dramatically as real. In spite of an election that promised hope and change, war and racism were still seen to ensnare and dominate. A president with an ethno-nationalist agenda came to office with a promise to "drain the swamp": worshipping Mammon openly, openly racist and misogynistic, a president proud to discount the rule of law and the boundaries of truth, espousing nuclear weapons as solution to geopolitical conflict—obstacles indeed!

During the course of this decade of gatherings by the edge of the woods, seventy-nine speakers and workshop presenters, including those whose essays follow, came to inform, challenge, and reflect on these daunting concerns. Strategies, practices, frameworks were offered, experiences and approaches shared, the interconnectedness among issues probed—the power of bringing shared minds and heartfelt concern to this quest affirmed and strengthened.

Direct action and civil disobedience were explored within the context of personal histories as well as the history of nonviolent social movements over time. Prison witness examined. Youth organizing considered. Principles of nonviolence studied. The inevitability of war challenged. The pain of the world's victims of war and injustice laid out. Mediation and meditation extolled. Native American spirituality held out as perhaps a path to grounding all work in harmony with nature. Organizing tools offered and, always, the witness of those who live their commitments placed front and center.

Taking center stage, manning panels, presenting workshops, these seventy-nine included anti-drone, anti-nuke, and antiwar activists. Others are prison justice, racial justice, anti-Islamophobia, human rights, labor, environmental rights, simple living, and political activists. Many are writers, spiritual leaders, or clerics. Also on board are scholars, prisoners of conscience, world travelers, risk takers, bloggers, Internet organizers, Veterans for Peace members, and a former diplomat.

Our presenters stood in picket lines and prison lines, under the gun and under the baton. They faced down falling bombs in brother/sisterhood with those bunkered who had no choice. Our presenters write, speak, march, protest, organize, and advocate unflinchingly for peace and justice, and they have come to the Kateri Peace Conference year after year to move and inspire.

The KPC roster includes many whose names are recognized nationally and internationally, earning some, in fact, Nobel Peace Prize nominations: Kathy Kelly, Medea Benjamin, Col. Ann Wright, David Swanson, Bishop Thomas Gumbleton, Ray McGovern. We were also honored to have shared the perspectives and experiences of many local and regional activists as well.

Through our roster of speakers, the experience of the KPC midsummer meetings connected those who attended to the work of a vast array of peace and justice initiatives. This broad nexus illustrates the "six degrees of separation" among peace and justice energies and the ever widening range of possibilities for networking. Old and new initiatives were made real through the presence of those whose own backgrounds were shaped by numerous initiatives: Pace e Bene and the Peace Corps, Fellowship of Reconciliation, War Resisters League, Catholic Worker Movement. Others came to us from the Green Party Shadow Cabinet, the Audacity of Hope Campaign, Iraq Veterans Against the War, the Afghan Youth Brigade, and more. (See Appendix B for a list of aligned organizations and initiatives.)

As this brief sampling of our annual calls to action makes clear, one of our evolving commitments was the need to feed both mind and heart in order to ground our activism in a deeply held understanding. We've thus done our best to incorporate a strong cultural component in recent conferences. The inspiring lyrics of both traditional and original folk songs and the rousing chorus of protest music served to punctuate many conferences. We were moved over the years by the work of many regional artists, including political satire and spoken word performances that sparked much laughter.

We had great fun in 2014 when the opening site for the event moved to a sightseeing cruise on the Erie Canal. Under the banner "Rise Up! Resist! Transform Now! Rock The Boat for Peace!" Our presenters laid out the challenges for the conference, while Green Party presidential candidate Jill Stein brought her band and a bunch of middle-aged (and older) peace activists truly rocked the boat. Our desire to help participants grapple with the despair that can accompany peace work led us to attach a day-long retreat to the conference.

In keeping with the conference site's proximity to New York's most thoroughly studied Mohawk archeological site, and in honor of the First Peoples whose land we traverse each August, the haunting sounds of traditional native flutes and drums stilled spirits and opened hearts and minds in 2012. We gathered that year to probe the imperative for truth telling. Kay Olan, a well-known Mohawk storyteller led us in the traditional "the meeting at the edge of the woods" ceremony, a ritual that invites us to open up to truth bearers. The words and ideas of great truth tellers such as Martin Luther King Jr., Mahatma Gandhi, and Dorothy Day were invoked for guidance and inspiration during this special Iroquois-modeled KPC meeting. A traditional Iroquois community dance followed the solemn ceremony, celebrating the circle of unified hearts and minds gathered to learn and grow.

The "Circle of Life" conference—where we tried again to link environmental concerns with issues of war and justice—opened with a community storytelling experience based on the work of visionary peace activist and psychotherapist Joanna Macy. Her work gave voice to multitudes of earth's creatures, allowing them to speak from the deepest planetary heart in the hope that all thinking and strategizing resulting from the conference would be grounded in planetary need and possibility. Participants listened to poetry, and were invited to write their own. Staged readings of issue-driven plays moved and engaged us. A regional human rights activist, James Ricks, recently jailed for his political action, "performed" Dr. King's "Beyond Vietnam" speech (an important guide for the KPC which can be found at: https:king institute.stanford.edu/king-papers/documents/beyond-vietnam).

The retreats initiated in 2012 offered the option to spend a quiet day together in preparation for listening, speaking, and confronting the often painful issues under consideration. They were based on the belief that "deep spiritual centering must be seen as the ground for our efforts to understand more fully and confront more effectively a culture of fear, militarism and war," and that "our work must flow from personal peace of mind and heart." Titles for these days of reflection included: "Moral Pain and Spiritual Struggles: Caring for The Soul in Peace Work," "Affirming Peace in The Face of Fear," Nurturing the Sacred," "Active Love and Nonviolence: The Only Moral Response to War."

These nondenominational events included an array of leaders from diverse spiritual traditions: retired Catholic bishop Thomas Gumbleton, known internationally for his commitment to social justice and peace; the internationally lauded peace activist Kathy Kelly, whose work is grounded in Catholic Worker tradition; a local imam, Djafar Sebkhaoui, who actively works with the regional Muslim solidarity movement, shared the day with Father Mark Steed, the director of the Kateri shrine and a Franciscan priest who considers Teillhard de Chardin his spiritual guide; the founder of the Revolution of Love ministry, Rev. Felicia Parazaider; and Unitarian minister and former military chaplain Chris Antal, renowned for his anti-drone activism.

Combining ritual, lecture, discussion, and quiet, our retreats aimed to strengthen community as participants together sought "to find a way to live and speak our deep concern for the world" through an affirmation of the "sacred grounding . . . in universal sisterhood and brotherhood . . . at the heart of why we care." Further details about the retreats, their presenters, and schedules are available at kateripeaceconference.org. Additionally, a number of the presenters' reflections are included in this volume of essays.

The Kateri Peace Conference springs from an organic reaction to the historical moment and an evolving sense of how best to engage in "bending the moral arc of the universe" toward peace and justice. Over time, this required experimentation as to how best to structure the time for maximum impact. How to offer a rich menu of information, ideas, and inspiration as well as opportunities for dialogue, and thereby build a community galvanized with strategies for action?

We tried a new design in 2012, moving away from our keynote, speeches, workshops format. We developed a series of questions we asked presenters to consider in their remarks. Presenters spoke in panel format; the panels progressed across the day in a cycle that moved from personal reflection to strategies for action, and which provided opportunity for discussion with attendees.

"Our [2012] conference is structured to create a continuous flowing dialogue among the presenters while maximizing [audience] participation throughout the day," read the guidelines for presenters. "Speakers will participate in a series of three sequential panels in order for each to consider their work, the issues and actions with which they are engaged, and their own personal journey" in the quest to "bend the arc" of history. We asked them "to look at priorities, obstacles and strategies and finally, ask them to help us imagine how true transformation might be realized." For each panel, speakers addressed "the same questions from their own diverse perspectives, motivations, insights, life story and experience."

These guiding questions included: (1) "Describe your work in terms of both issues and actions that engage you" and explain "why you care, what compels you to act?" (2) "What is the greatest priority demanding our attention; if we are to move forward, what should we be working on?" and "What are the greatest obstacles before us?" (3) "What are the most strategic actions and campaigns we should embrace" for the greatest "transformative change," and finally, "Do you see reason for hope? Is a global order premised on peace and justice on the horizon?"

We borrowed a modified version of this framework to unite the reflections that follow in this volume.

The Moral Arc

I smile now when I recall the sense of surety that accompanied my early activism in the run-up to the 2003 Iraq invasion. How could George Bush possibly move ahead when millions in streets around the world marched in opposition?

In detailing the history of the Kateri Peace Conference, I smile again. This annual peace gathering is an effort both persistent and passionate. It may, in fact, be one of the longest-running conferences of its kind. But has it been "successful"? Have we transformed the world through "revolutionary love"? Have we found the way forward to shared planetary sustainability where war is seen as abomination and justice and equality rule?

Of course not. Instead, the minute hand inches forward on the Doomsday Clock, environmental degradation proceeds at breakneck speed, America is wracked by partisanship and fragmentation, a new Cold War broke out, the U.S. defense budget increases obscenely, eating away at the nation's capacity for social uplift, and global inequality grows rather than shrinks. The number of attendees at the KPC annual conferences always disappointed. John W. Amidon's deeply felt hope that these gatherings would attract and galvanize more active-duty religious leaders was thwarted. We can point to no grand or transformative initiative springing directly from the nearly two decades of conferences.

And yet. And yet. Summer after summer in Fonda, New York, like the Mohawks before us, we proclaimed: "We are still here." We are peacemakers. We still share Dr. King's view that "the calling to speak is a vocation . . . a vocation, beyond all, to brotherhood." "We must enter the struggle . . . must raise our voices . . . [must] match action with words, finding every creative form of protest." We are still here. Participants come, season after season, to seek the wisdom to expand what Dr. King called "the field of their moral vision" so that rather than being "mesmerized by uncertainty" and suffering the "apathy of conformist thought" they can be confirmed in their determination that "I must be true to my conviction." They are to show "overriding loyalty to mankind," "an all embracing unconditional love" in order to conquer "the giant triplets of racism, materialism and militarism." Every year they return from this little verdant space to the world and ripples move forth, toward the future. We are still here.

In the essays that follow, please find narratives that detail the lives, work, and reflections of some of those who aim to "bend the moral arc of the universe" toward peace and justice, and in them find inspiration and encouragement.

Specific details on the speakers and presenters who have participated in the conference can be found in the conference archives at: kateripeaceconference.org

Chapter 3

The Road to CODEPINK

MEDEA BENJAMIN

The Vietnam War shaped my life and political beliefs. Growing up in a suburban, Jewish household on Long Island, I was in high school when my sister's boyfriend was drafted. When he left for Vietnam, he was a sweet guy, the quarterback on the football team. A few months after he was stationed in Vietnam, he sent my sister the ear of a Vietcong fighter to wear as a souvenir. She went into the bathroom to throw up.

It hit me that there was something horribly dehumanizing about war. War took good kids and turned them into crazed killers.

Shaken, I decided to get involved in antiwar activities, and I set up a peace group at my high school. We organized protests and walkouts. We learned to play the guitar and sing peace songs. We mobilized and networked around the state, we campaigned for antiwar candidates, we marched on Washington, and, finally, we won. Ever since then, I've been trying to stop my government from involving us in wars we shouldn't be in.

Growing up in the 1960s, my rebellion was not just against war. We also struggled against the ills of racism, sexism, environmental destruction, and consumerism. We thought it was really possible to build a radically different world. Self-identifying as hippies, we experimented with different ways of living communally. We tried to build cooperative economic models, direct forms of democracy, new ways to encourage people to take an active role in determining how we functioned as a society.

I also had wanderlust and realized I could travel around the world as a hitchhiker, doing odd jobs here and there to pay my way. I spent years traveling throughout Africa, Asia, and Latin America and eventually used the knowledge I accumulated to get a job with the United Nations in Africa, where I spent many years working with malnourished children in war-torn countries.

Some of my most formative moments came from living in poor villages in Africa and working in rehydration camps for malnourished children. Many were tiny babies whose mothers had stopped breastfeeding them—convinced by infant formula companies such as Nestlé that powdered milk was better than breast milk. The women would spend the little money they had on a can of formula, and their breast milk would dry up. Meanwhile, they would water down the powdered milk to save money, and mix it with contaminated water. Their babies got dysentery and severe dehydration that would lead to death.

I watched children die just because some corporation wanted to squeeze profits out of poor villagers. There is nothing like having babies dying in your arms to convince you that something is profoundly wrong about the way we, as a global society, prioritize profits over human life.

Determined to stop this kind of corporate malpractice, I joined a budding international campaign against Nestlé. We took the issue to the United Nations as a grave human rights violation, and the campaign resulted in the first ever international Code of Conduct to regulate the practices of multinational corporations.

I was struck again by the callousness of large corporations when I was living in Central America and discovered how the fruit companies had stolen the lands of poor farmers. Working as a nutritionist, I discovered that most of the impoverished parents I was supposed to advise on how to feed their children had previously been farmers. They would have been able to feed their families with their crops, but they had been forced off the land by U.S. banana companies. This made me question the policies of my government and the corporate interests it promoted.

I was also outraged by all the money flowing into the arms trade. I saw war raging from Africa to Latin America, and realized that my own government was often on the wrong side of the fighting, fueling the arms trade and supporting repressive regimes instead of people's movements. I learned how my government, in the interest of U.S. big business, had helped to overthrow democratically elected leaders from Guatemala and Chile to Zaire and Iran, and I became passionately opposed to this kind of intervention.

I felt that one of the ways to stop wars—and prevent new ones—was to take people to the conflict zones to see the world through the eyes of local people. Once there, I was certain they would reflect on the consequences of U.S. policies and return home as "citizen diplomats." With two colleagues, we started a group called Global Exchange that has, for more than thirty years, been organizing what we call "people-to-people" travel opportunities, often to places that have an antagonistic relationship with the U.S. government, such as Cuba, Iran, and Venezuela. Over the years, we created thousands of citizen diplomats who returned to their communities to advocate for negotiations and nonviolent ways of resolving conflicts.

We also began focusing on the kinds of trade that would not benefit big corporations and foster a race to the bottom in terms of wages and environmental regulations, but could be beneficial to workers and sustainable for the planet. We joined forces with unions, environmentalists, and faith-based groups to oppose the "free trade" agreements. We even managed to shut down the meeting of the World Trade Organization when it met in Seattle in 1999. Instead, we pushed for national and international regulations that favor workers, farmers, and the environment.

On the positive side, we introduced the "fair trade" label, starting with coffee and moving to tea, bananas, and chocolate. Today, there are hundreds of fair trade businesses that ensure that the producers get paid fairly for their products. This is part of a larger effort to build businesses with good social and environmental values.

I was deep into this work when the 9/11 attacks happened. While I did not lose a loved one that day, it did change my life, like so many others', forever. As the Bush administration immediately retaliated by invading Afghanistan, I turned my attention away from economic justice issues and focused on the war. I remember watching, transfixed, as the television stations showed the planes taking off for Afghanistan and the "smart bombs" dropping. But we never saw where the bombs landed; we were never told how many civilians were being killed as part of "collateral damage."

I decided to go to Afghanistan to see for myself. I was heartbroken by what I found—thousands of civilians killed, wounded and displaced by our "smart bombs." I came back from that trip deeply disturbed, but discovered to my horror that the drumbeat had already started for launching another war: this time in Iraq.

Shortly after my return from Afghanistan, when the threat of war in Iraq was imminent, I was in a retreat organized for women environmentalists. We were complaining about President Bush's color-coded alert system—red, orange, and yellow—which we felt was designed to keep people in a state of alarm to justify the impending war. Someone said in jest that we should create a "CODEPINK" alert for peace.

So we did. We felt that it was important to create a women-led response to counter all the male, testosterone-raging energy we saw from Osama bin Laden to Saddam Hussein to George Bush.

We started with a few actions in Washington, D.C., but with no intent to create a new organization. We all had our hands full with other work. We had planned on simply joining other groups that were mobilizing to stop a new war in the Middle East, and once the war was averted, we would go back to the work we'd been doing before. But quickly, CODEPINK took on a life of its own. Before we knew it, the group had grown to two hundred thousand people with about three hundred local chapters. In coalition with other organizations, we organized huge demonstrations, including the February 15, 2003, global day of action that went down in the Guinness Book of Records as the largest demonstration in the history of humankind.

Unfortunately, Bush ignored us and invaded Iraq anyway, and to this day, we still find that there's a need for CODEPINK.

We had a very vibrant peace movement during the Bush administration, when we could rally hundreds of thousands of people to protest Bush's military aggression. But all that evaporated when Obama was elected. It was hard to criticize President Obama because it was so monumental for our country to have elected the first African American president. Some people were also just burned out from eight years of protesting the Bush administration. Others were caught up in the domestic economic crisis, fighting to keep their jobs or save their homes from foreclosure.

Still others were certain that Obama would be a peace president—after all, he'd just won the Nobel Peace Prize—so we didn't have to put pressure on him. A lot of people read into Obama their own hopes and dreams for a peace president. Despite the Nobel Peace Prize, he never said he was against war. He was against the war in Iraq, but he was not against the war in Afghanistan, which he called "the good war." He subsequently oversaw the surge in Afghanistan—sending more troops and tax dollars into a quagmire. He then launched secretive drone attacks in Pakistan, Yemen, and Somalia that have killed thousands of people, including many women and children.

We also realized that many people who were part of the peace movement were Democrats who were ready to protest George Bush, a Republican, but were unwilling to protest Obama, a Democrat.

The reaction to continuation of the Middle East wars is a perfect example. If President Bush had been responsible for these wars, progressives around the nation would have been fighting vigorously against them. But they refused to criticize Obama, a fellow Democrat. I understand it's hard to criticize people we share values with, but it's a real disservice to our cause, as well as to our country, if we don't speak out against policies we think are wrong, no matter who is advocating them.

The whole point of a successful democracy is constant vigilance by citizens to hold their elected officials accountable. Otherwise, power tends to corrupt—no matter who it is. Democracy isn't about "being a good soldier" to a party, it's about being an independent thinker and actor.

The movement environmentalists built up against the Keystone XL Pipeline is a good example of how a grassroots movement should work. Environmentalists started out very friendly toward President Obama, giving him the opportunity to join them, and then building the pressure and taking him on when it became apparent that pressure was necessary. After months and months of petitions, rallies, meetings, and even mass arrests, Obama finally succumbed to pressure and pledged to veto the pipeline if Congress approved it. That's an example of realizing we will only get the policies we want if we mobilize and keep the pressure on. And it's also an example of the fragility of environmental victories, as President Trump reversed Obama's decision upon taking office.

One of the worst foreign policies of the Obama administration has been the widespread use of drone warfare. I was appalled when I saw a poll back in 2012 revealing that the majority of Americans—a whopping 83 percent—supported the killing of terrorist suspects with drones. These "suspects" were people thousands of miles away in countries such as Pakistan and Yemen who had never been accused, tried, or convicted of anything. Yet most Americans approved of incinerating them with Hellfire missiles launched by remote control from the comfort of bases in the United States.

The use of drones allows the U.S. military to expand wars without congressional approval, behind the backs of the public and without putting U.S. troops at risk. This "risk-free" intervention makes it easier to keep our nation in a state of permanent warfare. We at CODEPINK realized that the first step to ending drone warfare was to change the minds of the American people. So I wrote a book called *Drone Warfare: Killing by Remote Control*, and traveled around the country mobilizing people against this new way of killing. We held two major Drone Summits in Washington, D.C., gave interviews, staged protests at drone bases and the White House, and took our message directly to the homes of the weapons manufacturers. We flew to Yemen, Pakistan, and Afghanistan to see firsthand the negative impact of drones and hear the stories of victims and their families. We brought victim families to testify, for the first time ever, before Congress.

All of our hard work started to pay off. As more Americans became educated, there has been an enormous shift in public opinion, from 83 percent in favor of drone warfare in 2012 to 60 percent in 2015. President Obama was forced to acknowledge and discuss the U.S. drone program, which had previously been a covert program, and to promise that his administration had taken steps to minimize civilian casualties.

Focusing on drone warfare pushed us to look at the issues of militarism and racism domestically. Drone warfare is an example of extreme racial profiling. Can you imagine the U.S. military sending drones to kill individuals living in a European country? No, we only use them in poor countries to kill people of color. The United States gets away with this extrajudicial killing precisely because we are using them in poor countries populated by people of color. This parallels what has been happening in poor communities of color in our own country for far too long. The police would never shoot an unarmed suspect in a white, affluent community. But police get away with murder in poor communities of color. There is a tremendous parallel between extrajudicial killings overseas and killing by police officers here in the United States, and the militarization the United States has fueled for a decade overseas is now fueling the militarization of our police forces. We see the Pentagon spending billions of dollars on equipment they don't need and pawning it off on police departments. Our police now resemble our military with armored vehicles, assault weapons, camouflage uniforms, and even drones.

Even before the nation's attention became focused on Ferguson, Missouri, and the Black Lives Matter movement emerged, we initiated a program to work with local communities to demilitarize their police forces. We brought mothers whose children had been killed by the police to Washington, D.C., to have meetings at the White House, Congress, and the Judiciary, and to hold press conferences and rallies. We continue to work closely with these women to keep the mobilizations moving forward and get their voices into the media.

Beyond militarism domestically and internationally, CODEPINK has also become involved in the ongoing Israeli-Palestinian conflict. We've been standing up for Palestinian rights and trying to move the U.S. government away from unconditional support of the right-wing government in Israel.

I first went to Israel as a teenager right after the 1967 War and lived in a kibbutz. There were many things I loved about the experience: the collective living, the working in the fields, the healthy lifestyle, the socialist values of working for the collective good. But at the same time, I was appalled at the tremendous racism against Arabs. The more I probed, the more uncomfortable I became.

On the other hand, my parents were great supporters of Israel, so I was reluctant to take it on. But in 2006, when the Israelis invaded Lebanon and caused so much damage to that country, I went to Lebanon and saw, firsthand, the devastating effects of Israel's bombing.

Then came the 2009 invasion of Gaza, which was a turning point for me. Arriving in Gaza a week after the invasion ended, I couldn't believe the level of destruction, the sheer brutality, the horror left in the invasion's wake. I devoted myself, full-time, to trying to stop my government from supporting the Israeli military.

Through CODEPINK, we organized seven trips to Gaza, delivering material aid, building playgrounds, and connecting with women's groups. We became involved in a movement to boycott Israeli goods, particularly those produced in the illegal Israeli settlements on stolen Palestinian land. We took on a very successful Israeli cosmetic company, Ahava, whose factory was located inside one of these settlements. We pressured stores not to carry Ahava products, affecting the company's bottom line, and eventually pushed the company to move its factory out of the settlement.

We also had success joining with others in a campaign against SodaStream and its settlement factory. Under pressure, SodaStream announced it was moving its factory. Our new campaigns focus on ReMax, a U.S.-based real estate company selling houses inside the settlements, and Airbnb, a home rental company that allows users to list rentals in settlements.

These campaigns are very tangible, very successful, and in the process we educate people about the plight of Palestinians. We are able to expose the fact that our government supports Israel with $3 billion of our tax dollars every year, money that allows Israel to keep building new settlements in Palestinian territory—making it impossible for a solution to emerge.

Our work in conflict areas around the world puts us in constant tension with pro-war forces inside the United States, or what President Eisenhower called the military-industrial complex. Weapons manufacturers and contractors that profit from war have powerful lobbies that provide them easy access to the White House and Congress. On the diplomatic side, the budget of the State Department and all our international aid programs is less than 10 percent of the Pentagon budget.

That's why peace activists are such an essential counterweight to the military mindset. But we need to be stronger, more effective, more determined. We have to build a movement independent of political parties.

To reach a broader audience, we have to convince the public that we will never have the funds we need for education and healthcare or for rebuilding our infrastructure and confronting the crisis of global warming if we continue to spend $750 billion a year on the military. We have to show the tradeoffs, while at the same time showing that the all the money we spend on the military is not making us safer. We can take just one unnecessary weapons system, the F-35, which will cost us a trillion dollars, as an example. According to the National Priorities Project, eliminating this one weapon could provide free college education for all young people for over two decades.

While reality proves that war is not a solution, our society glorifies the war machine and the warriors. Those who fight wars—including unjust wars such as those in Vietnam or Iraq—are considered heroes. "Thank you for your service" is a constant refrain for soldiers, as if military service is the only kind of service that is valued. Peacemakers, on the other hand, are usually belittled, rejected, or ignored. If you are trying to bring in a voice of compassion, caring, and peace, you're often treated as a crazy person— even downright un-American—and marginalized. We at CODEPINK have received heaps of hate mail and dozens of death threats over the years. We've even been physically beaten up—at home and abroad—by those who see peacemakers as threatening.

When I am feeling demoralized, I think of my peasant friends in Central America struggling to rebuild from the ravages of war, surviving on a couple of dollars a day. They don't have the luxury of giving up. I think of my friends in Iraq who, because of our invasion, have been killed, maimed, displaced, and made refugees. If they have survived, they don't have the luxury of giving up. I think of political prisoners in places like Egypt, rotting in sordid cells, not knowing if they will ever be freed. They don't have the luxury of giving up.

I remind myself of the terrible suffering that others throughout history have endured in their fights for justice, such as Nelson Mandela, who spent twenty-seven years in prison. My sacrifices have been nothing compared to that! So I try to keep pushing myself to do more.

Some people, who see CODEPINK going to dangerous places like Afghanistan or Yemen or confronting war criminals such as Henry Kissinger or Donald Rumsfeld, say we are fearless. That's not true. We are afraid. One of my dearest colleagues, Marla Ruzicka, was killed by a roadside bomb in Iraq. We don't want to pay that price.

When a group of us visited the tribal areas of Pakistan to meet with family members of people who had been killed by drone strikes, we were fearful. The U.S. ambassador told us that the Taliban were going to try to kill us by loading explosives onto camels and sending them into the rallies we would be attending. We were all afraid, but after long discussions, we decided to take the risk because we wanted the Pakistani people to know that we were so opposed to our government's policy that we would risk our own lives to tell them so. We also reasoned that while we could turn back and not take the risk, the people who lived there, the people being targeted by our drones, didn't have that option.

When we disrupt meetings of war makers or interrupt high officials, we're also afraid—afraid we'll get hurt by security guards or angry attendees at rallies, afraid that it might not be the right thing to do. The time I interrupted President Obama during a foreign policy speech in 2013, my heart was pounding so hard I thought it would jump out of my body. And there was a little voice in my head saying, "Don't do it; don't do it." But I went ahead and stood my ground, criticizing the president for the death of so many civilians with drone warfare and for the Guantanamo detentions. "That woman is worth listening to," Obama responded, as I was escorted out of the room.

We push ourselves to find the right balance between fear and courage. Fear would have you sit home and do nothing. You have to step out beyond your comfort zone. That's the only way you realize, "OK, I did that, and it was helpful to our cause. I think I could do a little more."

Some of the bravest peacemakers are those who put their bodies between warring factions, without waiting for the green light from bureaucratic UN agencies. Christian Peacemaker Teams have done this in Palestine; Peace Brigades International has groups in Honduras. We need to multiply these efforts. I envision that one day we will have creative, unarmed peace forces that can mobilize quickly to intervene to stop conflicts before they spiral out of control. Consider the carnage going on in Syria. Wouldn't it be wonderful if we could mobilize a hundred thousand people to converge on the borders of Syria and start linking arms to demand that all sides stop the madness?

I love my work. I don't get up every day thinking, "Oh no, today I have to try to stop war again." I'm excited each day to participate in movements to make the world better. It's a tremendous honor and privilege. I know that my friends overseas also do their work with tremendous joy. It's amazing how much joking and laughter you hear among human rights activists in places such as Bahrain, or Honduras, or even Iraq. I take inspiration from the people I work with. My colleagues are literally the best people in the world—from Archbishop Desmond Tutu, to the young Pakistani Nobel Peace Prize winner Malala Yousafzai, to countless unnamed grassroots activists. Working for peace allows you to interact with some of the most wonderful people on the planet.

Some people say that we are fighting a battle we can never win. "War has always been with us and will always be. It's human nature," they say. But people said similar things about slavery, the oppression of women, and all kinds of injustices of the past. Certainly we can evolve beyond war. At some point in our evolution as a human species, people must rise up globally and declare, "We've had enough of war; it's time for peace." Being part of this evolutionary process is indeed a great gift.

Chapter 4

Liberation Theology

BLASE BONPANE

At the end of World War II, I was sixteen. There was near-zero opposition to that war from the public. Serving in the high school ROTC, we thought much of our training was funny. Can you imagine the huge mob of service people and civilians at Hollywood and Vine as we celebrated victory on August 15, 1945? The cities of Japan had just been firebombed to annihilation, followed by two atom bombs at Hiroshima and Nagasaki. Everyone was cheering.

"Those bombs saved so many lives!" The military propaganda of that day has been repudiated internationally by scores of scholars for more than seventy years. On the contrary, this was the beginning of a military holocaust that has since taken some thirty million lives. Prophetic words spoken by a highly interventionist former general and then President of the United States, Dwight Eisenhower, expressed the reality of perpetual war to the present.

> Every gun that is made, every warship launched, every rocket fired signifies, in the final sense, a theft from those who hunger and are not fed, those who are cold and not clothed. This world in arms is not spending money alone. It is spending the sweat of its laborers, the genius of its scientists, the hopes of its children. This is not a way of life at all in any true sense. Under the cloud of threatening war, it is humanity hanging from a cross of iron.

Then it was off to college at the University of Southern California. I had expressed my desire since tenth grade at Loyola High. I had told my parents of my intention to become a Maryknoll priest. They would have none of it. My mother thought that nothing could be worse than a vow of celibacy. Anticlericalism is strong among Southern Italians. My dad said, "If I had five sons and one was an idiot he could become a priest. You belong in my law office!"

So I became a member of Kappa Sigma Fraternity in the midst of a triumphalist return of veterans and a hyped-up fraternity row. Having played football at Loyola High I went out for spring practice at USC. Suddenly, I began to receive a check. What is this? It's for erasing a blackboard in room 247. I was beginning to understand money and football. I began engaging in practice with All-American champs. I was totally out of my depth. After one of many failed efforts at fullback I heard the famous coach Jeff Cravath say, "We are going to have to prune off some of the dead wood." He was talking about me and perhaps a few others. That was one of many times that being fired was a great blessing.

But an interesting thing happened before I left that team, the Marine Corps arrived in the locker room after practice. "We are going to recruit Marine officers from the finest football teams in the U.S.," they said. So I joined the U.S. Marine Reserve as a member of the Platoon Leaders Class. We trained at Quantico, Virginia, during the summer months. I received my honorable discharge on February 21, 1950. I put in an application for Maryknoll Seminary.

The Korean War began on June 25, 1950. Many of the young men I trained with at Quantico had not received their discharge. They were sent to Korea, and a substantial number never came home. Seminary studies required eight years after college. I was happy to be away from parental control and to be preparing for international service for peace and justice. Ordination was on June 14, 1958. Cardinal Francis Spellman of New York was our ordaining prelate. He was also Military Vicar of the United States and supported the Korean War, and later supported the Vietnam War. I was not yet aware of the enormous harm the so called Just War Theology had done to the human race. I am delighted with the Vatican gathering of April 2016, which literally bombed the Just War Theology as centuries of approval for imperial holocausts.

My first priestly assignment was to recruit seminary students and funds for Maryknoll. I covered the Midwest area of the United States, speaking in high schools and colleges and begging for funds at Sunday Masses. I finally received my mission assignment. Maryknoll leadership had determined that much of our history had been in the service of really poor and uneducated people. They decided it was time for us to go to those who just might be leading their nations in the future. The determination was to send some missioners to serve the university students in the third world. Therefore, my assignment included first going to Georgetown University in Washington, D.C., to get an advanced degree in Latin American Studies and then going to Guatemala to serve the students at the National University of San Carlos.

This experience was a great boost to my consciousness of the military industrial complex. Classes were in the evening and often taught by moonlighting members of the State Department or the CIA. Many of the Jesuits were in complete sync with the war in Vietnam. The few exceptions included people such as Father Richard McSorley and his close friend Father Daniel Berrigan.

The stench of the Indochina disaster raised our consciousness, and by 1965 we were demonstrating in front of the White House. We were immediately labeled as Reds, people cursed at us, gave us the finger, and determined that we were traitors. A half-century later we find a far more conscious citizenry . . . but at what a great cost!

I began to understand that many issues labeled as "Left" should simply be called ethical. Peacemaking is called Left. It is not Left; it is the essence of the Beatitudes. This game had gone on for years in Latin America. Those fighting for the poor were categorized as subversives and killed by the hundreds of thousands. Our government is completely aware of this game and continues to play it with a few new words, including *terrorist*. Free translation of Communist: OK to kill. Free translation of Terrorist: OK to kill. It's tragic that our government institutions are not credible. The CIA tells us that our drones don't kill noncombatants?

Arriving in Guatemala, I was mentored by the great Sister Miriam Peter of Maryknoll. She was the most knowledgeable person regarding the armed revolution. Talk about sexism in the Church. Because I was a priest, Cardinal Casariego gave me official papers to direct the University Catholic Center (El Crater) and Cursillos de Capacitacion Social (Workshops on Social Justice) throughout Guatemala. I told Sister about this document and assured her that she was in charge. I was simply a newcomer with a piece of paper. Together with very dedicated students we brought those workshops to the indigenous people of Guatemala. The focus was on literacy, health, and labor organization. The armed rebels were aware of our programs and warned us that we would never be tolerated by the military. They were correct.

After many successful programs in the departments of Huehuetenango, Quiche, and elsewhere, our Center was bombed; our students were listed as subversives. Some left the country and some joined the armed revolution. I was expelled from the country by church and state. My book—*Guerrillas of Peace: Liberation Theology and the Central American Revolution*—a popularization of my doctoral dissertation, tells this story in detail. I was ordered to appear at the Maryknoll Headquarters in New York. Under threat of suspension, the Superior General assigned me to Hawaii. Landing in Honolulu, I was informed that the gag order the superior gave me was not a threat. It was a mandate: no speaking regarding Latin America, no writing regarding Latin America, no organizing regarding Latin America. This order was unacceptable in conscience. Lives in Guatemala were dependent on my speaking and writing. My response to the superior in Hawaii was, "When is the next plane to the States?" I took that plane and went to Washington, D.C., where the *Washington Post* had expressed interest in my story. After a meeting of several hours with the editorial board, the *Post* published a major front page report (February 4, 1968) with my byline: "A Priest in Guatemala." I explained that Guatemala was our Latin Vietnam. A few days later, I read in the same newspaper that I had unilaterally separated myself from the Maryknoll Fathers.

That same month, February 1968, Dan Berrigan invited me to spend a week speaking to the students at Cornell University where he served as a professor. I was honored to get to know him as a very sensitive and compassionate person. At a host of campus gatherings my talks were titled "The Guatemalan Guerrillas and the Revolutionary Priest" and "The Gringo and the Guerrillas."

Dan was thoroughly disappointed with the performance of Church and State at that time. He had recently returned from Hanoi with Howard Zinn and brought some U.S. captives back to the homeland. We developed a friendship there at Cornell. Dan was an intellectual giant, superb poet, and moral revolutionary. Sometime after Dan completed his prison term, Theresa and I had dinner with him, together with a leader in Physicians for Social Responsibility and his wife. Dan had written a widespread media piece chiding his fellow priest, the former Trappist Monk Ernesto Cardenal, for serving as Sandinista minister of culture in Nicaragua. "No, No, Ernesto," wrote Dan Berrigan making it clear that he opposed Ernesto's participation. Of course, Pope John Paul II also chided Ernesto Cardenal publicly when he visited Nicaragua. But Theresa and I were working regularly with Ernesto Cardenal and considered his work with the Sandinistas as very positive and effective in making the revolution humane.

Dan was so upset at that dinner that he left the table and departed. What we failed to consider was that whenever his brother Phil was in prison Dan was very upset. Had we known that, we might have avoided a difficult discussion about Ernesto's role. And painful discussion. This incident was later followed by *abrazos* and our continuing love for Dan.

The action of that amazing year, 1968, was unending. Phil Berrigan asked me to attend a meeting to discuss a major action. Thirteen of us met and discussed the matter of attacking the Catonsville, Maryland, draft board. Nine agreed. I was not one of them. I explained that I had requests from universities all over the country to explain what was going on in Guatemala and that I did not care to risk years of silence in prison. I have never regretted that decision. Many of us served on the Berrigan Defense Committee and were present at the famous Catonsville Trial.

It is hard to reject an offer to participate in a historic action but personal discernment is critical for everyone in the movement to avoid peer pressure. "Can you top this?" While on the road speaking in St. Louis, Professor Donald Bray approached me asking if I would consider teaching at California State University, Los Angeles. So after a year of nationwide speaking I began my position as professor of Latin America Studies in Los Angeles. It was January 1969. The faculty were very cooperative in covering any classes I was unable to teach because of speaking engagements during 1969.

As the school year came to an end in June, I was asked to meet with a group of four students from UCLA. They said, "We are hiring you." I said, "You have no authority to hire me." They said, "Yes, we do." Then they explained a new Ford Foundation program called The Humanistic and Educational Needs of the Academic Community (HENAC). This was a fifteen-unit course of "student directed learning" and the students were allowed to select the faculty. So I accepted a full-time teaching position at UCLA. Peace demonstrations were loud and constant on campus. At one anti-draft demonstration, I saw the LAPD breaking windows from inside the campus draft office. I immediately reported this provocateur action to radio news. Then there was the Black Panther shootout in Los Angeles. The *Los Angeles Times* reported my presence at the scene. Oh yes, our governor Ronald Reagan was not happy with five of us on the University of California faculties. As a member of the Board of Regents, he asked that Angela Davis, Mike Tiger, Richard Flacks, William Allen, and I have our positions "reexamined." That was the end of my UCLA position.

But there is a blessing next to the wound. I had met former Maryknoll Sister, Theresa Killeen. She was the blessing and with stunning courage, graciousness, and unsurpassed organizing ability has been my wife of forty-six years. I have eternal gratitude for her constant love, child-raising mastery, and fearlessness. Theresa heard of my being "not rehired" at UCLA just after our three-day honeymoon. Not having a job, I decided to run for U.S. Congress in 1970 as a Democrat. Several of us determined to challenge any Democrat who had not come out against the war in Vietnam. My choice was to oppose incumbent Edward Roybal in the primary. I was his only opponent. Looks like he won.

I sought out my Freedom of Information files from government agencies. A host of material was forthcoming from the FBI, CIA, DIA, and other agencies. I discovered just how active J. Edgar Hoover was at spreading malicious gossip. I would apply to a university, a faculty position was offered, and I was told to order books for the upcoming semester. Alas, after a few more days the administration would call to say that, "The courses have been canceled." "The department could not afford another member." I even expected them to say that the department was eliminated. J. Edgar had signed chits in response to academia's investigations. The governor's denunciation of my work against the draft gave state approval to the federal opinion that I was a "bad guy."

I was hired by the Santa Paula School board as community coordinator of the bilingual-bicultural program for the district. They were enthusiastic about this new role in a bilingual community. Just before reporting to work at the school district, I received a call from the United Farm Workers asking me to celebrate a Mass in the field for a farmworker who had died. I accepted. Santa Paula is the lemon capital of the world. It immediately became a huge lemon in our newly married lives. Congressman Teague circulated negative material about me to his constituents. The *Santa Paula Chronicle* had headlines on the radical background of the new bilingual coordinator. Major newspapers picked up the story.

Theresa and I began what might be called the "Novitiate Year" of our marriage. We were pariahs in the white community that ran the city. I was to report to the district office every day to "count paper clips." My work as community coordinator for bilingual-bicultural education was greatly curtailed. School board meetings that generally had an attendance of four or five people were now drawing five hundred citizens. "Get these communists out of town," was a basic theme. I probably made things worse when responding to the board speaking first in Spanish and then following with an English translation. Theresa suffered terribly during this painful period. Petitions were signed to rid the community of our kind. She was insulted while shopping as well. We had an unexpected visitor. "I'm Rev. Chris Hartmire from the United Farm Workers Union." What followed was an invitation from Cesar Chavez to move to the new headquarters of UFW at La Paz, California. "Cesar would like you to start a Farm Workers University at the headquarters."

Leroy explained that it would be a place where farm workers could study anything they wanted. "They will select the subjects; you will make every effort to see that they get what they asked for." For me, this was an invitation to liberation from an oppressive position. Theresa was less enthusiastic but accepted the challenge. We moved with our year-old baby Colleen to a miserable shack on a hillside at the La Paz headquarters. It was not free from rodents, wind, or rain. It trembled each time the freight trains rumbled through on nearby tracks. And what about the Farm Workers University? Well, these were some of the most tumultuous years of the UFW. Each day involved some serious crisis. The most treasured part of this was unexpectedly to work on a face to face daily basis with Cesar Chavez.

First he asked me to reestablish the UFW newspaper *El Malcriado* (The Brat). We tried various formats. Who is it for? Well, it's for farm workers and their supporters. Let's do bilingual. First we must do many different leaflets for farm workers and their supporters. We have to deal with daily attacks from the Teamsters Union, the growers, the government, the police, and a racist environment here in the San Joaquin Valley and elsewhere. In spite of endless leaflets and information sheets the newspaper was published. Theresa managed the Taller Grafico, the graphics department. Bumper stickers, posters, buttons and all promotional materials of the union. What happened to the Farm Workers University? Just one urgency after another.

I became a troubleshooter for Cesar. "Romolo Avilos has just been shot and killed by the Migra in Livingston. Go up there with Dolores Huerta and find out what happened." "Let's you and I leave tonight for San Francisco and buy the Chapman Press. We can move the whole thing down here and print all of our own material." We made the trip and bought the Chapman Press chauffeured by former police officer Andy Anzaldua and a few police dogs for added security.

Federal agents made a call to visit our headquarters at La Paz, California. They explained that $30,000 had been paid to assassinate Cesar. They urged us to establish an armed security team. Andy Anzaldua was in charge of that. My assignment for security was to drive a Jeep around the property during the wee hours of the night. I was armed with a pistol and a shotgun. Guard duty was shared with other members of the administration. Ironic? I was never armed during a bloody revolution in Guatemala and now I was armed to protect a major nonviolent revolutionary.

Cesar asked Theresa and me to travel to the San Fernando Valley to establish a UFW promotional center for funds and volunteers. We did that until a despondent Cesar told us that he no longer could pay our rent or even the five dollar a week "salary." The Teamster battle and the grower animosity were devastating. While I was leafleting in a parking lot at California State University, Northridge, a professor approached me and said, "Why are you not teaching here?" I realized that it was time to go back to academia. Our work in the San Fernando Valley for UFW continued but now with some income from teaching. My old friend and seminary colleague Father Miguel d'Escoto visited us and explained what was going on in Nicaragua and how he was now foreign minister for the rebel forces (FSLN). "I have two superiors, one at Maryknoll and the other in the Sandinista revolution." We remained in touch with Miguel during the 1970s and invited the rebel minister of culture, Father Ernesto Cardenal to speak on campus.

Sandinista demonstrations began in Los Angles and continued until July 19, 1979, with victory. I celebrated Mass that day at St. Joseph's Church in Los Angeles. The leader of the demonstrations in Los Angeles, Manuel Valle, went up to the consulate of the Somoza government and reminded them they had just lost their positions. Unbelievably, the newly defeated officials gave Manuel the keys and walked out. Shortly thereafter, Manuel approached me and said, "Blase, let's go to Managua and I'll get my papers as the new Consul in Los Angeles." We went. Managua was full of joy. We met with the victorious comandantes and knew that Nicaragua would have a major role in our lives thereafter. Rosario Murillo, the wife of Daniel Ortega, asked us to bring people to visit the revolution. She also knew that a brutal mercenary army was formed by the Reagan administration to destroy the Sandinistas. Theresa and I immediately began to send delegations to Nicaragua. In short order, our home was uninhabitable by virtue of political activity. Theresa gathered some of our best organizers to get us out of the house, form an organization, and get an office. We opened the Office of the Americas at St. Augustine's Church in Santa Monica in April 1983.

A solidarity movement unlike previous peace movements began sending thousands of people to witness the Contra War in Nicaragua. The founding of the Office of the Americas was Theresa's doing. Her organizational ability made the impossible possible. We began with no funds at all. The response to our request for delegations was immediate. We did not seek out celebrities, they just came and offered their help. Martin Sheen, Haskell Wexler, Edward Asner, Jackson Browne, Kris Kristofferson, David Clennon, Oliver Stone, and many others. Haskell Wexler did a full-length feature film during the fighting in Nicaragua, *Liberation*. Oliver Stone spoke to us before making the film *Salvador*, Edward Asner had recently lost one of the most popular programs on TV, *Lou Grant*, because he submitted a check for the wounded rebels in El Salvador. Martin Sheen insisted on giving blood in Managua. He came with us in spite of family opposition. Theresa, always the bravest, brought teenage delegates to see the war after getting detailed approval from their parents.

The Committee in Solidarity with the People of El Salvador (CISPES) was in charge of visits to El Salvador. We joined them and had the honor of meeting the Jesuits at the University of Central America who were subsequently murdered with their housekeeper and her daughter. The greatest challenge in my life was the International March for Peace in Central America, 1985–86. A Norwegian doctor contacted me and said, "We would like you to lead the U.S. contingent of a march from Panama to Mexico for Peace." I accepted. We had a planning meeting in Vienna, Austria, with representatives from Europe and Latin America. All of the experts, including Nobel Laureate Adolfo Perez Esquivel, said it was an impossible venture. Shortly thereafter some four hundred of us from thirty nations met in Panama City and the march was on. The U.S. delegation was by far the largest. A documentary film of the march, *Viva la Paz*, was produced and directed by one of the marchers, Kelly Holland. It received a gold medal at one of the great film festivals. The march is also covered in various books listed near the end of this chapter.

We were in Managua the night that Mrs. Chamorro won the election in 1990. The message of the United States was so very clear, "Elect Mrs. Chamorro or the Contra War will continue!" The Nicaraguans voted with a gun to their heads. There was no cheering in Managua that evening. As the UN participated in Central American peace accords, we were jarred by another war, this time in Iraq. Global Exchange asked us to join them on a delegation to Baghdad. As 1990 turned into 1991, we met Yasser Arafat, who explained how Arab leadership had been excluded from the discussions and that the United States wanted this war for the benefit of its corporations. Most scholars today would agree with everything Arafat said to us in that five-hour meeting in Baghdad. Why did the Office of the Americas turn its attention to the Middle East? Because our mission is to address the foreign policy of the United States.

Returning from Baghdad included the one time that Theresa and I together with our son Blase Martin were all arrested at the same time and place. It was in front of the Federal Building in Los Angeles. Hundreds had gathered to say no to bombing Iraq. We blocked the doors of that stately place. So we found ourselves hogtied and on our bellies on the polished marble entrance floor. We were finally taken to holding cells where word of mouth reports told us that the bombing had begun in Iraq. Once again, our government was making clear its frequent motif: "We don't care what you want, we want war, perpetual war." Such was the message I discerned in scores of previous arrests.

It was January 16, 1991. Eighty-eight thousand tons of bombs were dropped on Baghdad, slaughtering children and other noncombatants. It was a massive war crime of the highest order, an aggressive war. It has continued to this day and represents a clear pattern in our wars since 1945. We have won every battle and lost every war. Some thirty million people have been killed in our endless holocaust. It is redux of the Vietnam disaster. The Iraqi soldiers we so carefully trained are in a state of mutiny. We have destroyed the cradle of civilization and given birth to ISIS in a classic case of blowback. A quarter of a century has wasted the lives of innocent people who had hoped to live in peace. It has wasted the lives and the minds of our combatants. It has destroyed any ability for our nation to deliver health care, education, services for the poor. But most of all, as the prophet Martin Luther King stated, "Any nation that spends more on armaments than on social betterment is approaching spiritual death." That death is obvious everywhere. It is no surprise to have candidates of little competence and much demagoguery rage about the need for carpet bombing, increased torture, collective punishment including capturing family members of "suspects." Such people are found half-drunk in every bar. What is overwhelming, however, is that millions of our citizens are cheering these blowhards. Yes, that is a sign of spiritual death.

The Clinton years did not stop the killing. Millions died as a result of brutal sanctions, which primarily took the lives of children. The demonstrations continued. The Democratic Party is not now nor has it ever been a party for peace. It is an integral part of the military, industrial, congressional, gun, prison, and pharmaceutical complex.

In the reign of an unelected George Bush, the Twin Towers were attacked by a group of international criminals. Sixty nations immediately asked to help us find any living members of the attack force. Instead of accepting help from the United Nations and the rest of the world, the United States attacked Afghanistan, undoubtedly one of the most stupid military actions in world history. Would we attack Chicago if we knew a group of criminals were hiding there? As in the case of the failed Gulf War, the Taliban of Afghanistan (a group we created to oppose the USSR) are now far larger than they were at the onset of hostilities. The world's largest source of heroin now haunts our nation. In some places heroin deaths outnumber deaths by auto accident. In the midst of the terror and fear of 9/11/01, Theresa announced the formation of the Coalition for World Peace on 9/12/01. She organized the first major demonstration opposing an attack on Afghanistan and she connected with those who had lost family at the Twin Towers, "Families for Peaceful Tomorrows."

From 1991 to the present, the Office of the Americas has fostered demonstrations, speaking engagements, radio and TV programs, and outreach on social media. Personally, I was struck with two cancers in 1999 and 2000. In the wake of surgery and chemo, I found the best therapy was to continue my work for peace as much as possible. Writing and media appearances were the available means. This meant less travel but actually led to far more outreach.

My writings in this post-cancer period include:

The Nicene Heresy—Christendom and War—Reverence and Critique (2016). Christendom refers to the sum total of nations in which the Catholic Church was established as the religion of state. This was a period of a holocaust based on acceptance of a creed. Crusades, Inquisitions, and Conquistadores took the lives of millions of "infidels." The book is also a denunciation of the so-called Just War Theory, which was also roundly condemned at the Vatican Peace Conference of 2016.

Commentary on the Encyclical of Pope Francis, Laudato Si, On the Care of Our Common Home (2015). This commentary sees the environmental concern as an evolution of Liberation Theology without implying that Pope Francis accepts this theological position.

Imagine No Religion (2011). This book is my autobiography.

Civilization Is Possible (2008). These are my collected radio commentaries and interviews about the formation of an international peace system that aired on KPFK (Los Angeles) for the Pacifica Network.

The Central American Solidarity Movement (2005). The Oral History Program of UCLA published this lengthy interview with me.

Common Sense for the Twenty-first Century (2004). Another collection of my radio interviews and commentaries on peace that aired KPFK, Los Angeles.

Guerrillas of Peace on the Air (2002). More peace-building radio commentaries by way of KPFK, Los Angeles.

Guerrillas of Peace, Liberation Theology and the Central American Revolution, third edition (2000). A book about my experience in Guatemala during the revolution of the 1960s.

The day that NAFTA went into effect, January 1, 1994. Jody Evans called and said that a revolution was underway in Chiapas, Mexico, that tanks were in the streets and the Zapatista Revolution was underway. We quickly put a delegation together and went to San Cristobal de las Casas, the scene of the revolt. Clearly, the Indigenous people knew much more about NAFTA than Mr. Clinton. Mexican President Zedillo abrogated section 27 of the Mexican Constitution of 1917, which protected the *ejido* system of community land ownership. Indigenous people began to lose their land to forced sales. When the Mexican government agreed to negotiations with the indigenous people, the Zapatistas agreed on the condition that Bishop Samuel Ruiz Garcia would be their negotiator. It was our privilege to work directly with this international leader for peace and justice during the turbulent times that followed. We never even thought of trying to tell the bishop what to do. He knew what to do. We simply accompanied him through the war zones and negotiating sessions.

February 15, 2003, saw the largest peace demonstration in world history. It was an attempt to speak to "Iniquity Lying to Itself," as is the formula for starting unnecessary, illegal, immoral, and planet-threatening wars. Some thirty million people demonstrated worldwide speaking to moral midgets and money-grubbing warmongers in Washington, D.C. I was privileged to address hundreds of thousands of people jamming the street of our nation's capital.

A translation of our government's response: "We don't care what you want, we want perpetual war." What is to be done? We must be proud of the peace movement and the heroic efforts made every day to end the useless, counterproductive evil of war. We are very pleased with the recent meeting at the Vatican denouncing Just War Theory. This sham had been used by Empire and Christendom for centuries to give approval to aggressive wars. Many who opposed such wars as unjust were called traitors or infidels. American Exceptionalism is simply a contemporary version of Just War Theory. The necessary marriage for this coming epoch is to join the peace movement and the environmental movement into one entity. Any movement that calls itself "environmental" without demanding an end to a trillion-dollar "modernization" of nuclear weapons is not worthy of the name. We see and accept the horror of global warming. But without confronting the impending disaster of nuclear winter, we fail to salvage planet earth.

While we appreciate the concern some in the corporate sector have shown for the environment, we must continue to tell the whole truth: the military at peace is the biggest polluter on the globe. The military at war is a planet killer. And what about the domestic scene? Black Lives Matter, complete reform of our police culture, respect for the rights enshrined in the Universal Declaration of Human Rights, and a total reversal of elements of the National Defense Authorization Act that President Obama says will not go into effect on his watch. The Obama era is over. What's to become of this dictatorial mandate in Age of Trump?

There is currently a coalition of progressive and conservative groups organizing together against this attack on democracy: PANDA (People Against the National Defense Authorization Act). Its mission is to nonviolently block and void Sections 1021 and 1022 of the 2012 NDAA. The lead plaintiff in *Hedges v. Obama* (the case challenging the NDAA), Tangerine Bolen, declared:

> We are no longer a nation ruled by laws. We are a nation ruled by people who have so steeped themselves in a false narrative that at the same time they are exponentially increasing the ranks of terrorists, they are destroying the rule of law itself. It is madness upon madness—the classic tale of becoming the evil you purport to fight while believing you remain righteous.

The BDS (Boycott, Divest, and Sanction) movement in solidarity with Palestine is another clear example of the power of nonviolence. It was a huge success in South Africa and is proving successful as applied to Israel. We must not allow frightened academic administrators, state, or federal governments to outlaw this time-honored, deeply American mode of protest.

Time is short. We must stop those who think the nation is something to be worshiped. It is not an idol and must not become one. Our nation must be a group of self-governing citizens who also see themselves as citizens of an interdependent world. Only then might we bring an end to the scourge of war.

Chapter 5

Paradigm for Peace

KRISTIN Y. CHRISTMAN

Ever since I was five, I've been interested in the international: dolls, languages, clothing, foods, history, music, geography. It was disappointing to learn that wars ruined the lives of people from these nations that I loved, nations that these dolls, so friendly and beautiful, represented.

It wasn't my nature to love one group and hate another. In third grade, nearly every girl in my classroom divided into two rival gangs that hated each other. Girls would ask me, "Are you in Marianne's gang or Lisa's gang?" I told them I was friends with both Marianne and Lisa and liked playing with both. I didn't see the point of the gangs.

The wisdom of animals made more sense to me. I loved how my dog was never mean, she didn't talk on and on, she never worried about abstract human matters, she didn't have to attend school, and her species never waged war.

My mom helped people feel good about themselves. I remember a field trip in middle school. My mom had volunteered to come along. When she got on the bus, I was dismayed to see her cheerfully sit down beside a boy who was unpleasant, mentally disabled, poor, and rumored to have lice. All the kids avoided him, and befriending him would only gain their ridicule.

I saw my mom chatting with him, and over the course of the ride my dismay faded away, and I felt quite proud of her. She later told me, "I thought he looked like someone who needed company." Apparently, they had a nice conversation about his pets. Without making a big deal out of anything, she helped someone who was rejected by others.

My dad, a physical education teacher, would figure out what was wrong with a car and fix it for a fraction of the cost at a garage. In the winter, he'd walk down the hill and help push cars up that were stuck on ice. And my mom, if she were president, she wouldn't have any forty million dollar inaugural ball or forty thousand dollar dress. She'd sew her own beautiful dress for forty dollars.

Once some neighbor's kids wrote mean things about my family on the road. I remember watching my dad walk down to their house. He didn't refuse to communicate. He didn't insult or attack. He spoke seriously with them and made sure they understood the hurt and anger they'd caused. Then he cleaned up the graffiti. I remember watching him clean it up and feeling so proud and safe that he was taking care of everything. They never bothered us again.

And when something broke in our house, like our sump pump, he wouldn't go down and bang around claiming he'd exhausted every resort and must attack the pump. He patiently focused on understanding the problem and fixing it. Instead of wasting mechanical minds designing weapons, we ought to be using a mechanic's mind to create workable, nonviolent foreign policy.

If my parents were leading foreign policy, they'd initiate fun activities to create international friendships: swinging on traveling rings, snowshoeing in the sunshine, outdoor games with laughing, friendly people. Joyful fun is an overlooked remedy to hatred, greed, and alienation.

As you read through my *Paradigm for Peace* model, I think you'll see my parents' values coming through, values unrepresented in our nation's policies.

School was also a major influence. It filled me with rage. I felt like a caged lion, forced to spend seven hours per day at school, working into the night on homework, and surviving on little sleep while sadly craving to play outside and pursue my hobbies. The endless daily grind of producing and receiving assignments felt like I was being forced to swallow my own vomit. Yet the system shames children into believing that to resist is irresponsible and wrong.

One useful experience was a huge middle school Revolutionary War project assigned over spring break in 1981. It ruined vacation, but one segment involved reading a British soldier's perspective. I'd never before read the enemy's point of view. Yet this enemy seemed so reasonable and likeable. It had never occurred to me before that the British had been anything but wrong.

Also relevant was a trip to the UN for a Nicaragua program sponsored by the Methodist Church. At the conference, a kind Nicaraguan woman explained that many Sandinista social reforms had been helping the poor, but reforms were undermined by U.S. support for the Contras. It sank in that the news doesn't tell the full story.

After majoring in Russian at Dartmouth College, I attended Brown University, but it was maddening to be learning material irrelevant to peace while bombs were destroying Baghdad in the 1991 Persian Gulf War. Extremely depressed, I cut short my studies, got a secretarial job, and began reading independently about conflict. After futilely seeking foreign policy work, I enrolled in SUNY Albany's public administration program and studied organizational behavior, cultural analysis, decision making, and negotiation, all relevant to peacemaking.

When 9/11 struck, I was frightened, but even more, I was enraged by the U.S. government's violent reaction and sickened by the animosity between Americans of conflicting views. When the United States began bombing Afghanistan, I ran out and ripped off the red, white, and blue decoration I'd had hanging on my mailbox since 9/11.

Fortunately, U.S. congressman Dennis Kucinich had previously proposed a bill to establish a U.S. Department of Peace. The bill was inspiring, but I thought the department's structure should be reorganized. So, shortly after 9/11, while my young sons were napping, I sat on the bed between them and drew shapes and scribbles as I considered which circumstances motivate killing and how to organize solutions to violence.

This list of motives suddenly reminded me of theories about why employees don't work optimally: their needs aren't being met, needs for appreciation, security, fair pay, caring, stimulation, freedom, etc. Employers can most effectively motivate workers, not through threats, but by meeting workers' needs. Similarly, while preventing violence sometimes requires force, threats, or physical barriers, policymakers can encourage peacefulness by changing circumstances to fulfill needs.

My model has four parts: Roots of Violence, Escalators of Violence, Three Facets of Solutions, and an underlying cooperative, open-minded "Quest" attitude of thought and discussion. After all, an effective Department of Peace requires productive inner dynamics, without rivalry, intimidation, and exclusion.

I named the model *Paradigm for Peace* and mailed it with a seventy-page U.S. Department of Peace Strategic Plan to Congressman Kucinich. I was thrilled when he called to express his gratitude! I didn't tell him, but since the mailing my husband had killed himself. In a bewildering time, the congressman's call meant a lot.

In 2003, I mailed a rationale against the proposed U.S. invasion of Iraq and an invitation to join in cooperative Quest Dialogue to a hundred acquaintances. Nothing happened until I directly asked a best friend from Dartmouth, Sandy, if she would do a Quest Dialogue by e-mail about our diverging opinions over the invasions. She kindly agreed.

Unlike antagonistic debates in which each side tries overpowering the other, cooperative dialogue involves working together as partners to access the truth. Our dialogue followed rules: uphold bold amiability, seek to understand the other, sincerely step in each other's shoes, state opinions freely and kindly, don't call each other "naive" or make snide remarks, question what we don't understand, talk candidly about disagreements, and if ideas have weaknesses, try to strengthen them together.

For weeks, we exchanged lengthy, amiable e-mails. We found we had similar values but differing assumptions. For example, I was furiously opposed to the invasion of Iraq, and Sandy was moderately for it. Yet we were both driven by compassion. She's hawkish about protecting people from torture and execution. I hate how war destroys people. Sandy assumed President Saddam Hussein wouldn't negotiate; I assumed he would. Sandy assumed U.S. policymakers were analyzing roots of violence, while I assumed otherwise, partly based on my graduate project on U.S. policy toward Angola. Rather than arguing over incomplete information, pro- and antiwar activists and reporters should cooperatively investigate facts. Would Saddam Hussein negotiate? Are policymakers analyzing roots of violence? Do Iraqis want help?

I then read numerous library books and sorted information through the *Paradigm for Peace* model. By day I'd play with my children and homeschool, at naptime I'd read and take notes, while washing dishes I'd jot down ideas, and through the night I'd type, sometimes while holding my sleeping baby.

In 2011, I finished writing *The Taxonomy of Peace: A Comprehensive Classification of the Roots and Escalators of Violence and 650 Solutions for Peace*. My focus, using a Quest attitude, was to run the U.S./Mideastern conflicts through the *Paradigm for Peace* model, but I examined many other conflicts and also ran the U.S. Civil War, World War II/Germany, and the Cold War through the model.

Help came unexpectedly when my Dartmouth advisor, Barry Scherr, kindly volunteered to review the 2,500 page project. After receiving his thoughtful advice and making modifications, I worked hard trying to get it published, but unsuccessfully. I wrote journal articles, but also in vain. I even presented the model to Senator Gillibrand's summer staff.

Fortunately, in 2014 the *Albany Times Union* began publishing my op-eds on a volunteer basis. I hoped these op-eds could reach people who might not normally read about peace. The editorial page editor, Jay Jochnowitz, took the time to coach me with my writing. Now I've begun condensing the *Taxonomy* to make it more publishable.

My work is deeply influenced by observations as a mother raising children, and I value topics of love, joy, play, adventure, parenting, friendship, meaningful purpose, self-worth, fear, and tension as relevant to international relations. Peace ideally begins in childhood; patterns of human relations can last a lifetime. It bothers me intensely to see hateful habits of adults toward children, as if children's behavior could ever justify this clouding over of the heart. To think that young children are taught they're bad for wanting to be held by loving arms but good for sitting isolated with toys.

So many are boxed in by negative tradition, doing what others do, doing what was done to them, releasing negative tension onto their children, and displacing goals of love with timelines of accomplishment. It takes great energy to break out of that habit and radiate loving strength, even while correcting a child's behavior.

Nations, too, require tremendous creative energy to break free from hateful habits. Now, that's what I call freedom.

Paradigm for Peace

ROOTS OF VIOLENCE

We wouldn't kick a car to make it go. If something were wrong with it, we'd figure out which system wasn't working and why: Are the wheels spinning in mud? How's the battery? Sparkplugs? Are air and fuel getting through? But in terms of dealing with so-called enemies, the United States is just kicking the car. It's relying on force without figuring things out.

Paradigm for Peace calls for us to cooperatively and impartially examine Aggressive and Defensive Roots of Violence on all sides of conflict. People will disagree over whether they're fighting aggressively or defensively, but it's not necessarily important to pinpoint who's fighting for which motivation. What's necessary is that our foreign policy have a standard approach that addresses both Aggressive and Defensive Roots of Violence in opponents and ourselves. Otherwise, U.S. policy will be either naive and vulnerable or unnecessarily hostile and inattentive to injustices.

Probably right-wing Americans are more aware of enemies' Aggressive Roots of Violence and see the United States as the defending hero. Probably left-wing Americans are more aware of enemies' Defensive Roots of Violence and see the United States as an aggressive bully. But we must examine all motivations, and if we significantly address both sides' Defensive Roots of Violence, it's more likely that those still fighting have primarily Aggressive Roots. We can then cooperate to humanely restrain their violence.

When we understand Defensive Roots of Violence, we shouldn't necessarily excuse the violence, but we should remedy legitimate grievances. When we recognize Aggressive Roots, we shouldn't necessarily respond with hostility. We may have to use force, barriers, or humane confinement to halt such violence, but we also need self-restraint.

As Debra Niehoff writes in *The Biology of Violence*, the particular brain neurochemistry of victims of violence and trauma is strikingly similar to the brain neurochemistry of perpetrators of violence.[1] So while many victims never become aggressors, many aggressors may have once been victims of physical or psychological trauma. In our response to violence, it's important to not create the trauma and fear that spawn aggressive mentalities.

When the United States invades, fires drones, sends weapons for killing, tortures, promotes coups, or imposes sanctions, it's heightening Defensive Roots of Violence by exacerbating injustices and it's heightening Aggressive Roots by brewing a toxic climate of fear and distrust.

Paradigm for Peace examines eight categories of Roots of Violence: life and safety; power and freedom; wealth and possessions; values; love, friendship, and worth; self-potential; joyful tranquility; and truth. To counter mainstream media, I'll emphasize below some key Defensive Roots of Violence in U.S. enemies and Aggressive Roots in the United States. But remember: A full analysis examines Defensive and Aggressive Roots on each side.

Life and Safety

Fear of death is a potent Defensive Root of Violence. Americans understand this with regard to their own fears. Nine-eleven and Iraq's alleged weapons of mass destruction were deemed justification for massive U.S. violence in the Mideast. What is much less understood by Americans is that our so-called enemies also have fears of death that provoke violence. Afghans and Iraqis, fearful of invading U.S. troops, kill in self-defense. But the United States brands them insurgents. Egyptians, fearful of torture and execution, rebel against tyrants. The United States calls them extremists.

North Korea, brutally occupied by Japan, carpet bombed to near obliteration by the United States, and forced to endure three decades of nuclear weapons in South Korea, develops a handful of nuclear weapons. The United States, never having been occupied or carpet bombed but nonetheless requiring four thousand nuclear weapons to feel safe, calls Kim Jong Un crazy and belligerent.

The United States expands NATO into former Soviet territory and sells new members Lockheed Martin Corporation's weaponry. Yet it is Russia that is considered aggressive.

The United States has got to recognize the defensive nature of enemies' actions and work to alleviate enemies' fears of death.

Power and Freedom

Who's fighting for democracy? Are we? Or are they?

In describing 9/11, New York City mayor Rudolph Giuliani claimed: "On one side is democracy, the rule of law, and respect for human life; on the other is tyranny, arbitrary executions, and mass murder. We're right and they're wrong. It's as simple as that."[2] Actually, Giuliani's wrong. Many terrorists are fighting for freedom from tyranny. They're enraged over U.S. provision of money and weapons to Mideastern tyrants, including tyrants of Saudi Arabia, the United Arab Emirates, and Egypt, the origins of eighteen of the nineteen 9/11 terrorists. These tyrants brutally abuse civilians, particularly Islamists, killing thousands and imprisoning tens of thousands.

Islamists are Muslims, some peaceful, some violent, who want to base their government upon the Sharia, a goal with a range of interpretations. Some simply wish for a government that supports Islamic values of fairness, humanity, tolerance, care for the poor, and honesty[3]—values many Americans would accept as secular. In fact, Islamic principles of *shura* (consultation), *ijma* (consensus), and *maslah* (choosing the interpretation of the Sharia that leads to the greatest good) are akin to democratic principles "of the people, by the people, for the people."

Islamists' methods range from nonviolent grassroots service to top-down authoritarianism. Osama bin Laden was loathed by some Islamists for his autocratic nature and stifling of internal debate.[4] And some Islamists call for adherence to strict pre-Islamic ethnic traditions pertaining to clothing, women, and punishments that are not universally accepted as Islamic.

Islamist men and women should be granted political rights and representation and engaged in dialogue. Continued oppression of Islamists is unjust and increases the likelihood that violent, authoritarian Islamists will emerge as leaders.

Wealth and Possessions

Nine-eleven terrorist Mohammad Atta was furious that Egypt's government neglects Cairo's extreme poverty while Egyptian "fat cats" live luxuriously.[5] Alleviating poverty is an Islamic principle.

Meanwhile, greed has been the paramount U.S. Aggressive Root of Violence that has driven U.S. foreign policy since settlement, mining, ranching, and railroad interests were deemed justification for destroying Native Americans and wildlife. With that destruction, land lost its dignity and became like a slave, sold to the highest bidder. Money became a god.

Prior to the Spanish-American War, American leadership became hooked upon Charles Conant's influential 1896 theory that U.S. capitalism will collapse unless the U.S. government works closely with powerful banks and businesses to continually force open foreign markets and investment opportunities to increase profits.[6] Accordingly, foreign leaders have become U.S. enemies simply for failing to conform to U.S. businessmen's desires.[7] Yet economic rivalry is always cloaked with a good versus evil drama. Even now, U.S.-fracked liquid natural gas is shipped to Europe to drive Russian natural gas out of the market, with the alleged noble goal of "rescuing" Europe from dependency on Russia.

For decades, powerful leadership positions in the departments of State and Defense, the CIA, and National Security Council have been intricately connected with social circles of certain wealthy families, including the Rockefeller and Morgan families and their foreign relations council, law firms, investment banks, railroads, airlines, oil, and weapons corporations.[8] The danger is that these social circles, so unrepresentative of Americans, have juxtaposed their obsessions with wealth and their blindness to broader concerns upon foreign policy.

Policymakers must have the guts to eradicate greed's claw in U.S. policy, but we must also caringly uncover the origins of this sickness.

Values

American CEOs may strive to continually increase sales and exports, but many people don't want to be on the receiving end of this, nor do they want the accompanying destruction of Earth and expanding population so necessary for increasing profits.

North Korea is determined to preserve traditional Korean identity and not become a fast-paced, Westernized South Korea. Nineteenth-century Russia experienced major inner conflict over Westernization, with some arguing that the Western emphasis on rationality and individuality severed mind from soul and individual from community.[9]

Hassan al Banna and Mawlana Abul Ala Mawdudi, founders of the Muslim Brotherhood and Jamaat-i-Islami, both perceived Western cultural infiltration as more malignant than Western political intervention. Islamists detest "the emptiness of secular progress represented by Western prosperity."[10]

Benjamin Franklin even noticed American colonists' attraction to Native American life: "No European who has tasted Savage Life can afterwards bear to live in our societies."[11]

Certain technological, social, and humanitarian aspects of Westernization are more greatly appreciated worldwide. Yet there are clearly aspects of non-Westernized cultures that appeal to many, including Americans. The values issue is broader than Americans may realize. With regard to Mideast/ U.S. conflicts, major topics of friction include: consumerism and luxury, urbanization and migration, women's rights and identity, sexuality, family, community, spiritual health, alcohol, and leaders' corruption and dishonesty.

The United States will not significantly progress in international relations if policymakers continue to assume U.S. culture is "exceptional"[12] and ignore how the imposition of culture grates on others' hearts. It must engage in cooperative dialogue, share differing perspectives on strengths and weaknesses of cultures, and discuss how to respect cultures. Cultural exchanges should be a two-way street, where underdeveloped and overdeveloped nations gain insight from each other.

Love, Worth, and Friendship

Alienation frequently appears in terrorists' and U.S. killers' histories. This prickly feeling of daggers aimed at oneself is an absence of caring connection with other living beings, with one's environment, or even with aspects within oneself. It is the feeling of a plant without roots, soil, rain, or sunshine.

Twentieth 9/11 terrorist Zacarias Moussaoui, 2001 shoe bomber Richard Reid, al-Shabaab member Omar Hammami, Algerians in Parisian suburbs, many foreign fighters joining ISIS: all have been targets of anti-Muslim, racist, or classist prejudice. Fifteen of the 9/11 hijackers were from Saudi Arabia's Southwest, an area high in unemployment and stigmatized as socially inferior by the Saudi elite. In Iraq, the Ba'th party attracted the marginalized: lower classes, religious minorities, those uprooted by modernization and urban migration.[13] Much of the Mideast feels alienated by U.S. hatred.

The entire U.S. arsenal doesn't have the power to alleviate alienation.

U.S. inactive indifference toward this alienation is reflected in its inactive indifference toward alienated children within our schools. This alienation factors into depression, anxiety, drug use, poor performance, self-hatred, suicide, and mass shootings. But who cares? Kids are expected to endure their feelings and perhaps eventually channel their rage in war against enemies. Some receive individual counseling, but what teacher is allowed to make friendship building in the classroom a priority over academics?

Nine-eleven terrorist Mohammad Atta, like many male suicide bombers, was misogynistic and alienated from women, viewing them as inferior tempt-resses. Adding to the alienation was his father's directive that his mother not raise Mohammad with affection, "like a girl."[14] There's a common link here with our U.S. policymakers who are alienated from their own and other's hearts and instead admire toughness in foreign policy.

As evidenced by hearts and peace symbols sewn on little girls' clothing and fierce animals and flames on boys' clothing, love and understanding are associated only with the feminine, and the feminine is associated with inferi-ority and weakness. Love and understanding, however, are human qualities, not only feminine qualities. They require great strength, not weakness. If policymakers weren't so afraid of appearing feminine, perhaps they could develop the strength of heart and mind required to actually secure peace.

Self-Potential

U.S. specialization in the arms industry inhibits the self-potential of numerous Americans whose careers are strangled by lack of funding. You want to cure cancer? Protect wildlife? Work for peace? You'll probably be vainly applying for grants or paying your own way. More than half of the federal government's research and development budget is allocated to military research.[15] And in the Mideast, where unemployment fuels violence, billions are allocated, not to job creation, but to U.S. weapons procurement.

Self-potential is also shattered when humans are raised in conditions contrary to human nature. Currently, Americans must sacrifice their child-hood to school, following a mass prescription for human development. Yet such a cookie-cutter approach to our species warps individuality, stunts freedom, love, and joy, and escalates anxiety, apathy, family disconnection, hatred, hopelessness, inner conflict, sedentary lifestyles, sleep deprivation, and violence.

But *that's* not considered psychological violence or an imposition of values. That's allegedly an *opportunity* all children should be grateful for. School doesn't threaten our freedom. *Terrorism* does, right?

And what does this "opportunity" do to inner peace? How does the emphasis on competition and grades help kids learn to value people more than profits? How does the emphasis on assignments and obedience help kids question propaganda and reject cruel orders? As kind-hearted as some teachers are, the underlying dynamics of school are those of a bully: kids must do what we want, even if it makes them unhappy. To what extent does this bullying dynamic provoke actual bullying?

School has the Midas Touch. Everything Midas touched turned to gold. It seemed wonderful until he touched his daughter, who turned into a lifeless gold statue. Forging people to be valuable primarily for their academic knowledge and workforce competence can turn them into numb machines.

Why not cut the day in half, make half voluntary, create small classes, place a priority on warm caring, and provide much more physical exercise, outdoor adventure, academic freedom, and opportunities for kids to meaningfully improve our planet?

ESCALATORS OF VIOLENCE

In response to defensive fears and aggressive desires, individuals and nations can select nonviolent action, no action, or violent action. Violent action is more likely to be chosen in the presence of Mental, Legal, and Physical Escalators of Violence. Note that some Escalators and Roots of Violence overlap.

Mental Escalators

Mental Escalators include conditions of mind and heart that distort our attitude toward truth and cripple our ability to connect with and care for others.

Examples include one-sided information and lack of media attention to enemies' suffering. If empathy is one-sided, if policymakers see graphic footage of only one side's suffering, their passion can incite them to inflict enormous suffering elsewhere.

Other escalators include top dog and underdog biases that assume the wealthy and powerful are either superior or inferior, beliefs that war magically leads to democracy or Heaven on Earth, and lack of creative thinking about nonviolent solutions to past and current wars.

A fascinating category of mental escalators is psychological patterns. In *The Nature of Prejudice,* Gordon Allport describes Prejudiced and Democratic Personalities, each with different modes of perceiving and thinking.

Prejudiced Personalities see conflict as right versus wrong, fault others but not themselves, require oversimplification, lack empathy, and prefer rules, authoritarian leadership, and hierarchical relationships. In negotiations, such personalities, feeling responsible and reasonable, use preconditions, a limited agenda, "diplomatic leverage," and intimidation to overpower others.

Democratic Personalities have 360-degree empathy, seek to understand all sides, are comfortable with complexity and ambiguity, and encourage questioning of rules. They support egalitarian, cooperative negotiations.

Allport, who finds Prejudiced Personalities already developing by age five, observes that what fosters this development most are family relationships that revolve around power rather than love and family dynamics that emphasize obedience, punishment, threats, and rejection.[16] Such family themes are strikingly similar to our foreign policy themes—and underlying school system themes.

In *Moral Politics: How Liberals and Conservatives Think,* George Lakoff describes a similar dichotomy, with the Strict Father Model similar to Allport's Prejudiced Personality and the Nurturant Mother Model similar to the Democratic Personality.[17] (I prefer to omit "Father" and "Mother.") Of interest, in the Strict Model, wealth and power are considered indicators of superior morality and fitness for leadership.

What's clear is that presidents, negotiators, preachers, parents, and pet owners will drastically differ depending upon their psychological pattern. The influence of these patterns on foreign policy seems more significant than gender, race, or creed. Yet since Day One, no matter who we elect, the Prejudiced Personality/Strict Model has been running U.S. foreign policy.

Why else would the United States lack empathy for enemies' fears, expect the wealthy and powerful to rule, and try installing peace through threats and punishment? We need fair representation of the Democratic Personality/ Nurturant Model in government, in negotiations, and in transforming the American childhood experience.

A related mental escalator is lack of cooperative dialogue. U.S. administrations repeatedly handle internal disagreements with shouting matches, intimidation, yes-men, dismissals, and reassignments. In Mike Mazzetti's *The Way of the Knife,* for example, one side within the CIA, typically the "We're going to sock it to the foreigners" side, dominates the other. Meanwhile, those who warn "Your drones are going to aggravate terrorism," and "You always throw guns and cash at warlords when you haven't a clue what else to do"—these people get sidelined.[18]

In *The Waxman Report: How Congress Really Works*, Congressman Henry Waxman demonstrates that cooperative discussion can be uncommon in legislative committees, and committee chairmen have a surprising amount of authoritarian power that nullifies any democratic impact of our right to vote for legislators. Moreover, party members badger each other to create unity by banishing individual thought.[19]

If many minds must conform to one, how is this different from monarchy?

We need cooperative dialogue in government, the workplace, schools, and within the peace movement. Whether we consider our opponents to be North Korea and Iran or our own belligerent U.S. leaders, we must sincerely step into their shoes to understand them and their fears. With that generosity of understanding, our relations can progress.

Legal Escalators

These pertain to the presence or absence of laws and policies as well as organizational structure, behavior, and incompetence that enable people to get away with violence or that encourage injustices that provoke people to violence. Legal escalators of U.S. violence include impunity for torture policies, drone killings, and invasions.

Weapons corporations' grip over the U.S. government and foreign policy is another legal escalator. No matter who's in office, like-minded individuals in government and the arms industry collude to replace democracy with their mission of feeding the addiction to expanding weapons exports, increasing profits, and creating a global system of threat-based "peace."[20]

Insufficient firearms regulation is a legal escalator. For example, President Trump intends to continue President Obama's deregulation efforts and transfer oversight of handgun, assault rifle, and sniper rifle exports, including the mass shooter AR-15, from the State Department, which considers weapon exports' potential effects on foreign violence, to the Commerce Department, which doesn't.

Another legal escalator is the absence of a U.S. Department of Peace. Different organizational missions require different types of intelligence. Destructive Intelligence is acquired through stealth, bribes, and torture: who's planning what, when to kill someone where. It serves CIA and Department of Defense missions.

Constructive Intelligence pertains to history, culture, human relations, language, negotiation, roots of violence, and compassionate familiarity with foreigners' daily lives. It's readily acquired through friendly interviews and reading.

A U.S. Department of Peace could gather Constructive Intelligence to create constructive solutions. Instead, the excessive dedication to Destructive Intelligence hamstrings foreign policy by burdening interrogators, troops, and drone pilots with the belief that their destructive actions are vital to American security. "I've got to waterboard him or there will be another 9/11!"

Physical Escalators

While lack of weapons could increase vulnerability to violence, a more severe physical escalator is weapons possession, particularly of powerful weaponry that is impossible to be used judiciously.

The United States is the world's No. 1 Weapons Exporter. It takes sides in foreign conflicts and arms one side against the other. Yet no surveys of conflict participants determine whether those killed by U.S. weapons deserved death. No social impact statements determine whether U.S. weapons helped promote peace and justice in communities.

What's the use of all that science in developing weapons if there's no science in evaluating the application of weapons to real world problems?

If we're taking it on faith that weapons promote better societies, if we're not interviewing affected communities, if we're not comparing the benefit of $1 billion toward violent policies and nonviolent, non-hostile policies, then paying taxes to fund weapons manufacturing is equivalent to paying taxes to support an established religion.

The arms industry gets free handouts of enormous government contracts with no democratic input, no evaluation, no responsibility for consequences, and no expectations that weapons will solve causes of conflict. Yet nearly every U.S. president since the 1969 Nixon Doctrine has been a salesman for the arms industry: deregulating it, increasing public subsidies to it, receiving campaign contributions from it, and swamping at least one hundred nations with its lethal products, despite foreign civilians' protests.

∾

When faced with conflict, the United States pulls out its tedious hostile array of solutions: sanctions, weapons shipments, drones, air strikes, boots on the ground. Not a single non-hostile solution appears. Yet nearly every Root and Escalator of Violence is exacerbated by violence and requires non-hostile solutions.

We've got to make an enormous shift of energy, resources, and talent to initiate dynamic peacefulness based upon trying to understand and care equally for all, including those considered enemies. Instead of taking sides, rejecting people, and kicking the car, why not empower, fund, and unleash the American spirit that is chomping at the bit to nonviolently resolve conflict, alleviate suffering, and create friendships?

Notes

1. Debra Niehoff, *The Biology of Violence* (New York: Simon and Schuster, Free Press, 1999), 50.

2. Sandra Silberstein, *War of Words: Language, Politics, and 9/11* (New York: Routledge, 2002), 136.

3. Noah Feldman, *After Jihad: America and the Struggle for Islamic Democracy* (New York: Farrar, Straus, and Giroux, 2003), 20, 140.

4. Fawaz Gerges, *Journey of the Jihadist: Inside Muslim Militancy* (Orlando: Harcourt, 2006), 55–56, 180, 210–211.

5. Jane Corbin, *Al-Qaeda: The Terror Network That Threatens the World* (New York: Thunder's Mouth Press/Nation, 2002), 120–21.

6. Murray Rothbard, *A History of Money and Banking in the United States* (Auburn, AL: Ludwig von Mises Institute, 2005), 188–233.

7. Thomas Paterson, J. Garry Clifford, and Kenneth Hagan, *American Foreign Policy: A History Since 1900* (Lexington, MA: D. C. Heath, 1991).

8. Murray Rothbard, "Rockefeller, Morgan, and War," from *Wall Street, Banks, and American Foreign Policy*; https://mises.org/library/.

9. Andrzej Walicki, *A History of Russian Thought from the Enlightenment to Marxism*, trans. Hilda Andrews-Rusiecka (Stanford: Stanford University Press, 1979), 94–101.

10. Gerges, *Journey*, 30–35.

11. James Loewen, *Lies My Teacher Told Me* (New York: Simon and Schuster, 1995), 109.

12. Lawrence Kaplan and William Kristol, *The War over Iraq: Saddam's Tyranny and America's Mission* (San Francisco: Encounter Books, 2003), 64.

13. Samir Al-Khalil (Kanan Makiya), *Republic of Fear* (New York: Pantheon Books, 1989), 203; Dilip Hiro, *Holy Wars: The Rise of Islamic Fundamentalism* (New York: Routledge, 1989), 88–89.

14. Corbin, *Al-Qaeda*, 6, 126–27, 133, 142, 208–209, 235–36.

15. National Conference of Catholic Bishops, *Economic Justice for All* (Washington, DC: National Conference of Catholic Bishops, 1986), 75; Susan Webb, "Blood Money? US Is World's Top Arms Dealer," *People's World*, Jan. 26, 2016.

16. Gordon Allport, *The Nature of Prejudice* (New York: Addison-Wesley, 1979), 395–443.

17. George Lakoff, *Moral Politics: How Liberals and Conservatives Think* (Chicago: The University of Chicago Press, 2002).

18. Mike Mazzetti, *The Way of the Knife: The CIA, a Secret Army, and a War at the Ends of the Earth* (New York: Penguin, 2013), 135, 142–43, 228, 262, 292.

19. Henry Waxman with Joshua Green, *The Waxman Report: How Congress Really Works* (New York: Hachette, 2009), 7–8, 25–30, 85.

20. William Hartung, *Prophets of War: Lockheed Martin and the Making of the Military-Industrial Complex* (New York: Nation Books, 2012), 180, 191–97, 208.

Chapter 6

The Struggle for Peace and Justice as a Way of Life

LAWRENCE DAVIDSON

Introduction

It is a bit of a cliché, but life really is like a journey down a road of varying length. The length of the road is represented by one's lifespan, and this in turn is most often a product of one's genes and the nature of the neighborhood (or country) you live in. For instance, in the "developed" world, the road has been extended by scientific medicine and the growth of the "middle class." Still, it is not propitious to be born poor in any country.

But what about the width of the road? The width is determined by our cultural and familial context and that, for most of us, limits the range of perception as well as behavioral options. Think of these as high walls on either side of your road. Even amid prosperity, this is where the problem lies. Society's dictates can transform what should be a wide highway offering diverse views into a narrow alley.

Roots

I was born in June 1945 in Philadelphia into a household the values and outlook of which were shaped by three sociocultural constants: first, a military culture. Even though World War II was winding down, my father was an officer in the Army Air Corps and identified with military ways and mores. Two, a secularized Jewish outlook which, in the last years of the 1940s, would metamorphose from a liberal posture that supported the rights of minorities to a more Zionist one that placed the interests of Israel above all else. And three, Cold War patriotism emphasizing the United States as a defender of the "free world." These were the walls, if you will, on both sides of the societal road down which I was expected to walk.

My family moved to Elizabeth, New Jersey, when I was two and it was there that I grew up. As time passed, things started to go wrong in ways that eroded my adherence to dictated norms. My father's authoritarian ways were alienating to me and failed to create a comfortable model for how to approach the world. By the time I was eleven, I was in a sullen stage of mental rebellion. Public school compounded the sullenness because it too proved an alienating and sometimes dangerous place for someone who was basically bookish and introverted. At the age of twelve, regular school was supplemented by Hebrew school—three days a week for three hours each of those days. Even more than public school, Hebrew school was boring, and there were soon problems with bullying by both other students and some of the teachers.

The whole scenario produced a conflicted approach to the world. On the one hand, I had a sort of conditioned reflex that pulled me in the direction of solitude and retreating from a world that seemed hostile. On the other hand, I had a lot of internal anger and resentment and I did not know what to do with it all. Two other results were a questioning of authority and an identification with the underdog. By the time I was a teenager, whatever the authority figures in my life—my father, my teachers, society in general—were telling me was the correct way of perceiving and acting, I did not believe a word of it. I had begun to dismantle those walls along my road and this enabled me to see beyond them.

It was during my university experience (first at Rutgers and then at Georgetown University) that I really broke free in a way that at once comple-mented my intellectual nature and also provided an outlet for my anger. That outlet was not the educational institutions themselves, but rather Students for a Democratic Society (SDS) and the struggle it mounted for human rights both abroad and at home.

SDS gave direction to my inclination to support the underdog. I actively participated in the efforts to end the Vietnam War and extend civil rights. I developed a critique of U.S. foreign policy that was anti-imperialist and against the militaristic exceptionalism promoted by the country's leaders. At the same time, I began a lifelong effort to understand the mass psychology of citizens that brings them to support governments that defy commonsense notions of fair play and the fulfillment of human needs.

It was also at this time that I began to actively support the Palestinian cause. This support evolved as a logical extension of my anti-imperialist and anticolonialist way of seeing. The post–World War II world was decolonizing and the establishment of Israel by tens of thousands of Europeans who happened to be Jewish made no sense to me. I admit that this was at least in part due to my negative experiences as a Jewish child forced to go a Hebrew school and listen to hours of Zionist indoctrination. It my case the process clearly backfired and this particular wall rapidly crumbled. After that, a historically accurate and justice-based perception of the Israeli-Palestinian situation took over.

Part of that perception entailed a recognition that a commonsense notion of justice is always linked to the search for peace. Thus, there can be no genuine peace until the Israelis can accept responsibility for the injustice they did to, and continue to practice against, the Palestinians. Taking responsibility means amending for the past and changing one's ways in the present. Peace and justice are two sides of the same coin. It is, of course, possible to misconstrue justice and falsely feel aggrieved. However, in the cases of recognizable aggression, ethnic cleansing, and other such practices, injustice is readily visible.

Working for Peace

By the late 1960s, my efforts to promote peace with justice had come to focus on two areas. One: Work against the Vietnam War, which entailed helping a coalition of Washington, D.C. area peace organizations plan for large antiwar demonstrations, as well as local actions that took place at various area campuses. This effort produced a personal crisis. My father was by this time a colonel in the Air Force. He was visibly upset and disappointed by my work against the war and this resulted in years of estrangement.

My antiwar stand in the sixties extended to opposition to other imperialist efforts on the part of the U.S. government in Latin America, and subsequently in Iraq and Afghanistan. This work also flowed from a growing understanding of U.S. history and the lobby-based nature of its government. In truth, the United States is not a democracy of individual citizens as much as a democracy of competing interest groups.

Two: Opposition to U.S. support for Israel. This opposition fit neatly with my position on the imperialist nature of U.S. foreign policy. It was my growing opposition to Zionism that produced yet another personal crisis. This was not family-based, but rather involved close Jewish friends in SDS. As SDS fell apart, many of the Jewish members with whom I had worked filled the resulting emotional void by converting to Zionism. They rationalized this move by denying Israel's colonial origins and identifying Palestinian resistance not as an effort to resist colonial conquest, but rather as anti-Semitism. For me, this way of seeing things seemed blatantly ahistorical. As a result, what had been close working relationships and friendships were ruptured.

Looking back at these times it seems amazing to me that, through it all, I managed to earn three university degrees—BA, MA, and PhD. The whole process really equated to holding two full-time jobs for more than two decades. In any case, getting the degrees led to an academic career and, by the 1980s, my work for peace and justice became focused on teaching, researching, and writing on U.S. foreign policy in the Middle East. I also began to do a lot of public speaking. In other words, I slowly moved from the arena of radical antiwar actions to the world of academia. I transformed into a "public intellectual."

Obstacles to Peace and Justice

This transformation was complete by the late 1980s and has structured my life ever since. Or, to get back to the metaphor of life as a road, it has allowed me a broad and objective view of the world around me. This broad perspective has also brought to fruition long years of study about why most people see the world as they do and respond so readily to the propaganda of their leaders.

Almost all people live in a state of "natural localism." This is a roughly thirty square mile radius within which they live, work, socialize, raise their children, etc. Sometimes this status resets itself when people are transferred or otherwise move, but it always, rather quickly, reasserts itself as a default position. In terms of world outlook, most people will conform their perceptions to those that prevail in this thirty square mile range. That is, they will conform their own outlook to those of their neighborhood and the community in general (those walls again). Information coming to them from official government and mainstream media about the world outside their immediate locale will be absorbed and result in a coherent, if not always accurate, picture of the outside world.

In the case of one's own locale, independent knowledge by which to judge government and media information is available by virtue of living in that very locale. But the farther one gets from one's home base the harder it is to exercise independent judgment. Thus, the great majority will have no way of critiquing or judging the worldview presented to them—they are bound to the propaganda being fed to them.

This condition of natural localism, which prevails even in an age of social media and the worldwide web (most people in the West use the web to shop or talk to friends) serves a stabilizing societal function by filtering outside information potentially disruptive of the status quo. This is why change, aside from the category of technology, is slow. Except in times of catastrophe, it is hard for social critics and reformers to get their message heard, much less acted upon.

Issues of war and peace are taken up within this system of natural localism. It is relatively easy to move a localized population toward war. Consistent war propaganda about an outside country or people about which there is no independent, reliable information can quickly shape mass perceptions. Peace usually comes when war has already been waged to the point that the horror sours the home population on the propagandistic official picture. This is particularly the case when causalities are high and war objectives fall too short to be hidden from the public. However, even the memory of failure can be short-lived and, given the right sort of propagandistic revival, policy mistakes can be repeated. Even in a country such as the United States, with its theoretical dedication to free speech, the population can be brought to support policies that only a generation earlier had been proven bankrupt.

This analysis does not paint a pretty picture. Myopic prejudices and nationalistic narrow-mindedness are much readier consequences of natural localism than are open-mindedness and tolerance. Within such circumstances the role of peace worker is an arduous one and demands almost infinite patience, for the struggle against nationalist elements for which war is ever popular seems never-ending.

A Vision of Peace

Peace is a vital concept. One might even say that, as a goal to strive for, the hope for peace is important to overall human sanity. However, seen historically, universal peace is little more than an ideal. The practical aim is to strive for influence over the policies of one's own government. Within a more or less democratic setting, this should be doable.

In the case of the United States, this requires the development of a serious, enduring peace lobby. Why so? As mentioned above, the United States is not a democracy of individual citizens. It is a democracy of competing interest groups that function as lobbies to pressure the government to treat their parochial interests as "national interests." The collective manifestations of the lobby that represents those industries that manufacture weapons, and therefore have a vested interest in war instead of peace, is good example of this reality. If, as the saying goes, peace is to be given a chance, those who want to see it realized must organize an interest group just as powerful, and just as permanent, as those that profit from war.

Conclusion

Learning to live without the cultural and social walls that conform one's values and perceptions to one's neighbors is at once a blessing and a curse. It is a blessing in the sense that, as one's eyes are opened, a more objective sense of reality comes into view. It is a curse because that objective sense alienates you from your immediate fellows. Either way you see it, bringing down the walls reveals the iniquities of interest groups and governments. Then you have a choice: cynicism or activism. And a dark sense of humor helps as well.

I have been an activist for peace and justice for more than fifty years. Will I see the ideal of peace realized in my life time? I very much doubt it. But then, the struggle for peace and justice has long since defined who I am, and I can no more stop acting in this way than I can stop seeing and talking. And so I value the struggle itself as a self-defining process that leaves me with a relatively clean conscience and sense of real satisfaction. For me, at age of seventy-three, the struggle itself is enough.

Chapter 7

The Old Tribalism and the Vision of Abraham

STEPHEN DOWNS

I was born in 1942, in the middle of World War II. My father was a Navy doctor who died in 1945 while training for the invasion of Japan. My grandfather was a minister who advocated pacifism from the pulpit; his brother supported the establishment of the United Nations and international agencies to help assure peace after the disaster of World War II. Our dinner table conversations often revolved around issues of war, peace, justice, Christianity, and religion. And often it came down to the question, "How long can civilization survive if we cannot learn to give up war and work cooperatively?"

In 1948, my mother moved to Geneva, Switzerland for two years. Europe was still recovering from the devastation of the war; even as a six-year-old I remember the sense of fear and shock that hung over Europe in the aftermath. I asked my mother how the war started and she said, "A man named Hitler came to power in Germany and attacked neighboring countries. There were many good people in Germany who could have stopped him but they remained silent and let him seize power." The phrase "Good people remained silent" has always stayed with me. I came to understand at a young age that my father and many other people died because good people remained silent in the face of wrong.

I was fortunate in my youth to spend considerable time abroad. In high school, I went to New Zealand for eight months as a foreign exchange student, and I spent the summer of 1961 in the highlands of the Cameroons in West Africa helping to build a hospital. The organizations I went with, American Field Service and Crossroads Africa, were created specifically so that people from different cultures could get to know each other and with heightened understanding become buffers against future wars.

After I graduated from college in 1964, I went into the Peace Corps in India, focusing primarily on youth work and beekeeping. I met my wife Wilhelmina there who was in the Dutch Peace Corps as a nurse. We began our married life together with a multicultural background feeling comfortable with friends of mixed ethnicities. We eventually helped resettle four refugee families from Poland, Vietnam, and Iran, and learned much about the pain and joys of the world from their experiences.

After I returned from India I became a lawyer and eventually became the chief attorney for the New York State Commission on Judicial Conduct, imposing discipline on judges who engaged in judicial misconduct. It was the perfect job for me because it involved principles of law and justice that reflected religious and moral imperatives of society. I loved the job for twenty-eight years until I retired in 2003.

Over the years I developed my own understanding how the world was organized into tribes under one universal "God" as described in the Bible and the Quran. When our Patriarch Abraham was living in Ur some four thousand years ago, each tribe worshiped their own tribal god in the form of an idol, and sought strength to prevail over rival tribes and their idols. Abraham had a different vision. He saw God as the creator of the universe—the sun, the moon and the stars. All people and all tribes on earth were children—creations—of that God, and all people were thus bound by a common human dignity. This was the gift of monotheism—the understanding that while tribes might war and fight with each other over their tribal interests, God was the universal parent who kept order in the house. Abraham's vision was eventually embodied in the Jewish, Christian, and Muslim religions

My favorite statement of our universal Judeo-Christian-Islamic tradition is Jesus's parable of the King (God) who gathers the "nations" (tribes) before him and separates out the "righteous" saying to them:

> Come enter into my kingdom. For I was hungry and you fed me, thirsty and you gave me a drink; I was a stranger and you received me in your homes, naked and you clothed me; I was sick and you took care of me, in prison and you visited me. The righteous will then answer, "Lord when did we ever see you [thus and relieved your suffering]. . . . The King will answer, "I tell you

that whenever you did this for one of the least important of my children, you did it for me. (Matthew 25:31–40)

All three Abrahamic religions offer versions of this inclusive, compassionate vision as an antidote to the tribal moral code that emphasizes survival of the fittest. (See among many examples, Micah 6:8, "And what does the Lord require of you? To act justly and to love mercy, and to walk humbly with your God," and the Quran, Surah 4-135, "Oh you who believe! Stand out firmly for justice, as witness to Allah, even as against yourselves (tribe), or your parents or your kin, and whether it be (against) rich or poor: for Allah can best protect both.")

Tribal law presupposes that interaction between tribes is a zero sum game. What one tribe gains another tribe must lose. In order to survive, a tribe would be wise to follow certain basic rules:

1) A tribe must take from weaker tribes what it needs to survive and prosper. It is far more important that your tribe prospers than that all tribes are treated equally or fairly.

2) It is very dangerous to appear to be weak and divided. It invites attack.

3) Dissent within a tribe is a sign of weakness and division. It must be forcefully suppressed.

4) Tribal members must always support each other, right or wrong, and show loyalty to the tribe. If you are not loyal you must be expelled.

5) A strong leader is necessary to unify the tribe, suppress dissent, and present a strong appearance to would-be attackers.

6) If an individual of another tribe offends a member of your tribe, it is necessary to retaliate against the other tribe to avoid appearing weak even if the retaliation falls on someone who was not involved; all members of the other tribe can be targeted not just the guilty one (collective guilt).

7) Alliances between tribes are good but only as long as the alliances help your interests and allow your tribe to survive. (As Kissinger famously said, "America doesn't have friends, it only has interests.")

8) Other tribes and their members can be stigmatized and demonized in order to build tribal unity and strength; a tribe that is peaceful and open to other tribes becomes weak and is easily attacked.

Most of us have inclusive compassion and tribalism hardwired into our thought processes. We desire strong leaders who can unite the country, prevent other countries from attacking us, and obtain benefits for our country. But we also tend to accept universal principles of law and agree that all people should live by the same rules. We admire dissenters who call for justice for groups who are demonized and treated unjustly, and we feel compassion for those who are marginalized. Our thinking tends to swing back and forth between the poles of tribalism and inclusiveness depending on the circumstances.

When I was growing up after World War II, the world had just gone through an enormous tribal bloodletting. Germany had picked on weaker countries (tribes) and other tribes had been drawn into the conflict until it became an unprecedented orgy of killing and violence. The world was desperately searching for universal rules to prevent this kind of tribal violence in the future. The United Nations was created and the Universal Declaration on Human Rights was adopted. It was said that we now lived under universal rules which applied equally to everyone and so tribalism had been vanquished. In fact, it was just a gloss to cover up the old tribalism lurking underneath.

Perhaps because of my background coming out of World War II, I believed strongly in universal principles of law eloquently embodied in our Declaration of Independence which stated: "We hold these truths to be self-evident. That all men [people] are created equal." The principle certainly seemed self-evident to me. I was able to ignore the old tribalism of the Constitution that accepted slavery and declared that a black man was three-fifths of a white man (U.S. Constitution, Article 1, Section 2). As a lawyer for the Commission on Judicial Conduct, I took on the obligation to make sure that the courts and agencies of government put aside tribalism and treated everybody equally before the law. The Rules Governing Judicial Conduct that the commission enforced required judges to be impartial—to be free of all tribal biases including specifically "age, race, creed, color, sex, sexual orientation, religion, national origin, disability, marital status, or socioeconomic status" (Rule 100.3[B][4]). There would be one universal law for everyone regardless of what tribe you happened to be in.

I retired from the commission in March 2003, just as the drums of war were beginning to beat for an invasion of Iraq. I believed that the invasion was a fraud. Bush said that Saddam Hussein had weapons of mass destruction, but Bush was unable to tell the UN inspectors in Iraq where the weapons were located. Bush was bluffing. It seemed obvious that the invasion of Iraq was a tribal response. We could not appear weak in responding to 9/11 or we would invite more attacks, and we could not attack Saudi Arabia whose nationals had largely launched 9/11 because we depended on them for oil. So we went after Iraq, the one country with almost as much oil as Saudi Arabia in order to show strength and control oil. It made perfect tribal sense.

The staff of the commission was supposed to informally follow the same Rules Governing Judicial Conduct as the judges, including the rule prohibiting a judge from activities that "cast reasonable doubt on the judge's capacity to act impartially" (Rule 100.4[A][1]). I did not feel I could do anything controversial but I wanted to go on record as opposing this insane invasion. Some peace activists described going to Crossgates Mall outside of Albany, New York, before Christmas wearing peace T-shirts, and being told to take off the T-shirts or be arrested. When they took off the peace T-shirts they were kicked out of the mall anyway. The whole fiasco seemed wrong and unconstitutional to me and I wanted to test the story, both as a way of protesting the war, and as a way of proving to myself that this kind of repression of dissent did not exist in America.

On March 3, 2003, I went to Crossgates Mall with my son Roger, and we each bought peace T-Shirts. Mine said, "Peace on Earth" and "Give Peace a Chance." Roger's said, "No War in Iraq" and "Let Inspections Work." I don't particularly like malls and I was not sure what to do next so we decided to walk down to the food court and eat. Within fifteen minutes, the security staff was all over us, saying that we had to remove our T-shirts or be kicked out of Crossgates. I refused, and to my surprise I was arrested and charged with trespassing. A few days later, when the news of my arrest was publicized, hundreds of people showed up at Crossgates wearing peace T-shirts and tried to get arrested. Crossgates backed down and withdrew the charges.

Being arrested for wearing a peace T-shirt seems incomprehensible until we recall that the incident occurred just as America was about to go into an unpopular war, and the tribalists were trying to rally patriotism and suppress dissent. As Amy Goodman pointed out, the significance of the event was not that some poor slob was arrested in a mall for wearing a peace T-shirt; the significance was that hundreds of people came out afterward to support him. Thus, after spending most of my legal career with the Commission on Judicial Conduct avoiding politics and controversy, on the eve of my retirement from the commission I was for the first time introduced to the Albany progressive community and the life of an activist.

Since the State of New York would pay me a large sum of money in retirement to do essentially nothing, I decided I would take on for free any case that seemed to need a pro bono lawyer. Many people had contributed to my becoming a lawyer, and it was now my turn to make my license to practice law available to the community.

The first case was a request to represent Save the Pine Bush (STPB) in a lawsuit to prevent a corporation from building a hotel on land that was part of the ecologically rare Albany Pine Barrens, which contains many endangered species. A colony of rare worm snakes lived on the hotel site, and a colony of endangered Karner Blue Butterflies was right next door. Eventually, the case went to the Court of Appeals where the issues were: (1) whether the City of Albany had adequately considered the snakes and butterflies when granting zoning changes, and (2) whether STPB properly had "standing" to speak for the environment.

In New York at that time, only those people next door—the most directly impacted by a proposed development such as a landfill—had standing to object to the project, because only they (supposedly) had the most at stake. However, this rule made no sense when applied to worm snakes and butterflies. Most neighbors would not know or care that worm snakes lived next door, especially when they were corporations seeking to develop the land. Developers are hardly the best people to speak for the environment.

The good news was that the Court of Appeals in its decision expanded the standing rule to include persons whose interest in the environment was greater than the public as a whole even if they did not live close to the area; as a result, we got standing. The bad news was the court decided that worm snakes, although rare, were not worth worrying about, and allowed the hotel to be built anyway. What I realized from this experience was that standing rules and other procedural hurdles in the law were intended to control who was heard. It was the Corporate Tribe's way of bending the law to its favor while seemingly the law applied equally to all people. And if procedural rules could be used to block legal consideration of the extermination of animal species, how much better would humans fare when we sought protection in the courts from global warming and environmental decay?

In 2006, I met Albany attorney Kathy Manley, and I worked with her and her law firm on a terrorism case brought against locals Yassin Aref and Mohammed Hossain. The case was unlike anything I had ever seen before; it was dominated by secret evidence, ex parte contacts between the prosecution and the judges, mistranslations and misunderstandings of foreign words and concepts, biased expert testimony, jury intimidation, and other such practices that in my eyes made the trial completely unfair. The government had deliberately targeted and convicted two men that were not involved in terrorism, apparently because the government thought the men might be open to unspecified terrorist plots in the future. Kathy and I soon found hundreds of other cases like it around the country.

At a news conference after the Aref-Hossain trial was over the prosecutor said that the government had "no evidence that he [Aref] was a terrorist but he had the ideology. To preempt anything from happening we [brought this case]." Kathy and I focused on the word *preempt* and began to call this "preemptive prosecution"—prosecuting ideologically suspicious people before they committed a crime. Kathy compiled a data base of preemptive prosecution cases and we formed an organization, Project SALAM, to document these cases and advocate against this misuse of the justice system (www. projectsalam.org).

With Project SALAM and later with the National Coalition to Protect Civil Freedom (NCPCF), Kathy and I, along with Lynne Jackson and Jeanne Finley and many others, traveled around the United States for close to a decade describing the injustices brought about by preemptive prosecution, and protesting the erosion of civil liberties, the use of fear and Islamophobia to demonize a religious group, and the abuse of incarcerated prisoners. We came to know the families of the defendants and saw how they were scapegoated to fulfill a political agenda. Their stories were heartbreaking. People were entrapped by the FBI, or were charged under new laws that criminalized charity, free speech, free association, peacemaking, and social hospitality. Absurdly long prison sentences were imposed, often in solitary.

In retrospect I would say that the Aref-Hossain case was my first experience with "tribal justice." But in the wake of 9/11, tribal justice was everywhere to be seen for those who were willing to look beyond the lies. Torture was authorized by the U.S. government and widely practiced. Targeted assassinations by the United States of American citizens were carried out. Guantanamo Bay was used as a place outside any legal authority to detain people indefinitely without charges. Routine invasive surveillance by the FBI and NSA was directed at everybody including their e-mail, bank accounts, phone conversations, and other forms of communication, which previously had been considered private. Justice to me is the art of treating equally people who are inherently unequal in circumstance (such as wealth, or birth, or other considerations). Justice is always inclusive. Tribal justice by contrast is always exclusive, focusing only on the good of the tribe by casting out dissenters or disloyal members, and by discrimination against member of "other" tribes which threaten our own.

As I saw how tribal justice was being inflicted on the Islamic community, I came to realize for how long America had practiced tribal justice on other "outside" groups including Native Americans, African Americans, Latinos, immigrants, Communists/Socialists, and women. In saying this, I must be clear that being tribal is not the same as, for example, being racist, or misogynist. A racist hates members of other "races"; a misogynist hates women. But being "tribal" does not require hating someone else. It only requires looking out for your own tribe at the expense of someone else's. You can like members of another tribe and even work with them until their interests clash with yours, and then they must be eliminated for the good of your tribe.

For example, spending tax revenues on the common good creates fear in rich tribes that their money is going to support poorer tribes, and this in turn creates fear that their tribe needs a stronger leader to protect the rich tribe's interests. Powerful tribes try to bully weak tribes into submission, raising fear in the weak tribes who must band together to resist. The country becomes polarized and a cycle of increasing conflict and even violence begins. Donald Trump is successful because he is an unapologetic bully for his own tribe at the expense of all the others. He calms the fears of his own tribe because they feel at last that someone is looking out for their own interests and not just the common good. Trump's presence has caused other political leaders to adopt the same persona of "tribal champion" and the struggle for top tribe has come into the open. If the Top 1 Percent Rich Tribe can accumulate 50 percent of the nation's wealth, why shouldn't it try to accumulate 75 percent or more? It is simply the logical result of the rules that govern unrestrained tribal behavior.

But who then speaks for the common good? Who speaks for economic cooperation to grow the economic pie for the benefit of all? Who speaks for the environment on which everyone depends for survival? Who teaches that we must value members of other tribes because their talents will benefit everyone? People remembered the U.S. military during and after World War II as a national unifying force for the common good. Defense was a shared sacrifice against the threats of fascism and communism. But as the United States emerged as the only remaining superpower, the military increasingly became a vehicle to advance private corporate interests, especially in petroleum and control of resources. The War on Terror—a war on a concept that can never be won—was created to enlist public support for defense against a mostly illusory threat, while stripping rights from the public and creating chaos abroad. It is the perfect tribal war that tries to advance corporate America's interests at the expense of everyone else.

Traditionally, religions, and enlightened governments, institutions, and ideologies that reflect religious values have advocated for the common good as the conscience of society. They are the wise parents in the house who keep the strong tribes (children) from bullying the weak, and permit all the children to flourish equally because each is loved and valued in their own way. But the dominant ideologies have failed. A united communism died with the collapse of the Soviet Union and broke up into competing tribes of Stalinists, Maoists, and Trotskyists.

Unrestrained capitalism actually permits the strong tribes to bully the weak, and accentuates the inequalities within society. The U.S. government has been captured by the very warring tribes that it was supposed to control, and it is paralyzed. Religion for the most part has thrown off its mantle as the parent in the room, and has formed a bewildering number of competing tribal faith groups that argue about who is better, while failing to address the diminishing sphere of common good that holds society together.

I grew up as a Protestant attending my grandfather's church. My grandfather had suffered under the rigid sectarianism of Christianity and he was determined to try to end this division within a religion that is supposed to represent the unity of a monotheistic God. He agreed to be his church's minister on the condition that all denominations would be welcomed. My wife Wil was a devout Catholic, while I, reflecting perhaps my upbringing, had no denominational preferences, and so I eventually became a Catholic also.

But the Catholics, like most religions, had split up into tribes themselves, especially on the axis of high church (a mighty God enthroned above) to low church (the spirit of God appearing in the community through the eyes of your neighbor). I was a low-church kind of guy and so I became an enthusiastic member of what I call the Catholic Left. Our heroes include people such as Megan Rice, an eighty-year-old nun who, in 2012, cut through a chain link fence, damaged a nuclear facility with a hammer, and sang hymns with her group until they were all arrested. (She was sentenced to three years in jail, essentially for exposing the government's astonishingly lax protection of nuclear materials.) Such groups and people in every religion keep alive Abraham's vision of a God who is truly worth worshiping; the creator of the universe who loves all people, as a parent loves children, and who moderates their furious tribal competition with love, compassion, and mercy.

The present War on Terrorism should be renamed, the War for the Narrative. Governments have cast the present situation as a war between religious extremists, with Muslim extremists against Jewish and Christian nations, Jewish and Christian nations against the Muslims. Lost in the scapegoating is the actual inclusive compassionate tradition that these three Abrahamic religions share; a tradition that for more than four thousand years rose above tribal extremism to moderate the excesses of the survival-of-the-fittest competition that tribalism brings.

It is not necessary that religions give up their own tribal tendencies in order to reclaim their prophetic voice; only that the world's religions recognize a sense of priority. First and foremost must be the prophetic vision—the joining of hands with other religious leaders to proclaim with one voice that our Abrahamic tradition is and always has been the welcoming of strangers, the feeding of the hungry, the release of prisoners from jail, the cessation of war and violence, the worshiping of God as loving children and not as warring enemies. To remain silent in the face of wrong, to allow others to silence the victims of tribalism are not options we can entertain. Our world is facing too great and too many perils to allow the voice of unity to be silenced.

Chapter 8

A Quixotic Vision of Peace

JAMES E. JENNINGS

A quixotic task is by definition an impossible dream, a hopelessly optimistic quest for an unrealistic goal, which may be truly noble but is so idealistic that it is utterly impractical. The attempt by a few groups of peace activists and human rights advocates to reverse the imperialistic U.S. military juggernaut in the run-up to the Iraq Wars of 1991 and 2003–11 may rightly be characterized as quixotic.

Yet there is different standard of measurement that applies to noble ideals: they stand the test of time when wars and conquests, blood, burials, and parades are long forgotten. The courageous acts and reasoned advocacy of these very few idealists will remain as a marker for future generations, who will look back to the 2003 Iraq War as the ultimate in imperial hubris and stupidity, with consequences so horrific and long lasting as to be indescribable.

Conscience International was one of those groups. Along with others, we vigorously opposed the Iraq War in the American media, on CNN, PBS, Canadian Broadcasting, Al-Jazeera, Japanese TV, and other radio and print outlets. We joined with others in the 2001 "Baghdad Airlift"—flying through the no-fly zone—and organized and led high-visibility protests in Iraq itself, including the "Peace Walk to Baghdad" over the hot Iraqi desert in 2002.

Before the Iraq War—and during its course—we engaged directly as "US Academics for Peace" with high-level officials and academics in Iraq, Syria, Iran, and Sudan. Our groups of professors from dozens of U.S. universities

counseled pursuing the path of engagement and negotiation rather than
"diplomacy by B-52s" as the U.S. government apparently intended.

In Iraq, successive Conscience International teams provided hospitals
blockaded by the U.S.-UN embargo with urgently needed supplies. We actively
trained physicians and nurses in child survival techniques during the time that
the draconian siege was literally choking the life out of countless infants—a
scene we witnessed repeatedly at hospitals in Baghdad, Basra, and Mosul.

Today it is no comfort to say that, although we did not succeed in
preventing war, we feel vindicated by subsequent events. These include the
sad descent of Iraq and Syria into terribly bloody internecine conflicts and
the universal worldwide repudiation of the *casus belli* behind the original U.S.
attack and occupation of Iraq. By 2016, even leading Neo-Con politicians
and pundits, and most Republican officeholders and presidential candidates,
have distanced themselves from the results of their hawkish war-mongering.

By the time Conscience International organized the first "US Academics for Peace" conference at Baghdad University only six weeks before the
"Shock and Awe" massive bombing attack on Baghdad began on March 20,
2003, it was of course too late to stop the gargantuan U.S. war machine that
was poised to rain death and destruction on the country and its citizens.

Even so, our first delegation of thirty-seven professors from twenty-eight
U.S. universities that joined more than two thousand of our Iraqi colleagues
at the conference at Baghdad University felt that a last-ditch attempt to
intervene was worthwhile. Even if it would not affect the outcome, at least
it would be a landmark, leaving a vociferous and visible witness that there
was indeed a genuine alternative to war.

Most of the strategic thinking for our activism in Iraq and the United
States, as well as the organizational tasks for the projects, fell to me as
founder and president of Conscience International. Much of the time, I
worked singlehandedly, but found encouragement from wonderful colleagues
such as Kathy Kelly of Voices in the Wilderness (later Voices for Creative
Non-Violence) and former U.S. attorney general Ramsey Clark of the
International Action Center. In a PBS interview, mine was one of the first
widely broadcast voices Americans had a chance to hear raised against the
crippling U.S.-led UN sanctions on Iraq. The UN Humanitarian Program
Coordinator in Iraq, Denis Halliday, who eventually resigned in protest, as
did his successor, confirmed my statements in the same interview against
the incredulous questioning of the host.

Looking back, there is typically a wellspring of early impressions that
guide our actions through the plethora of experiences that make up the

flow of our lives. For me, that was when I was five or six and my father, a Baptist pastor in the coal mining camps of West Virginia, took my hand and led me down to a hobo jungle beside the railroad tracks. "These men need our help," he said, as he proceeded to hand out food and clothing to homeless men squatting around a small fire and heating coffee in a tin can.

Years later as a college graduate and young archaeologist in the Middle East, I felt the same kind of empathy toward the numerous beggars I encountered on the streets of Cairo, Damascus, Baghdad, and elsewhere. The first woman I saw begging alms in the street late at night with a baby in her arms made an unforgettable impression on me. I also learned to empathize with and care for the Arab people, especially the Palestinians among whom I worked, and to appreciate their rich culture, strong sense of honor, colorful personalities, and more often than not, their genuine commitment to peace and justice.

These elements were blended with a deep conviction that, as Daniel Webster once thundered, "The greatest thought that ever crossed the mind of man is the awareness of his responsibility to God." As a young man I felt an unalterable obligation to follow the golden rule and "do unto others as I would have them do unto me." How this led to my organizing Conscience International and the US Academics for Peace is a long story that began with the Siege of Beirut in 1982, when I found myself on the deck of a ship sailing into Lebanon's active war zone to deliver medical aid. This in turn led to decades of humanitarian work in Iraq, Iran, Syria, Gaza, Afghanistan, Darfur, and elsewhere.

To become an activist for peace and an advocate for human rights was out of character for those in the more or less quietist religious tradition from which I came, and definitely outside the boundaries of behavior for a sober academic, a professor at Wheaton College, a small, conservative Midwestern school. My colleagues were shocked when I vigorously defended Palestinian human and political rights. Few of my acquaintances understood when, in 1982, I traveled to an active war zone in the midst of the bloody Israeli siege of Beirut to deliver medical aid to those injured and dying.

Having a keen sense of justice and injustice requires that a person act. It is an essential part of our humanity to follow the sensitive gyroscope that is our conscience. Somehow many people, although tugged this way and that by feelings of right and wrong, never arrive at the point of action. It is a dramatic and determinative event in a person's life when that moment occurs. I can remember the exact time when I saw on television the crushed and lifeless body of an infant being lifted out of the ruins of a bombed house in South Lebanon. I instantly got up from the couch, began to make phone calls, and within two weeks was in Beirut harbor with five tons of medical supplies, sailing directly into a city under constant and fierce bombing assault.

At the outbreak of the first Gulf War in 1991, I again acted quickly when images of multitudes of Kurdish people fleeing to the rocky crags of the mountains in Northern Iraq and Iran were flashed around the world. Within days I was on the flight deck of an old C-130 landing in western Iran, having helped organize a humanitarian airlift from Rhein-Main airbase in Germany. "Active faith," Helen Keller said, "knows no fear." My life has been guided by similar experiences in many places over the years since. Realizing that acting quickly purchases time and saves lives, I have generally tried to move right away into the vacuum following a disaster.

My chief exemplars were sacrificial humanitarians like Albert Schweitzer, "Burma Surgeon" Gordon Seagrave, and other heroic pioneers such as high profile explorer Roy Chapman Andrews. My brilliant but somewhat arcane archaeology professor, Joseph Free, demonstrated what persistence can do in crossing borders, implementing projects in exotic locations, dealing successfully with local governments' Byzantine bureaucracies, and triumphing over petty critics in academe. By joining his excavations at Dothan in Palestine as a young college graduate I gained abilities that later allowed me to successfully implement an Indiana Jones–type of excavation at the Pyramids of Giza some five years before the film of that name was released.

Spiritually, I was influenced by studying and absorbing the Bible, which I read through three times before graduating high school. Other influences were biographies such as those of John Wesley and David Brainard, and devotional books like Thomas á Kempis's *Imitation of Christ*, Charles Sheldon's *In His Steps*, and *The Acting Person* by Karol Wojtyla (Pope John Paul II).

My college roommate Dale Rhoton and his friend George Verwer fearlessly campaigned for greater religious freedom by traveling behind the Iron Curtain and throughout the Muslim world. Within a very few years in the early 1960s they organized two thousand young people to sell Christian literature throughout Europe and to trek overland as far as India. Eventually, the group Operation Mobilization purchased four large ships all filled with dedicated and enthusiastic young people from every nation fanning out to sell literature at each port around the world. This activist milieu engaged me in possibility thinking, and the belief that no obstacle was too great to overcome with determination and persistence.

Intellectually, I was first challenged by the idea of philosophy itself, which urged radical thinking apart from faith in scripture. What was at first a shock—the ancient Greek Sceptics—became a feast in philosophy, as I devoured master works from Plato to Kierkegaard and Barth. In practical terms, widespread poverty and the inequality of the existing economic system posed a challenge to my thinking. Although I read and rejected the ideology of Engels and Marx, radical protests during the Cold War sharpened my perception of social injustice and its relation to poverty.

A major influence on the direction of my life came after I was already a young college professor. I met personally with Charles H. Malik, one of the drafters of the Universal Declaration of Human Rights and the former chair of the General Assembly of the United Nations. He urged me, if I really want to understand politics, to spend one year studying Thucydides and two years studying Aristotle. I took his advice and have never regretted it. At the time I was enrolled in a program in Archaeology and Near Eastern Studies at the University of Chicago's famed Oriental Institute, but subsequently switched to classics and earned a PhD in history under the University of Illinois' provost, Dr. Ron Legon. In 2013 I was honored by the University of Illinois Alumni Association as Humanitarian of the Year.

Later, as a professor of Islamic Civilization at the American Islamic College, the first Muslim institute of higher education to gain initial accreditation in North America, I became absorbed by Ibn Khaldun's *Muqaddima*. As the acknowledged founder of the discipline of sociology, his insights were, and are, magisterial. In sum, the two major intellectual influences on my subsequent peacemaking and humanitarian work would necessarily be, first, Thucydides, who taught *realpolitik* in his famous Melian Dialogue, and second, Ibn Khaldun, who illuminated *asabiyeh,* or group solidarity in social systems, as a way of understanding political events. Whereas one's motivation for action may be philosophical, it also must be practical in order to succeed.

Catalyst

In the case of the Iraq War, one catalyst for action was the inescapable clash between the two realities of capitalism and collectivism, a struggle that had occupied most of the twentieth century. By the year 2000, Marxism as a revolutionary philosophy was certainly fading but still cast a long shadow. Thomas Piketty's *Capital in the Twenty-First Century* (2014), a magisterial response to Marx's *Das Kapital*, has subsequently made it clear that inequality remains the most important economic issue in today's world, driving political campaigns, incidents of domestic strife within countries, and much that we see of international conflict and domination.

Another catalyst that motivated the peacemaking efforts by the delegations I led to Iraq, Iran, and Syria was the realization that false motives and jingoism lurked behind many of the smooth political arguments of many of the talking heads on television and of those in power in Washington. At the core of their cleverly contrived talking points there was always to be found an ugly, raw assertion of a political agenda backed by money and power. Our delegations recognized, and were motivated by the fact that the situation was urgent and demanded taking risks.

In the United States there existed the gargantuan military-industrial-economic-political-academic-journalistic-entertainment-social-religious complex on the one hand, and a nationalistic-jingoistic tendency on the other. In Iraq, there was a kind of false bravado linked with a contrived nationalism, this coupled with a servile, almost abject, fear of the ruthless Saddam Hussein dictatorship. Neither of the protagonists, the United States or Iraq, ever understood its opposite.

We felt that it was incumbent for those who had long experience in Iraq, who had been on the ground and had come to know the people in their homes, shops, mosques, churches, and offices over the previous decades, and who had studied, taught, and written about its history and cultural legacy, to get involved to turn the tide of the nation's mad and inexorable rush to war.

In addition to these more overt motivations for engaging in a one-sided battle against the forces driving the American war machine, there was another, more low-key but persistent, reason. That was the nagging dissatisfaction that many of us in the academy and the church felt for the failure of these institutions to stand up with courage to the obvious lies and manipulations of government and media.

Government, we understand, practices deception as part of its repertoire of tricks in "the art of the possible." But why should journalism, a noble profession, kowtow to those in power and shield the public from the truth? And what other purpose do universities and the massive scholarship they produce have besides searching out and revealing what is true? The same could be said for the legal profession and the men and women of the cloth. Yet all these institutions can be said to have significantly failed in the run-up to the Iraq Wars of 1991 and 2003–11. Most did not raise their voices at all, and those few who managed to do so, did it timidly.

Link together the massively one-sided imbalance of wealth and poverty in today's world, the devastatingly cruel and bloody exercise of military power in the search for dominance, and the nearly wholesale failure of supposedly civil and moral institutions, and you will understand the forces that drove some of us to risk plunging into the maelstrom of wars in Palestine, Gaza, Iraq, Syria, Afghanistan, Sudan's Darfur region, and Iran, with the goal of peace, and if not peace, at least witness.

"What did you do in the war, Daddy (and Mommy)?" is a question asked by each generation of children of their parents. They have every right to do so. It is civilization's task to pass on values, and only humane values are worthy of being acted on if the future is to be preserved. In a crisis it is not words but deeds that count. Therefore, we were moved to act. For some of us, the motivation to become peacemakers was a religious one, for religion properly understood is about peace. Synagogues, churches, and mosques that teach otherwise are alien from the spirit of religion.

For others, the motivation was a crystal clear understanding of what we have learned of history, philosophy, the arts, politics, sociology, and anthropology—in short, the intellectual life of humankind as preserved and promulgated in institutions of learning. How, we asked, can destruction of civilization advance civilization? How can destroying human beings be other than an attempt to destroy their creator, or at the very least, the creativity residing in the persons themselves? Consequently, those of us who took risks for peace did not do so hopelessly, even if the odds may have been considered impossibly long. We lived in hope and in the conviction that right prevails over might in the long run.

For many of us, standing on principle and opposing the multitude cost us jobs at the universities or churches to which we were affiliated. Some were imprisoned or fined for breaking contrived administrative rules of a partisan and myopic government, but in each case, a quiet satisfaction—even joy—was our reward. By standing firmly for what is true and honorable against great odds, often at great cost, we could proudly show our children, and others who would listen, the value of acting on conscience.

Yet at the time the truly prophetic voices that challenged the war fever went unheeded. As the years went on, however, the overwhelming majority of American citizens—and even the politicians that had unthinkingly supported the Neo-Con War in Iraq—reversed their positions. By 2016 it was hard to find a leading political figure or conservative think tank in Washington still maintaining that Bush and Cheney's war on Iraq was a good idea. The realization came late—but at what a cost in lives and treasure, both in the Middle East and in our own country!

Historical Background

It is impossible to clearly understand the rigorous demands and incipient possibilities for peacemaking in the world of the early twenty-first century without an examination of the current economic and political situation and how we as Americans have arrived where we are both as national and world citizens.

A decade-by-decade overview of the American experience in the second half of the twentieth century is instructive. By the American experience, I mean the social and psychological evolution of the U.S. electorate over the more than seventy years since the end of World War II, since citizenship is a theoretical, not an organic, concept. The United States with its Constitution is simply an agreed framework for civic identity and deportment, but not a necessary one. Among other examples that could be adduced, the Civil War was a failed attempt to construct a different set of values. It is therefore obvious that the mindset of citizens in a democracy can, will, and must, change over time.

Among the most impactful changes that have occurred over the last three-quarters of a century are those of communications and technological innovation. Television was not common in American homes until the mid-fifties. Computers as a workforce aid, and the internet as a vehicle for a vast explosion of knowledge, were not widely available until the late eighties and mid-nineties. That almost everyone in the developed world, and increasing numbers in the developing world, are personally connected wherever they happen to be by hand-held devices, has created a stunning expansion of power, both individual and corporate. These inventions have profoundly altered the economic and political landscape of the entire world, meaning that the climate for peace has never been better, nor at the same time more fraught with danger.

What all this has meant to the growth of American military power leading its current world hegemony is both complex and instructive, but the real issue is twofold: the transition to an oligarchic political system and the rise of radical conservatism in a large segment of the U.S. electorate. Much in American life has fundamentally changed from the unique social and political solidarity of the years 1941–45 to the discordant politics of the early twenty-first century. This is where a retrospective over the past several decades is useful.

Unlike Germany and Japan, the United States came out of World War II with its cities intact. As the world's most powerful nation, the U.S. in the following decades experienced an era of cultural confidence expressed in the growth of trade and international involvement, as well as in its determined resistance to the Soviet Union and its allied nations. Under the threat of nuclear missiles and challenged by the space race with the Soviets, patriotism was high. Middle class expansion appeared favorable as jobs and housing became more plentiful, even in the face of troubling inequality in race relations and the incipient civil rights movement. The fifties were therefore an energetic time, as expressed in the worldwide popularity of American films and music, particularly jazz and rock and roll. Americans were known the world over as having a "can do" spirit. Eisenhower, the European war's victorious general and a kind of paternal figure, was president, and all seemed right with the world.

The sixties burst on the scene with an altogether different type of energy: the disruptive Vietnam War that pitted children against parents and helped to spawn the hippie movement and the popularity of recreational drugs. For the first time since the early-twentieth-century women's franchise and temperance movements, the decade's vigorous antiwar and civil rights movements philosophically challenged the political status quo. Americans were forced to reexamine their unthinking patriotism, their largely fear-based militarism, and even the ages-old morality that had once been taken for granted. Some considered this period the "Greening of America," others its downfall. Like the Civil War in the nineteenth century, the Vietnam War in the twentieth tore the country apart significantly and still casts a long shadow today. Most analysts consider the counterculture sixties a definitive time in changing the direction and even the nature of American citizenship.

Perhaps it was inevitable as a follow-on by natural progression that the seventies became known as the "me" decade, a phrase coined in 1976 by novelist Tom Wolfe in *New York* magazine. Its excesses marked the period as an era of rampant individualism, hedonism, and materialism. The 1980s saw the beginning of materialism run amok, typified by the 1987 movie *Wall Street*, starring actor Michael Douglas as an amoral corporate raider with the famous line, "Greed is good." The insights provided by this fictional analysis nevertheless exposed two things that characterized the 1980s in America: wealthy excess and corruption. Clearly, the strengthening of the oligarchic class and the marked decline of the middle class dates from this period.

In the 1990s, the long shadow of the collapse of the Soviet Union and failure of Marxism generally as an economic and political philosophy led to a turn to neoliberalism in economics and neoconservatism in politics. By the year 2000, complacency with the status quo seems to have failed to motivate American voters to differentiate between the two political parties, and by the narrowest of margins and an unprecedented Supreme Court ruling young George W. Bush became president. The Neo-Cons in Washington and fat cats on Wall Street were ecstatic. However, the 2000 election presaged ruin for the country in the next decade, with the September 11, 2001, terrorist attacks, the disastrous Iraq War, and the economic meltdown and collapse of major banks. In combination, these events managed to trash both the Constitution and the economy.

The years following 2010 saw gradual improvement under the Democratic administration of Barack Obama. Several national election campaigns touched on the theme of inequality, but it was not until the Occupy Movement began protesting against Wall Street in 2011 that the evident inequality in American society was widely exposed. By 2016, the alarming reality of the economic dominance of the 1 percent became the central claim of Democratic presidential aspirant Bernie Sanders. But millions of Republican conservatives endorsed the meteoric and chaotic rise of billionaire Donald Trump. His presidential campaign was sometimes accompanied by violent clashes, a scenario that had played out before in the streets of Italy and Germany during the 1930s.

Action

The first step in antiwar activism is always rejection of the prevailing jingoistic mindset. In the case of the 2003 Iraq War, the first step taken was necessarily a repudiation of the facile and superficial claims put forward by Washington's political leaders and their sycophants, who at times included not only the entire government bureaucracy, but also many supposedly independent think tanks and revered journalistic institutions. It was therefore no surprise when a high percentage of the public followed these prestigious institutions wholesale in supporting the Bush administration's evident eagerness for war.

The few voices that dissented were from higher education, from churches with a strong peace tradition, and from several veterans' organizations. Consequently, groups that coalesced around rejection of the war were typically made up of people from the intellectual, spiritual, and experiential-activist traditions. This fits the pattern of those who, a generation earlier, had marched in civil rights protests and resisted the war in Vietnam, most of whose leading figures were those with deep knowledge, sincere faith, and relevant experience.

Determination

The second step in taking action was determination. It required firm resolution to pursue a course that was overwhelmingly unpopular, being against the tide of almost all public opinion. Those few public intellectuals who constantly rubbed public opinion the wrong way found it necessary to have strong philosophic roots and a deep well of resolve that would enable them to stand like a rock against the so-called "muscular" foreign policy of the Neo-Cons.

Risk

Next was acceptance of risk. It is normal for humans to avoid risk, and almost all universities and churches are excessively risk averse. Not only was advocating peaceful diplomacy rather than war, and understanding rather than confrontation, uncertain of success, it could be downright dangerous. Among the risks to war dissenters were the actual physical danger to life and health from being in a war zone, and other dangers such as being arrested or fired from a job, or in a lesser way, becoming unpopular or misunderstood. Yet our groups of activists persisted, taking arguments for peace to the halls of Congress and to those rare media outlets that would listen, but also to the borders of Iraq, trekking on foot across the desert from Rutba to towns under active aerial bombing, including Ramadi, Falluja, Tikrit, Balad, Baquba, and Baghdad itself.

Courage

Those who took risks for peace had little protection; it was requisite that they hold nothing back. The kind of activities our groups engaged in required a person to go all out and "all in" for peace. This was an especially challenging step for academics to take. Living in an ivory tower surrounded by ivy-covered walls, enjoying the quiet prestige of an elevated profession, and in some cases having the security of a sinecure beneath chapel bells, it was a shock to suddenly find yourself in a war zone sleeping on the floor beneath the rocket's red glare. But it was a necessity if our convictions were to hold true.

Practical Steps: Dealing with Officialdom

There were many practical steps to be taken before vision could become reality. For American citizens there were official barriers from our own government. The Department of State regularly issues travel warnings and posts them online as well as at U.S. Embassies abroad, which, if they were read and believed, would be extremely intimidating to those intending to travel to war-torn countries.

In addition, Congress passed the Iraq Sanctions Act, a blanket prohibition for American citizens to engage in any sort of transaction with that country. This was reinforced by the Treasury Department's Office of Foreign Assets Control (OFAC), which exercised a tyrannical, and as some of us believed, unconstitutional, control over a U.S. citizen's First Amendment rights. Even so, this presented legal and bureaucratic obstacles that had to be overcome. In a few cases, individuals—and one group—were found in violation of these provisions and given large fines.

Then there were the obstacles from the Iraqi side. The government and security services were naturally suspicious of Americans, given the hostile political climate, always fearing penetration by the CIA. Visas were notoriously hard to get, and were almost always slow in coming. The shortest time required was six weeks, but it could take as long as six months if they were to be granted at all. Under these circumstances it was extremely demanding to make travel arrangements for a large group of delegates, secure airline tickets without being sure that the visas would be awarded, and prepare a meaningful program involving academics from numerous universities in the United States and Iraq, while simultaneously dealing with stodgy and duplicitous bureaucracies in both countries.

We came to realize gradually that borders are permeable, that even the most obdurate wall can be breached by persistence and trust. Bureaucracies are much the same everywhere. High officials and power elites are similar in every country. All are human, and despite the fact that they often dwell within a security bubble surrounded by sycophants and imbued with self-importance, they become amazingly accessible if they perceive that it is in their self-interest to do so. Our slogan was always, "Dialogue is essential or conflict is inevitable."

The magic ingredient is sincerity. People, especially political people, often have an openness to and are quick to recognize the disarming simplicity of sincerity. We tell our story in a few words: our motivations, our desire for fairness, peace, and justice, and intention to help change the situation. We have almost always been met with reciprocal expressions on the other side, whether from presidents, kings, dictators, warlords, or ordinary people. Of course, diplomatic niceties are required in meeting high-level people, but deception doesn't work. Maybe that's why we could get into places and secure interviews and arrange meetings that the intelligence agencies couldn't.

Outcomes

In dealing with the media, we learned that high-sounding policy papers, impressive venues for holding press conferences, and other such lures do not attract coverage, even though the subject of war or peace is vitally important. Broadcasters will generally ignore the bland ideology of peace in favor of covering dramatic or bloody events. So we set out to create events that news directors and reporters could not afford to ignore. By the simple expedient of initiating direct action, we faced many television cameras in the United States and abroad, often being besieged for numerous TV, radio, and newspaper interviews, sometimes up to a dozen a day. We also held teach-ins and were continually interacting with the "enemy," which created opportunities for ongoing dialogue leading to two-way understanding.

Principles

Our principles were based on several basic convictions. We felt it necessary to act on conscience, to connect on the human level, to recognize and celebrate the humanity of the other, the "enemy." We acted in order to create trust by our sincerity, to cut through the typical political hypocrisy and double-dealing by simply being honest. We had to ignore political and legal barriers, even though they were intimidating. We came to realize that conscience is higher than law.

On the practical side, we discovered that we had to keep going back time after time, to develop solid friendships, and to keep our objectives in mind, which allowed us to make progress incrementally. This process helped us to design outside-the-box solutions. Sometimes we had the opportunity to show key policymakers that there might be openings for a peaceful resolution of conflicts other than those they currently imagined.

It was our goal to help the people we met, whether foreign ministers, parliamentarians, academics, clerics, or party leaders, to envision a better future. But first we had to lead them into a position of trust through a demonstration of our friendship. We refused to see Sudan or Iran as an enemy country, thus opening a dialogue with their leaders that might have been unimaginable to them before we proposed it. By being willing to personally become the missing "bridge across troubled waters," we made inroads for peace. In this way we were able to meet and hold discussions with Deputy Prime Minister Tariq Aziz in Iraq, President Bashar al-Assad in Syria, Former president Nimeiri and vice president Taha in Sudan, the prime minister of Lebanon, and three successive presidents of Iran, Sayyids Khatami, Ahmadinejad, and Rouhani.

We met with many parliamentarians and cabinet members in several countries. In addition, we met with Islamist parties, including the Muslim Brotherhood (*Ikwan Muslimin*) in Egypt, Hezbollah and HAMAS in Jordan, Lebanon, and Gaza, and with radical groups such as the Janjaweed in Sudan and the Taliban in Afghanistan and Pakistan. We tried to help these diverse actors realize that options were available that they might never have thought of. We were thus able to achieve meaningful connections and active engagement with influential forces in the opposing country, a necessary precursor to peace. This pattern may be useful for other groups seeking a peaceful way forward. We must continue to believe that, if pursued with dedication, energy, and persistence, peace advocacy will be effective. The cost of doing nothing is too great not to try.

Chapter 9

Voices in the Wilderness

KATHY KELLY

"Now, Kathy dear, don't be actin' too big for your britches!" Truthfully, growing up on the southwest side of Chicago, I wasn't sure what my mom's gentle warning meant. But the peace activism that eventually drew me into prisons and war zones most likely qualified for what my mom had in mind. And, at times, my actions drew an exasperated critique from others in my family: "Look what you're doing to Mom!" Fortunately for me, my siblings tried hard to understand me. They can laugh good-naturedly now at the notion that the IRS has become my spiritual director. They share my dismay over the overcrowded, cruel prison system.

Recently, I was asked to speak with a group of foster grandparents in Buffalo, New York. About eighty-five people, predominantly people of color, had assembled. Feeling awkward about being the fourth white woman to make a presentation that morning, I decided to begin by imitating the mechanical voice that begins every phone call made by a federal prisoner: "This is a call from a federal prison. This phone call will be monitored. If you wish to accept this call, press one. If you wish to reject this call, press three. If you wish to reject all future calls, press five." As soon as I began intoning the all too familiar tape, a majority of people shared a groan together. All of them knew the frustrations associated with phone calls from federal prisons. A familiar, perhaps even familial note had been sounded.

I wanted to give the foster grandparents some sort of credentials for being in front of them, and so I described what I had done to land myself in a federal prison. I told them that I had resigned from the increasingly posh Jesuit College Prep school where I had taught for six years and begun teaching English in my neighborhood's alternative school, where many of the students belonged to rival gangs. Tragically, at this school, annually, three or more students were killed. Often the cause was gang violence or a drug-related crime, but essentially these youngsters died because of poverty. I longed to be part of an action that would raise consciousness about the U.S. arsenal of nuclear weapons maintained at the expense of funding for social needs.

In 1988, a sturdy group of Midwestern activists settled on a plan to plant corn on top of nuclear missile silos. Calling ourselves "Missouri Peace Planters," we repeatedly planted corn at sites across Missouri where Intercontinental Ballistic Missiles were buried under the ground. This action "earned" me a year in prison, one of the most educational years of my life. In prison, I met kindly women who taught me about how poverty contributes toward rising rates of incarceration. I also gained perspective regarding fear. Punishment meted out by the U.S. courts could be fearful, but it would be far worse to become intimidated into cooperating with reckless elites ruling the United States that pursued criminal foreign and domestic policies.

The foster grandparents nodded in agreement when I said that I believed the wars we've waged were criminal, that my actions didn't represent crimes, that the prison industrial complex and mass incarceration were crimes, and as the United States poured resources into wars, there could be nothing left to meet the needs of vulnerable young people at risk of being caught up in the "rail to jail" system. What alternative did the U.S. government offer them? They could loan themselves to kill other people or possibly be killed themselves by enlisting in the U.S. military.

I was fortunate to be taught, in high school, by a progressive group of educators who were part of two religious orders, the Christian Brothers and the Sisters of St. Joseph. They taught us that the Rev. Dr. Martin Luther King Junior was a saint and a prophet of our time; that when the U.S. Air Force sprayed defoliant on trees in Viet Nam, it also fell on the backs of children; our teachers showed us the film *Night and Fog*, which French artist-historians created to document the terrible remains of Nazi concentration camps. This film made me wish never, ever to be sitting on the sidelines in the face of an unspeakable evil.

Nevertheless, I went through most of the Viet Nam war without ever involving myself in protest or nonviolent direct action. After earning an MA in religious education and teaching for a few years, I reached a point at which I could no longer teach about "the preferential option for the poor" and live in a neighborhood, Hyde Park, where I seldom encountered poor people. I moved to Uptown, one of Chicago's poorest areas, in the summer of 1979. New friends encouraged me to volunteer at the local soup kitchen, to take a turn staying overnight at the shelter, and to spend free time visiting with guests in the local house of hospitality and at a drop-in center for women living on the streets.

I grew close to neighbors, many of them desperately poor, or, as Black Lives Matter activists teach us to say, historically looted. Those encounters made it easier to eliminate from my personal budget expenditures for weapons. Why would I direct money toward payment for hideous weapon systems and ongoing war when my own neighbors slept in shelters, ate at soup kitchens, and struggled to meet their children's most basic human needs? Some of those children wouldn't survive their teenage years without becoming addicted, imprisoned, or, in all too many cases, being murdered. The "war on poverty" that had made so much sense just one decade earlier was turning into a war against the poor; levels of mass incarceration began to rise while programs such as Head Start were closing down. Meanwhile, weapons makers and war profiteers prospered.

Karl Meyer, an architect of war tax refusal during the Vietnam War, lived in Uptown. Soon after getting to know him, I asked my employers at St. Ignatius College Prep to lower my salary beneath the taxable income. That was in 1980, and since that time, thanks to Karl's careful advice, I've been a war tax refuser. In other words, I've successfully resisted paying all forms of federal income tax. Had I ever owned a car or a house or any seizable property, the IRS might have taken it. Living in Uptown, befriended by Catholic Workers and inspired by Karl's perspective, I grew enamored with prospects of living simply, sharing resources with others, and trying not to let inconvenience interfere with acting in accord with my deepest beliefs.

Some months after release from my first federal prison sentence (one year in maximum security for planting the corn on nuclear missile silo sites), I joined a twenty-eight-day water only fast in front of the U.S. Army School of the Americas. Our group of about one dozen people fasting believed this school shouldn't exist because graduates of the training had been indicted and convicted of committing massacres, assassinations, disappearances, torture, and other human rights violations. The fast offered time for reflection. Shortly after that fast, Saddam Hussein invaded Kuwait.

I was one among many U.S. people who, in 1990, could spell the word *Iraq* and find Kuwait on a map, if given a few minutes, but I knew little more than that. However, Ammon Hennacy's words had a great influence on me: "You can't be a vegetarian between meals and you can't be a pacifist between wars." With growing likelihood that the United States would soon go to war against Iraq, I felt increasing interest in a group called The Gulf Peace Team, which was planning a nonviolent interposition between the warring parties. The Gulf Peace Team began accepting volunteers and eventually sent word that I could join them.

We camped in the Iraqi desert during the first weeks of the Desert Storm bombing until Iraqi authorities decided to evacuate our tent encampment, fearful that we actually might be in the way of a U.S. military maneuver. We were taken by bus to Baghdad and from there, after a few days of intense aerial bombing; we were bused out of the country to Amman, Jordan. Some of us were given visas to re-enter Iraq. Traveling out of Iraq, we saw mangled and destroyed vehicles, including an ambulance, on the roadside. In Amman, we realized that if we traveled back and forth along Iraqi roads, we might help safeguard the only route available for refugees fleeing the war and the only road that could be used for delivering humanitarian relief to beleaguered Iraqis. We declared our intent to travel along the road between Amman and Baghdad, carrying medical relief supplies, and quickly turned to people in Amman, Jordan, for help in securing medicines, vehicles, drivers, and public support for our hastily arranged convoy, hoping to protect the roads from U.S. bombing. The Desert Storm war ended in mid-March 1991, but our convoy efforts continued for several more months.

When I returned to the United States in August 1991, Iraq seemed to have dropped off of everyone's radar screen. Eventually, I too stopped paying much attention to Iraq and became more absorbed in teaching, in caring for my aging dad who had moved into my apartment, and in promoting various other peace team efforts. But by December 1995, several friends and I who had been in Iraq either before, during or after the first Gulf War realized that the war had never ended—it had changed into a terrible economic war waged through the most comprehensive sanctions ever imposed in modern history.

We decided to launch Voices in the Wilderness, a campaign to end the economic sanctions against Iraq. On January 15, 1996, we announced to the U.S. Attorney in Chicago that we would carry medicines and medical relief supplies to Iraq as often as we possibly could in open defiance of the economic sanctions against Iraq. The U.S. Office of Foreign Assets Control and the Treasury Dept. notified us that if we persisted with our plan we'd face severe financial penalties and possibly twelve years in prison. We thanked the government for the clarity of the warning, assured officials that we wouldn't be governed by unjust laws, and invited them to join us in going to Iraq.

In August 2002, about a dozen Voices activists met in Chicago and decided to launch the Iraq Peace Team with the objective of bringing internationals to live alongside ordinary Iraqis before and during what increasingly seemed to be an imminent war. Bonds had developed, over the years, between ourselves and Iraqi friends who had given us help and hospitality. We didn't want to let war sever those bonds. Forming the Iraq Peace Team was our way of helping to encourage rising resistance to the U.S.-led bombing and invasion of Iraq.

∿

I think courage is the ability to control our fears. Everyone feels fear. But when our fears steer our actions, or when we become reactive and lose our composure (often because we feel insecure), it's difficult to regain equilibrium and to control our words and actions so that we don't hurt others or violate their basic rights.

One way to develop equilibrium and equanimity, as members of the human family, is to keep one foot firmly planted among those who are most oppressed or disadvantaged in our society and the other foot firmly planted in nonviolent resistance to oppression. I think this helps us overcome fears that governments sometimes cultivate and promote. For example, oppressive and greedy elites can sometimes control the resources of other people and profit from the weapons industry if they can convince people that their security lies in allowing the government to make war against certain people who are considered to be enemies. The belligerent country will then emphasize frightening and demonic threats posed by the so-called enemy. If citizens of one country are sufficiently frightened or feel terribly threatened, they are more likely to go along with waging war against the so-called enemy.

What do these wars accomplish? We lose our sense of equanimity, and we find out later that we have caused havoc, destruction, suffering, and smoldering resentment. People who have been bereaved, maimed, displaced, and traumatized by wars understand that "war isn't over when it's over." Had the general public in developed countries been better informed and educated, they could have done more to resist the wars waged in Iraq and Afghanistan.

Gaza is another case in point. In 2008, when Israel launched Operation Cast Lead against Gaza, I was well aware that U.S. taxpayers had funded Israel's military and that the United States had helped Israel develop the arsenal of weapons being used against Gazans. I felt it was important to live alongside people who could not escape these attacks and at least try to tell U.S. people about experiences of Gazans who were trapped and terrorized. Gazans were living under siege. They struggled with the inability to protect their children from constant attacks. From 11:00 at night until 1:00 in the morning, a bomb exploded once every eleven minutes. There was a lull until 3:00 a.m. and then three more hours of bombing. Some of the bombs were Hellfire missiles fired from Apache helicopters. Some were five hundred–pound bombs dropped by F-15 fighter planes. Children in the family I stayed with helped me distinguish between the different explosions. Because they were living under a state of siege, Gazans could not easily acquire materials to rebuild their homes and infrastructure.

I particularly remember going to the village of Al Atatra, after sitting at the bedside of Sabah Abu Halemi, a woman who had survived an Israeli attack on her home. The troops used tank-fired white phosphorous bombs, killing her husband and several other family members. The nightmarish accounts she gave of what happened left me wondering how she would ever cope with such trauma. My young friends and I went to the home and met one of her surviving sons. He showed us that he had collected his father's remains for proper burial. Then he took us inside the home, which the Israeli troops had completely ransacked. On the wall of one room, in green spray paint, someone had written, "From the Israeli Defense—We're sorry." When I returned to the United States, I read a full accounting of Sabah Abu Halemi's story, written by Sabrina Tavernise, in the *New York Times*. I feel very troubled still, wishing that I had volunteered to stay at the bedside of Sabah Abu Halemi, in the hospital, during a time when she suffered terribly and must have felt acutely alone. Later, the kindly doctor who introduced me to her told me that she had recovered from the burns she suffered.

I felt that I was as vulnerable as anyone else in the neighborhood where I stayed. We were living in Rafah, very close to the border and to the area where the Israelis were intent on destroying a network of tunnels.

As regards the possibility of being killed, I felt the same recognition that I first experienced in 1991 when I joined the Gulf Peace Team. Now, as then, it seems to me that I've been exceedingly fortunate in life, having been blessed with many joys and satisfactions and having been able, for much of my life, to live in accord with deeply held beliefs. If participation in a team demanding an end to a war while attempting to accompany people trapped in a war zone occasioned the end of my life, I could honestly say that I'd had many good years of life.

I first traveled to Afghanistan in May 2010. The Emergency Surgical Center for Victims of War allowed me and Josh Brollier, also a co-coordinator from Voices, to live in their guest rooms at two of their hospitals, in Kabul and Panjshir. Through firsthand observation and the dramatic accounts of these brave health care professionals, we learned more about the plight of Afghans whose basic needs for food, water, health care, jobs, and education often went unmet. By phone, we reached the Afghan Peace Volunteer mentor, Dr. Hakim, who lived in Bamiyan at the time. He encouraged us to visit Bamiyan, and three of us were able to do so in October 2010.

The Afghan Peace Volunteers, a group of teens who were working together, inter-ethnically, on various peacemaking projects, welcomed us warmly. We have built lasting relationships with this group, which now bases itself in Kabul. Their visions, projects, disappointments, and successes are documented extensively at a website called ourjourneytosmile.com.

Voices delegations that have stayed in Kabul as guests of the Afghan Peace Volunteers have done their best, when they have returned to their home countries, to speak and write about realities Afghan people face. The United States and its allies have exacerbated warfare, squandered resources, and fueled corruption. By telling what we've seen and heard, through articles, presentations, videos, photos, and interviews we've tried to educate people in the United States and the United Kingdom to accept responsibility for causing harm to Afghans, to people who meant us no harm. We also call for the United States to pay reparations for the suffering caused.

Peace movements are outspent and outmaneuvered by small groups of elites that control other countries. These elites insist that if people in other lands don't subordinate themselves to the autocratic interests of certain more powerful countries, the powerful elites and their militaries will smash and destroy the countries that defy them. The military-industrial-congressional-media complexes, which are now transnational, have a vicelike grip on education, and they consistently persuade their populations that there are no alternatives to war, that the wars serve humanitarian purposes, and that jobs will be lost if the wartime economy is threatened. The public should become educated about the consequences of war and the alternatives to war, but the task of education is very, very difficult. It certainly won't be accomplished through reliance on mainstream institutions that are already compromised and controlled by major forces loyal to the "defense" establishment.

A friend of mine recently acknowledged, using a baseball analogy, that he was "born on third base" as regards privileges and security. My friend is a well-educated white male who just finished law school and who lives in Manhattan with his spouse and two children. The income inequalities in our world are stunning. Why should the worth of one hour of one person's work be regarded as ten or even one hundred times more valuable than the worth of another person's work when both are performing necessary tasks to help societies grow and flourish? Why should people who already have so much be entitled to get more? My friend who mentioned that he was born on third base has devoted much of his life to creating, as the Catholic Worker movement puts it, "a new world within the shell of the old." He and his spouse are dedicated to sharing resources and serving the needs of the most vulnerable people in their area. They also have coordinated Witness Against Torture efforts, working to close Guantanamo, for the past six years.

We need communities of nonviolent resistance to defy the cultural norms that accept callous and dangerous inequities. It's interesting, to me, that some of the happiest people I know live in such communities.

I'm glad to be living in a time when people are reaching for new vocabulary to express right relationship with the world around us. Maybe we should seek adherents to "being-ism," to feeling empathy for all beings, human and animal, as well as grateful desire to sustain planetary life. Of course we cannot refrain from harming every being on the planet. But to whatever extent possible, living with compassionate regard for all beings seems wise and fulfilling in this precarious time when the environment has been so damaged by human overconsumption and the recklessness of human pollution and waste.

Thinking about human beings, I believe the neediest and most impoverished should always be our top priority. How do we build empathy and compassion? The counsels of personalism are helpful. Start with personal relationships, seeking equality and learning ways to refute the idea that one person's life is more valuable than that of another person. I think it's helpful for peace activists to live alongside people trapped in war zones and in prisons so that the victims of war and of the prison industrial complex can educate us.

I often feel hampered by language and inexperience when trying to hear what other people desperately want to tell us when they are aggrieved and enduring great suffering. We can listen better when we are accompanied by people who are trusted interpreters. This works in personal and political life, but a deep desire to listen to the cares and concerns of others should,

I think, be cultivated in every society. I have a young friend in Kabul who likes to run in the early mornings. I fret over anyone running in a city so beset by polluted air, but Abdulhai likes to stay fit and exults in the dawn adventures. Two years ago, he introduced me to Habib, a youngster who helped his mother, grandmother, and little brother by carrying a scale through Kabul streets and inviting people to weigh themselves on the scale. He held his little brother's hand, when I met him, and the two of them did their best, as child laborers, to bring bread home each day. Home is a set of poles covered by a blue tarp. Their grandmother tries to help by going out to beg. She wears the steel blue burka and sits on a curbside, hands outstretched. Abdulhai told me that one morning, as he ran, he heard a woman's voice, begging, and he realized that it was Habib's grandmother under the burka. He stopped to greet her and they exchanged good wishes. Abdulhai showed us the kind of listening and care we need. And, somehow, I feel sure that my mother would never have felt he was acting too big for his britches as he stopped to greet Habib's grandmother.

Chapter 10

The Quiet Revolution

JIM MERKEL

Being a recovering engineer, I'm haunted by curves—two in particular. Since 1800, world population grew from 1 to 7.4 billion people while world GDP grew from $660 to $13,000 per capita. These two exponential curves multiplied yield a 140-fold increase in human activity over two hundred years. The results include climate destabilization, wars, extinctions, and pandemics, to name a few. And in 2015 we added another 85 million more people—the population of Viet Nam or Germany.

Scientists at the Global Footprint Network led by Susan Burns and Mathis Wackernagel annually measure human ecological footprints. Through a massive data analysis of country-by-country use of raw materials, they arrive at the land and sea area needed to produce what a person consumes and needed to absorb her wastes. And each year they determine Earth Overshoot Day. In 2015, August 13 was the unlucky day when humanity's demand exceeded earth's capacity. From August 13 until the end of the year, earth's systems were in decline. We'd need a planet and a half to sustainably support the 7.4 billion living now as they do and by 2030 we'd need two planets. With world population set to reach 11 billion by 2100, it is obvious that we are the generation that gets to watch humans devour the planet. Before concluding that population is humanity's biggest challenge, let me share one more data point: the world's wealthiest billion alone consume the entire planet's annual yield.

As part of my work toward world peace and sustainability, I began an experiment in 1989. I turned in my top secret clearance, stopped selling military electronics and simplified until my consumption was in the ballpark of average world GDP—around $5,000. And to slow population growth, I delayed fatherhood into my fifties and then stopped at one child.

World peace seemed unlikely and unpalatable if I continued the lifestyle of a North American. My experience inside the war machine left a putrid taste that Bruce Cockburn's song "This is Baghdad," captures, "Car bombed and carjacked and kidnapped and shot. How do you like it, this freedom we brought?" I feel such sadness over the holy horror I contributed to for five years while designing and marketing military electronics. And after that experience, even paying taxes compares to hiring assassins. Keeping income below the taxable level offers a taste of the choices available to the majority of the world's people. But it also means I can be a full-time volunteer and a war tax resister without having my home taken away.

Unlike Snowden, Assange, and Manning, I lacked the courage to expose what I knew, not wanting to rot in a prison cell, hole up in an embassy, or live on the run. I did, however, commit my life to peace, human rights, and the environment and attempt daily to forgo the privileges that one-world-superpower status offer its citizens.

By taking on the challenge of living as a global citizen, nearly all my behaviors needed transformation. Twenty-seven years into this experiment it never grows old. Each year I grow more food, get better at fixing and building things and get better at saying no to things I don't need. I also get better at saying yes to things that add value to my life—such as becoming a father.

This experience solidified several things for me. First, I value having time to contribute to a better world. I've put on a tie and walked the halls of Congress and served on local government committees. I've gotten arrested and founded and directed organizations. And for a few years, I nudged Dartmouth College toward sustainable practices as their first sustainability coordinator. I've come to appreciate the infinite ways to work toward peace from mindfulness to direct action.

Secondly, I feel urgency in creating a peaceful world but attempt to remain present and unstressed. Without self-care, I spiral down. A certain amount of yoga, meditation, play, fresh air, and exercise keeps my keel somewhat even during this crazy period of human history. I've heard it said that if you haven't felt depressed lately, you should see a doctor.

Thirdly, world peace seems unlikely to be fostered or brokered by the United States while we maintain one-world-superpower status and use that status absorbed in self-interest. Our role must be to secure the well-being of the marginalized and future generations, and this will require a serious spiritual maturation. I know from firsthand experiences that good people do horrible things. I did. This spiritual awakening appears to be happening and grows with encouragement.

My latest project is the making of a documentary film with a working title *The Hundred-Year Plan* that optimistically lays out the essentials for defusing the population bomb, easing climate change, and averting the sixth great extinction. It tells the quietly dramatic story of educated and empowered women around the world who choose small families while creatively living with small ecological footprints. These conditions played out over one hundred years could return a healthy balance between humans and nature.

Biologist E. O. Wilson explains the sixth great extinction this way: "not an asteroid or volcano this time, rather human impact—a death of a thousand cuts—a little bit taken here, a little bit ceded to an oil company there." Added together, we are losing about thirty thousand species a year, where fossil records indicate background rates of ten per year.

On the side of hope, Wilson adds, "Our species might just luck out, with enough dropping population, improved production, and shrinking ecological footprint that we can win the race to save the rest of life." Wilson's book *Half Earth* suggests that by leaving at least half of the earth's areas intact, we could avert the sixth great extinction. The *Hundred-Year Plan* seeks to show how Wilson's "Half Earth" solution could come about by taking control of two things that you and I actually have control over: How much we take and how many children we make.

To unfold this story, I'm in the process of journeying to three exemplary societies: Cuba, Slovenia, and Kerala, a state in southern India. Through conversations with three generations of women, we will learn if the decades of social movements for family planning, gender equity, universal education, and healthcare improved their lives. Although these societies are poor by American standards, they now exhibit exceptional longevity, low infant mortality rates, and high literacy. In a world of increasing class division, battles over dwindling resources, and an economic system that demands continuous growth, the *Hundred-Year Plan* will explore how these societies have begun to model a sustainable future.

Due to gains in women's status around the world, eighty-two countries, totaling almost half of the world's people, now experience fertility levels below replacement and populations are set to retreat. But just as population pressures are easing, the stakes are raised as leaders in fifty-six countries work to develop policies to encourage women to have more children. Fears circle in the heads of multinational corporations, bankers, and politicians: Who will buy all the junk they want to keep making profits from, who will pay the taxes and who will pay for retired people's services?

The obvious benefits of naturally and compassionately encouraging small families and small footprints for the next hundred years are clear—we can set our planet on a course of restoration and pass a healing planet onto each generation. Every issue we face eases. We'll figure out how to love and care for our elders without growth economics. All we have to do is have zero, one, or two children, and shrink our footprints to about a quarter of the average American's. For comparison, a person in the United States uses seventeen acres, in Slovenia eleven acres, in Cuba four acres, and in Kerala, just two acres.

After filming low-footprint societies abroad, we'll return to home to focus the camera on the movements and people pushing the sustainability envelope within the small, increasingly progressive community of Belfast on the coast of Maine. We will see how, in the land of plenty, people have radically simplified while improving their quality of life. But the global, many-headed Hydra of unsustainable policies and habits will not give up easily. Steeped in the ether of consumerism, many see the chance to secure a livable and peaceful home for the world's children slipping away.

Part of the solution to the problem is for my son Walden, now six years old, and his generation to learn twenty-first-century survival skills from places not as mesmerized by the spell of consumerism. Seeing the low-impact, day-to-day realities in imperfect but quite sustainable societies kindles the imagination as to what is possible.

In early 2016 I traveled to Cuba, meeting filmmakers and women that have compelling stories to tell of their motivations and struggles to live simply and invent a fresh society with smaller family units. Through traveling and meeting people, I identified four areas to film, Havana, Playa Larga, Medio, and Sancti Spiritus—two urban and two rural locations. And I met amazingly hospitable real Cubans away from the tourist areas.

Cuba's forced isolation led to lifestyles and systems with dramatically reduced ecological impacts. Like the forbidden fruit, I wanted to see what my country forbid me to see and learn what Cuban women have to share from their decades of experience in gender equality, family planning, health care, literacy, and organic, small-scale food systems, all with scant fossil fuels.

To bring context to what Cuba might offer, of all the nations on earth it is the only country that has achieved a high level of human development while living on a globally sustainable footprint level. I wanted to find out for myself if there is another side to the "failed state" analysis of mainstream media. Could the (then) thawing of Cold War tactics by the United States be an opportunity for the overdeveloped world to recapture its soul?

Pedro Martin and I hopped off a trailer pulled by an old Russian tractor, paid the farmer and set off down a dirt track. We headed toward a windmill and a green oasis on a gentle hillside outside Sancti Spiritus, Cuba. The track became muddy and rutted through a cool hollow then rose into a sunny field of tomatoes.

We trekked past a small clapboard home, where a friendly couple was harvesting their February crop. They confirmed we were headed in the right direction: "See that gate up ahead? The Casimiro farm."

Through strings of contacts of empowered Cuban women, we were directed here, to one of Cuba's own permaculture giants, Leidy Casimiro Rodríguez, who returned to her family's degraded tobacco fields at the age of ten during Cuba's deepest recession, known as the "special period."

Through the gate in a living fence of thorns and coppiced trees, we entered the shade of a tropical food forest. Leidy's younger sister, Chavely Casimiro, greeted us and called off the pack of barking dogs. We walked past banana and mango trees up to the family compound of vine-covered whitewashed domes, among a permaculture playground including a large open cistern fed by a windmill-powered water pump, two biogas digesters and a rabbit house. We entered the dome used as a kitchen and dining area and met Leidy, now thirty-five, who had her laptop open working on her PhD in agroecology.

When I secured an invitation to their *finca* or family farm, I explained that our film tells the story of empowered, educated women around the world, who are leading society toward a more sustainable and peaceful future by having fewer children and learning to live well with small ecological footprints. Leidy, who has two siblings and is mother to one boy, Darío, let me know that almost any Cuban women from her generation would have something to say about this topic.

According to Cuban demographer Marisol Alfonso de Armas, the demographic transition in Cuba began in the 1930s—before it began in Latin America. An influx of immigrants, contraception, and public health initiatives dealing with mosquito-borne illnesses, along with the Great Depression, are thought to have instigated declining birth rates.

By 1978, fertility was below replacement levels and by 2008 it stood at 1.59, a rate comparable to the most developed social democracies in

Europe. For more than fifty years, Cuban women have had universal access to education, healthcare, contraception, and safe, legal abortion. These are the leading conditions demographers suggest improve the health and survivability of children, improve women's health, and lower birth rates.

Leidy's father and mother, Caridad and José, were raising two young children in 1989 as Cuba faced a tough test—the dissolution of the Soviet Union. As Cuba lost its primary trading partners in the Eastern Bloc, the impact of the U.S. embargo amplified. Without markets for its sugar and without imports of fuel, pesticides, raw materials, and food, all sectors of the economy screeched to a halt. During this "special period," the average Cuban lost twenty pounds.

José left his job as a traffic cop and returned to his parent's abused tobacco land. With a few tools he set to work with a deep commitment to not see his family go to bed hungry. He describes his return to the land of his childhood in mystical terms. The wonder and enthusiasm of a child returned and his days filled with meaning. In the beginning, they used conventional farming methods but soon the yields were falling, the family was overworked, and the land wouldn't respond. At about this same time, permaculture and agroecology methods were spreading across the island. After taking a course, José saw the shortage of energy and pesticides as an opportunity and began experimenting immediately.

The systems of permaculture originated in indigenous and pre–Green Revolution agrarian societies around the world. Dozens of fruits and vegetables are interplanted and assisted by intelligent interaction into a food forest that restores soil and ecological health. As José deconstructed the formerly extractive and poisonous Green Revolution practices, the land slowly responded.

Harnessing neighborly support with a bulldozer, they built a sizable pond below the old clapboard home site and installed a homemade hydraulic ram that pumps water without fossil energy to the top of their site.

Leidy walked us down to the pond, a human-made natural paradise budding with wildlife and tilapia—fish that wind up on the dinner table. After reveling in the stillness, Chavely led us further down the spillway and switched on the ram pump. With sprays of water and rhythmic clicks, the diaphragms began miraculously pulsing water uphill. Chavely explained that the water is piped to the land's height into a giant tank that overflows into a deep round cistern she helped build while in her teens.

As we walked back up the hill, the keyline design, which slows and directs the water flow laterally across the slope, was apparent, with gently terraced fields alternating with fruit trees and annual crops, all watered from above.

Before heading to Cuba on this "scouting" trip, my last visit was in 2009. I was nervous about how my topic of small footprints would be perceived and received. After all, billboards around Cuba then and now show a hangman's noose, with the caption "Blockade, the longest genocide in history," calling for an end to the U.S. embargo. The intent of this American policy has been to make ordinary citizens suffer to such a point as to call for a regime change toward free market capitalism.

Intellectually, I understand the severity of one of the strongest and longest embargos in history. And, having had a top-secret clearance in the 1980s, I'm not naive to the hundreds of covert assassination attempts and terrorist acts on Cuban soil funded and supported by the United States. So, to be from the United States and making a film about their small footprints seems thorny. Just as the developed nations complete their most consumptive and destructive fifty-year period in all of human history, from which Cuba was excluded, a North American comes to Cuba to glamorize their suffering in a film.

My twenty-five-year exploration of "Radical Simplicity" inspired by my travels to Kerala, India, was voluntary—a reaction against our imperialism and ecological exploitation. It was also around action—creating and living inside my wildest dream of a sustainable future.

Now, after weeks of hitchhiking, making friends, and experiencing real people's lives, homes, and daily decisions, I see the embargo's effects up close and personal. Their involuntary simplicity, with all its creativity and austerity, might, after fifty years, feel "normal" to them, but to me, the sheer scarcity of income and availability of goods is shocking.

Like a thorn in a sock, the irritation and frustration of the noose comes and goes. Nonetheless, a rural generosity and hospitality is present, similar to Kerala or Mexico or rural Maine. Most Cubans know that our incomes are twenty times theirs, and when in popular tourist areas, a gringo like me can become a walking dollar sign. This radical inequity is painful to witness and takes time to digest.

The night I left Havana for the countryside, I visited the home of Mabis Dora Álvarez, one of three hundred thousand literacy volunteers who trekked off to the countryside armed with backpacks filled with pencils and notebooks in 1962, on the eve of the Bay of Pigs invasion. As the United States stood up for the rights of the United Fruit Company to exploit another nation, Castro was delivering on his promise of education and health care for the most underserved.

Now in her eighties, Mabis tends her ailing cat and dozens of vibrant plants covering her veranda in the Vedado district of Havana. I ask about her plants. She explains that she was trained in Russia as an agronomist and spent her life working with women farmers across Cuba from the time the first agrarian reforms were signed into law on May 17, 1959.

When I explained my film project to Mabis, she responded that the agrarian reforms of Cuba were, in her mind, the most important beginning to improving the lives of women and children.

The Agrarian Reform Law limited land holdings to 993 acres and distributed the expropriated lands to the peasant farmers and the government. Families were encouraged to grow food for their families and produce for the market. Expropriated lands were to be compensated by bonds based upon assessed values used for taxes. The United States was not happy.

Fidel Castro commented, "They [the United States] are practically telling us that if we go ahead with agrarian reform, they will strangle us economically. . . . No country can have political independence if, when it issues a law, it is told it will starve to death."

The Casimiros returned to their seventeen-acre farm, determined not to starve. They had a vision of building a beautiful and sustainable subsistence life, swearing off growing sugar cane and tobacco or using chemicals.

We regroup in the communal kitchen as Leidy's brother, José, now thirty-four, comes in from his work harvesting bananas with his son and offers a bunch of ripe bananas. He quietly joins the conversation. Behind him, stacked on the counter, are sacks of rice and dried beans—several hundred pounds. Behind the counter, the hiss of the pressure cooker, fueled by homemade biogas and the quiet preparation of dinner goes on while our team sits down and describes our documentary film project to the family.

As we explained the small footprint part of the film, they told us about their twenty-five years of work and transformation. They broke out the before and after pictures—from a barren grassland to a food jungle. As they described their process, the father José strayed quickly from the practical to the philosophical and global, providing a context for the diverse motivations and contributions they see their lives offering Cubans and the world. Subsistence farms offer tremendous food security, but also healthy and creative work when done sustainably.

My worries that the small footprint topic would be thorny evaporated as we discovered our shared synthesis and understanding of humanity's peril and the power of putting forward a practical demonstration of the possible. Pedro Martin, the young filmmaker who hitchhiked around Cuba with me, insisted that I show them some of my slides of building my home from the trees on site in Belfast, Maine, and my own permaculture gardens. He translated my story of how I limited my income to world average at the same time they were entering the special period. As we recognized our kinship at a deeper level, we dove into tougher conversations, doubts and opportunities for creating a sustainable future.

After years of working to promote small footprints in North America, I've recently noticed a heightened recognition that we must create the alternative reality, in both our families and our communities. And more people understand that if the world's people lived American lifestyles, we'd need four planets.

The Casimiro family clearly conveys agency and sustainability. Against all odds, their resourcefulness, artful functionality, serious research, and dexterity unite this family. Their biogas digester, built by young Chavely, produces methane to cook their food, provides light and refrigeration, and the effluent fertilizes the crops through gravity-fed pipes.

Where locavores in the United States argue over favorite "wildcards" of coffee, chocolate, bananas, and olive oil—items that we cannot produce in our climate—I wondered what this family was not able to produce. They had dozens of fruits and vegetables, sacks of rice and beans, raised chickens, pigs, rabbits, fish, and dairy cows, pressed their own oil, made soap, and yes, ground their own coffee.

The Casimiro family was one of a half-dozen families we were invited to share rice, beans, and yes, homegrown coffee with, who have contributed to our documentary film.

Osmany Acosta's family were peasant sharecrop farmers before the revolution. They now live in an extended family compound and grow the bulk of the family's food. Their daughter Madaysi is studying medicine in the nearby city.

Lusay Miranda is a twenty-six-year-old family doctor in a clinic in the village of Soplillar. She laughs that some parents complain that their child learned to say her name before saying their own. For three months after a child's birth, Lusay will stop in on the family daily. Being born in the village, at first some of the older people used her childhood name, but now she has earned their respect. Her community can come to her twenty-four hours a day, seven days a week, although she keeps regular consulting times Monday through Friday. We asked her if there was domestic violence in the community. She responded, "Yes, there is." We then asked if women come in battered and she said, "No, no, I've not seen that. Some men won't help with the house work."

Yeni Ramos works in a health clinic conducting tests during pregnancies in Playa Larga, along the Bay of Pigs. She couldn't recall when the last child or mother died in the birthing process. Her daughter Roxanna competes in national math competitions and enjoys time with her friends. The younger daughter, Rosaly, loves art and dance. Rosaly's teachers, Lazaro and Suzana, work as popular educators teaching art, song, and dance in the school. Rosaly is among the many children they feel lucky to learn from.

Madelaine Vazquez is the director of Slow Food Cuba and edits Cubasolar's journal *Energia y Tú*. A renaissance woman, Madelaine started the first vegetarian restaurant in Havana in the botanical garden in 1994, and for years had a television show highlighting healthy and sustainable cooking. She seems to always be at the leading edge of societal movements, recently becoming involved in the Slow Meat movement that addresses the massive impact of industrial-scale meat production. The movement encourages eating less but higher quality meat along with ethical treatment of animals.

Yuliet Alfonso lives in La Conchita, a town centered on a food processing facility. She forgoes jewelry to purchase bricks and mortar for the house she is building, while teaching at a university. Speaking of her relationship with her seventeen-year-old daughter Alexandra, she says they share everything. Then emphasizes, "everything." Alexandra has gotten national attention for the documentary and fiction films she makes with a team of neighborhood friends. Her films delve into the social issues of their community.

Each person is ordinary and extraordinary. Each graciously opened their life to me, a stranger from the "evil empire." Each held no grudge. Each offered a sacred piece of their humanity to my consciousness. My most profound moments in Cuba were of being on the receiving end of generosity and hospitality by warm people with a fraction of the income, assets, diversions, and stuff that my countryfolk and I take for "normal." What is most clear, as I am back and again swimming in a sea of excess, is that this excess isn't making us any happier.

What else is clear is that the 1,001 ways that the United States dominates the world is truly upsetting and hurts real people. I could analyze and critique Cuban policy, systems and culture, its shortcomings and mistakes. However, I'll leave that for the Cuban people. Don't worry, they actively discuss all that and more and get on with their lives. The biggest fear I heard from the tourists I met in Cuba is that the island will quickly be ruined by consumerism and the decadence of modernity if the U.S. corporations come there. My biggest hope would be that the tourists return home from Cuba inspired to live more simply, dance a bit more, and lighten up.

I'd hope too that they'd return home and work for the embargo to be lifted and for Guantanamo Base to be returned to Cuba. Let the Cubans

Table 10.1

	World	USA	Slovenia	Cuba	Haiti	Kerala	India	Afghanistan
Ecological Footprint	6.5 Acre	17 Acre	11 Acre	4 Acre	1.5 Acre	2.2 Acre	2.2 Acre	1.2 Acre
GDP/capita Atlas, 2014	$10,858	$55,200	$23,220	$5,910 (2011)	$830	$1,120	$1,610	$680
Fertility or # Children	2.6	1.9	1.5	1.5	3.2	1.4	2.5	5.1
Infant Mortality Rate	40.9	6.7	2.9	4.8	54	15.3	52	165
Life Expectancy	66.6	79	80	79	63	75	66	61
Literacy, rt	82	99	99.7	99.99	60	91	71	47
Ranking	(NA)	(#35)	(#12)	(#4)	(#130)	(#60)	(#117)	(#148)

direct their own destiny. When I asked people if they thought Cuba could avoid the mistakes of the "developed" world's last fifty years, many could visualize that path, but also internalize the complexity and uncertainty of our moment in time.

One thing the embargo did teach Cubans is how to live well at a fraction of the footprint of the developed world. If the world's people birthed at the Cuban rate of 1.5 children, on average, in one hundred years world population would retreat to 3.8 billion. And if the world's people consumed at the Cuban four-acre ecological footprint, humanity would consume 15.2 billion bioproductive acres of the thirty billion acres available worldwide, leaving half the planet for nature.

Those in Africa, Asia, and Latin America who are stuck in the grip of poverty, could glean a few ideas around universal education and healthcare from Cuba—healthy, educated people on a shoestring. Those whose stomachs ache from too much and whose spirits sag from not enough of what matters might find that Cuba offers a breather, along with 1,001 practical ways to live lightly and still have fun.

Chapter 11

Becoming a Counterterrorist

Ed Kinane

"Terrorism" and "terrorist" are words oft invoked, but seldom defined. Not only nationalists and propagandists, but critics of U.S. policy abuse or misuse these words. Even those who should know better invoke, without quotation marks, the phony "war on terrorism."

What, then, is "terrorism"? For me *terrorism is violence—or the threat of violence—directed at civilians for political, military, or economic ends.*

The definition cuts to the chase, cuts through the layers of jingoism and obfuscation. It has implications:

- Contrary to U.S. mainstream media usage, terrorists aren't inevitably sallow or swarthy or people of color. Here in the U.S., "terrorism" has a strong racist tinge, somehow applying only to what *they*—nonwhites—do, not to what the U.S. does.

- Most terrorism is wholesale, not retail; most is *state* terrorism. Most terrorism is perpetrated by uniformed military. In the twentieth and twenty-first centuries most war casualties—in the tens of millions—are civilian. They aren't "collateral damage"; they are human beings, victims of terrorizing militarism.

- During the last two centuries, much of that terrorism has been *aerial*: V-2 rockets, atomic bombs, hydrogen bombs, neutron bombs, Cruise missiles, Hellfire missiles, napalm, white phosphorus, cluster bombs, depleted uranium, weaponized drones . . .

- Since at least August 6, 1945, the Pentagon has been the world's most relentless single purveyor of terrorism.

Bottom line: the "war on terror" is a war *of, by,* and *for* terror—terror for hegemony, terror for profit.

༄

I came from an intact middle-class Nixon Republican family. My parents were devout, though not ostentatious, Christians. They seldom raised their voice, rarely let us four kids see their infrequent fights. They always tried to set a good example. Physical punishment was rare.

Maybe peace and justice activists have a special gene. Some of these good folks seem disposed toward that way of being. I don't think I'm one of them. As a youngster I relished snowball and rock fights—the guys on our block versus the guys one block over. One time our rocks sent two of them to the ER. In school yards and on the streets, I was bullied . . . and, like my buddies, I was a bully. In that era, in that neighborhood, unless you were a goody-goody, that just seemed the way things were.

My fifth grade teacher, Mrs. Wasley, for whom I had high regard, once got to thinking my pal Benny and I were too big for our britches. Without explanation, she took us both out to the art supply room, had us lean over, and delivered ten bruising whacks on each of our backsides. Maybe that beating made me a lifelong skeptic. Thereafter maybe I began embodying the bumper sticker, QUESTION AUTHORITY. Maybe the incident was behind my eventual sensitivity to injustice.

I went to Catholic junior high school. Having read Bertrand Russell's essay, "Why I am not a Christian," by my late teens I had stopped going to Sunday mass. I had grasped that the church didn't provide moral guidance. Even so, I chose a Jesuit college in the Bronx. I figured if anyone could justify my accident-of-birth Catholicism, it would be those reputedly cerebral priests. Disappointed, after two years I left Fordham.

Nonetheless, my Catholic background had its value. It encouraged, perhaps only by rote, "examination of conscience"—assessing the right and wrong in one's thought and action. Heeding conscience was a way, not without pride, of accessing and activating an internal moral compass. In time, conscience helped consolidate my identity.

Around age twenty I read Thoreau. His essay on civil disobedience planted seeds. *Walden* was an antidote to the prevailing conformity, materialism, other-directedness, mindless acquisition, and striving for worldly success. Vance Packard's remarkable series—*The Status Seekers, The Hidden Persuaders, The Wastemakers*—offered an updated, more explicit critique of U.S. culture.

After a year working construction, not keen on a working-class destiny, I transferred to Syracuse University, majoring in anthropology. Anthro provided cross-cultural perspectives and tools for questioning U.S. life and society. Such studies began, haltingly, my escape from the "bubble" that blinds and desensitizes U.S. people. Once I started thinking—and traveling abroad—the prevailing U.S. exceptionalism silliness had little chance. I came to see that nationalism—like sexism and the other "-isms"—was a moral blight.

∾

The mid-sixties were the early years of the U.S. terror attacks on Laos and Viet Nam. After graduating, and thereby exhausting my student draft deferments, I had to go before the local draft board. Thanks to "severe *pes planes*"—flat feet—the board rated me "1Y," exempt from the military. Lucky me.

Those next few years I was caught up in what I call "privatism." To the extent I thought about it, I sensed that the Viet Nam invasion was heinous. But with my free pass, it had barely occurred to me to get involved in the antiwar activism then agitating campuses.

Post-college, I lived out of a backpack. I led a hobo-like life, sleeping out in fields and under bridges. I hitchhiked all over the country, thumbing north and south, east and west, working transient and menial jobs. Thoreau's "simplify, simplify" was my beacon. Recently, reading Temple Grandin, I've come to wonder if, like her, I operate on the high end of the autism spectrum.

In spring 1969 I was a deckhand aboard the SS *Jupiter*, a marine salvage ship bound for offshore Colombia. Turns out the captain and his son, the first mate, were latter day pirates. In Belize, having gotten the elderly watchman drunk, they looted a shipyard, ripping off every tool they could lay hands on. Later, learning about the long, long tradition of Yankees preying on our southern neighbors, that heist seemed to sum up generations of U.S./Latin American relations.

Being very out of step, at the next port, the island of San Andreas, I quit the *Jupiter*. Denied my back pay (did I mention that Captain McCrory was larcenous?), I flew to Costa Rica, then hitchhiked up through Central America and Mexico back to the States.

En route, a young Guatemalan employed by a U.S. corporation took me out on his rounds, supervising *campesinos* who were raising tobacco for a dollar a day. Carlos pointed to their shacks on the steep hillsides. It perplexed me that these semi-slaves could be so poor, expending their lives in their richly fertile land, working a cash crop for foreign bosses.

That mystery partly underlay my eventually doing graduate work in New York City at the New School for Social Research. Intellectually, my New School years were the best; they taught me to think critically and politically. Then for two years, I taught anthropology at a community college near Seattle.

By now, with my raised critical consciousness, my anger about the United States and Viet Nam was hard to contain. My classroom ranting often overtook my instructing: my adjunct contract wasn't renewed. That summer I did archeology in the Alaskan Arctic; that winter, flush with my Alaskan wages, I lolled on Mexican beaches with my younger brother and sister. Then I thumbed—point of pride: I've never owned a car—back to New York and the New School.

With the death of my father in 1976, despite my PhD work, I realized, "I need to get serious about life." Having told myself that activists were more essential than academicians, I put aside my scholarly pleasures. I joined Cesar Chavez's United Farm Workers Union, then boycotting grapes.

The UFW flew me out to La Paz, its HQ up in California's Tehachapi Mountains. The union provided its volunteers a shared dorm room and $10 a week strike wages. Pooling our food stamps, we ate in small collective kitchens. We worked long hours six days a week. After a year I resigned, disillusioned with Cesar—a charismatic but flawed visionary. Invited to the Philippines, Cesar had come back to La Paz praising that wily strong man and U.S. creature, Ferdinand Marcos. Aaarrrrgh!

∞

Skipping ahead: in mid-1979, bruised by a broken romance, I lit out for Africa. For thirty-three months I wandered and worked on that unknown (to me) continent. From Morocco I hitchhiked across North Africa, made my way south by rail on a freight car through Sudan's Nubian Desert. Then it was on to Juba by deck passage for twelve days on the now-defunct Nile steamer. And from there by lorry over the dirt road down through Turkanaland to Nairobi.

Finding Kenya to my liking, I signed up to teach in a one-room school on the northern frontier. George Fox Friends Secondary, nominally Quaker, was about six hours upcountry in the former "white highlands," in a hamlet eleven miles down a dirt road, impassable during the rainy season, from the town of Kitale. GFF was founded on a shoestring a couple weeks earlier.

Having gotten a work visa as a "missionary," I spent that school year teaching Form 1 (eighth grade) English, math, geography, and biology to about twenty fee-paying youngsters aged fourteen to nineteen.

After their various tribal languages and after the lingua franca, Kiswahili, English was their third language. These peasant kids had little use for English (learned [sort of] in public primary school) in rural everyday life. But throughout Africa people often spoke several languages. Knowing the colonial language was key to upward mobility.

Class met in the loft of a sturdy barn, once owned by white settlers, now long gone. Some students came each day from a couple hours' walk farther out in the *shambas,* the cultivated fields. At GFF there already was a Kenyan physics teacher and a Kiswahili and religion teacher. But there was no supervision, no set curriculum, few textbooks or other school supplies—except a blackboard and chalk. No electricity or plumbing.

My pay was skimpy and erratic. Like the locals I got by on two meals a day—greens and *ugali,* homegrown maize meal (ugh!). But there was esthetic compensation: to the west, outside our glassless window, in the Ugandan distance was the majestic Mount Elgon; eastward, across a misty valley, were the purple Cherangani Hills, home to spear-carrying cattle rustlers.

Life in this outpost, with no other native English speaker for miles, was lonesome. But the classroom was lively, the kids bright. Their English improved as they found they could ask me *any* question, no matter how impertinent, and I would respond honestly. Their favorite themes: sex and outer space or astronomy (a subject I know little about). Mostly I responded, "I don't know." That unfamiliar candor spurred more questions—and sustained thinking in English.

My sententious remarks about the power of nonviolence met with skepticism. But my breaking the cane—a fixture in the front corner of the room—over my knee caught their attention. So did my passing around a condom in class. (A Kenyan woman, often not a man's only wife, bore an average of eight children. With each short generation, the family *shamba* kept subdividing. Hunger was rife.)

Second semester, their English got a boost after the kids lobbied to have us devote every Friday afternoon to debate. Typical topics: "Resolved: Polygamy is no good," or "Whites should leave Africa," or "Boys aren't as smart as girls." On Monday they brainstormed the week's topic, then for homework wrote an essay about it. On Thursday they read those essays aloud in class. On Friday, the self-selected, opposing teams gathered on either side of the room to debate. Revved up, throughout the afternoon students readily switched sides to express evolving takes on the issue.

I had read Paulo Freire's *Pedagogy of the Oppressed* and felt the GFF air alive with critical consciousness.

∾

After my Kenya year, I hiked up Mt. Kilimanjaro. I roamed on foot and rode in the back of lorries over mostly dirt roads—Uganda, Zaire, Rwanda, Burundi, Tanzania, Zambia. Zimbabwe, Malawi, Lesotho, Botswana. I crossed the Kalahari and Namib Deserts. My Africa days exposed me to broad swaths of the human condition.

In the Serengeti and in the Ngorogoro Crater and other national parks of East and Southern Africa I encountered lions, elephants, rhinos, hippos, and giraffes. In Rwanda, I met up with mountain gorillas. In the Gombe Reserve, reached only by launch on Lake Tanganiya, I met up with Jane Goodall's chimps. (I used to assign my college classes Jane's book *In the Shadow of Man*.) And in the Ituri Forest I met with Pygmies, the subject of Colin Turnbull's *The Forest People*, which I had also assigned.

There and elsewhere I met tribal people utterly unWesternized and barely covered by a loincloth. The material scantiness was beyond Western imagining. Life was lived at a walking pace. There was little obesity. The earth's abuse was far less accelerated. To this day, I appreciate the luxury of toilet paper.

In rural areas there seemed less anomie, less social dysfunction than back home; people had an easier sociability. Religion, sometimes Animist or Islamic, but mostly Evangelical Protestant, was laced with fervor, music, and dance. (Someday, I thought, it would be Africans who would come to Christianize the West.)

As I hiked through one of South Africa's rural Bantustans, a young woman danced up to me, delighted, declaring she had never before seen a white person on foot. Earlier, in central Africa I had encountered people who—judging by their startled reaction—had never before seen a white man, on foot or otherwise. What deeply impressed me throughout Africa were the women and children hauling buckets of water on their heads, often over long distances. (Here in the water-squandering States I wince when I see a faucet running needlessly.)

I had vowed to steer clear of Apartheid South Africa. But then I realized I would never understand Africa and the Frontline states until I had seen the place for myself. In the cities of that regional superpower I felt right at home. I was back in the Anglosphere. Johannesburg might just as well have been . . . Cleveland.

Finally, with easy access to bookstores and newspapers, I studied Apartheid, in full force in those days. Elements of South Africa's major English-language press were highly critical of that scourge. In the United States it was the era of Reagan's "constructive engagement," his wink and a nod support for Pretoria's state terror—a total system of militarized white supremacy.

As I was to witness firsthand years later, South African Apartheid has its avatar in Israel's ethnic cleansing of Palestine. The Israeli model, more lethal and more lavishly subsidized by the United States, features drone and other aerial terrorism—"cutting the grass," the recurring systematic demolishing of Gazan infrastructure.

ᐁ

Returning to the States in the early eighties, I got prolific about writing letters to the editor exposing the misconceptions and rationalizations here so tolerant of Apartheid there. (In the United States, de facto systemic apartheid was then, and remains, barely on white radar screens.) Then, for the price of a postage stamp, such letters reached multitudes.

Ann Tiffany, a local public health nurse and Latin America solidarity activist, was intrigued by my letters. In the mid-eighties we eventually met, were arrested together occupying a congressman's office, and have been partners—both domestic and political—these past three decades.

Inspired and educated by Ann's Sanctuary Movement work, in 1988 I joined Peace Brigades International in Guatemala. PBI fielded teams there and in El Salvador during their brutal civil wars. PBI volunteers served as unarmed bodyguards accompanying nonviolent indigenous human rights workers, journalists, teachers, and labor leaders. Absent such accompaniment, government-linked death squads had a way of disappearing or assassinating such activists. In these client states the killers often got their training and marching orders from U.S. agencies.

The death squads used terror to crush grassroots empowerment, to undermine democratic initiative, to extirpate hope. Leveraging our white privilege, the very presence of Peace Brigade volunteers deterred them and drew U.S. and international attention to death squad mayhem. Any harm done to us could generate publicity, jeopardizing their U.S. funding.

In certain contexts, especially in the U.S. imperium, accompaniment is a powerful tactic. Accompaniment protects lives and allows brave souls to continue their risky and essential missions. Although PBI insists on its nonpartisanship, in doing PBI counterterrorism work over several years in Central America and in Haiti and Sri Lanka, I saw myself fostering liberation.

∾

PBI work led me to Father Roy Bourgeois's persistent direct action campaign to close the Pentagon's School of the Americas at Fort Benning, Georgia. Known to its critics as the "School of Torture" or the "School of Coups," since the 1940s the SOA has taught "anti-insurgency" tactics (in Spanish) to Latin American military personnel.

In 1996 SOA Watch, Roy's organization, exposed the SOA use of "torture manuals" for indoctrinating its trainees to extirpate "commies" on behalf of national oligarchies and U.S. corporations. The scandal forced the SOA to close. But within weeks, cosmetically changed, it reopened, rebranding itself as the Western Hemisphere Institute for Security Cooperation.

Resistance to the SOA/WHINSEC is ongoing. Until 2016, when that resistance moved to Nogales on the U.S./Mexican border, every November thousands from all over the United States and beyond came to Ft. Benning's gates to protest its training state terrorists and to demand the school's final closure. Each year the protests entailed nonviolent civil disobedience as activists broached Fort Benning's perimeter. Scores of prison sentences have ensued, totaling about two hundred years.

Thanks to my several Benning arrests, I once spent two months, and another time twelve months, in federal minimum security prisons. Given my lifestyle over the years, I was preadapted to penal austerity. Prison was a kind of sabbatical—I got in lots of reading. As a greybeard I seemed, by virtue of irrelevancy, exempt from risks that might beset younger prisoners.

Prison was eased by my having no dependents. It helped that my activist "career" outside, such as it was, was innately interruptible. Unlike many prisoners, I had outside support. The two Syracuse dailies ran editorials condemning the SOA. One was titled, "Going to Prison for a Good Cause." I got oodles of solidarity mail. Supplementing my eleven cents an hour wage as the landscape department tool clerk, my local anti-SOA group, the SOA Abolitionists, provided a generous monthly commissary stipend.

It certainly helped that Ann, now retired, had herself just finished six months in Danbury federal prison for "crossing the line" at Fort Benning. Ann knew the score, and was immersed in SOA Watch activism. With my two prison terms, each in the hills of Pennsylvania, about five hours' drive from home, she would visit me for a few hours every few weeks.

I spent a couple weeks in the SHU—Segregated Housing Unit, i.e., isolation. This wasn't "solitary" since I had a bunk mate. T. and I were the only whites there. T. was an extreme right wing guy who had done two combat tours in Viet Nam. When I asked why he had chosen to reenlist, he said, "For the exhilaration of killing." T. had a skill set: stalking and then garroting Viet Cong sentinels. (In the U.S., few activists take such risks for our causes.) After Nam, T. trained Contra terrorists in Honduras. When I asked what became of the trainees who got weeded out, T. sliced his finger across his throat.

Being in minimum security prisons, my experience was "soft time." The disruption in my life was as nothing compared to the suffering that SOA grads inflicted on Latin America's poor and upon their allies. I knew exactly why I was in prison and knew it was where I needed to be. Such "prison witness" publicized the SOA issue, swelling our ranks at Fort Benning every November. It deepened my commitment to antimilitarism and to future resistance actions.

Prison showed me firsthand the "New Jim Crow" and mass incarceration. I would encourage any white middle-class activist *who can* to have such an experience. Or one might do resistance actions leading to spending at least a night or two in the local slammer. It is a good way to learn local reality.

∾

For months, in 2002, my aging mother had been bedridden; Ann and I were her caregivers. On Christmas morning mom died. In early February I flew to Amman, Jordan, to join the Iraq Peace Team, a project of the grassroots human rights group, Voices in the Wilderness. From Amman an Iraqi ally of the team drove me nine hours through the desert to Baghdad.

The Iraq Peace Team had a couple dozen volunteers of all ages, mostly from the United States, but also from South Korea and Australia. The idea was that we'd stay in Baghdad through the impending U.S. invasion, our publicized presence possibly lessening its havoc. We saw ourselves in solidarity with the Iraqi people, victims of both Saddam Hussein and George W. Bush. Given that then, by U.S. law, it was illegal for us to be in Iraq, we were committing protracted civil disobedience. We compounded the crime by bringing medical supplies to Iraq, thereby violating the genocidal U.S. sanctions.

In the wee hours of March 20, 2003, the much-ballyhooed U.S. "Shock and Awe" began. Often we dove to the floor as shells burst nearby. It was a three-week-long aerial terror attack on Baghdad, less intense but akin to the 1945 Allied firebombing of German and Japanese cities and the atomic bombing of Hiroshima and Nagasaki.

Overlooking the Tigris River, our hotel, the Al Fanar, was fifty yards from the Palestine Hotel, where all international journalists had to stay. On April 9, the U.S. Marines poured into Baghdad. They surrounded the two hotels with tanks and machine gun nests. Hours before, they had shelled the Palestine, killing two journalists, friends of our team. That same day the Marines shelled the *Al Jazeera* office, killing one journalist. It seems invaders frown on unembedded media. Ordered to evacuate by their editors, many of the journalists scrambled to enlist taxis for the dangerous drive back to Jordan.

Anticipating the U.S. Marines' arrival, in March our team had posted large photo portraits of ordinary Iraqi people several stories up on the outside of the Al Fanar. These images were to remind the invaders—and the media—that the invasion was primarily maiming and killing civilians. We also draped a banner over an outside second-story balcony: "COURAGE FOR PEACE, NOT FOR WAR."

Throughout Shock and Awe our team shared our observations and experiences via Internet or satellite phone with both mainstream and alternative media elsewhere. After my visa expired and I came home, I went on speaking tours with Voices with the added credibility of having survived.

∾

In 2009, the Syracuse *Post-Standard* ran several page-one articles by reporter Dave Tobin. Ignoring legal and moral issues, these hyped the new MQ-9 Reaper Drone hub at our local Hancock Air Force Base. Hancock now hosted the New York State Air National Guard's 174th Attack Wing. The 174th, otherwise locked in secrecy, proudly announced that its hunter/killer Reaper drones—armed with Hellfire missiles—operate 24/7 over Afghanistan.

In 2010 anti-drone activists and grassroots groups from throughout New York State and beyond mobilized as Upstate Drone Action, aka the Ground the Drones and End the Wars Coalition. Inspired by SOA Watch actions at Fort Benning, over the years this decentralized, nonhierarchical network has engaged in direct actions periodically blocking Hancock's main gate. Our actions have sometimes been accompanied by attempts, rebuffed at the gate, to hand deliver a "People's War Crimes Indictment."

We are arrested and charged with some combination of violations and misdemeanors: trespass, disturbing the peace, interfering with government administration, or contempt of court. We're tried, in both bench and jury trials, in the DeWitt Town Court. There have been dismissals and acquittals, but mostly we have been found guilty and have been fined (always the max, $375) and, some of us, incarcerated. In a country with little respect for treaties, our legal defense based on international law—which according to the U.S. Constitution is "the supreme law of the land"—gets no traction.

At Hancock's behest the DeWitt judges have imposed "Orders of Protection" on dozens of us, forbidding us from returning to the base. On the pretext of protecting the base commandant, these OOPs are crude devices to deny our First Amendment right to petition the government for a redress of grievances. The surreal fiction that the commander of a clandestine operation terrorizing civilians in Afghanistan (and probably Pakistan) needs "protection" from scrupulously nonviolent peace activists jolts the imagination. To use Orders of Protection, designed to protect abused spouses and children, to suppress dissent shows the DeWitt Town Court's connivance with the military and exposes its contempt for law and justice. A further irony is that Reaper victims are often women and children.

As I write a number of us await further trials. Hancock has yet to press federal charges, preferring that local police and courts deal with us. The Pentagon may pretend not to see Upstate Drone Action's efforts, but were there none, drone criminality would be further normalized.

At Hancock we aren't engaging in civil disobedience, but in civil *resistance*. We aren't breaking the law, we're seeking to *enforce* law—the UN Charter, international humanitarian law, and Article 6 of the U.S. Constitution. We are keenly aware that the post–World War II Nuremburg Principles, signed by the United States and other nations, require citizens to expose their government's war crimes or be themselves complicit.

Besides our over a dozen arrest actions, our group has deployed a range of tactics to alert the public to Hancock war crime. These include, weather permitting, twice-weekly demonstrations around busy intersections in Onondaga County. Among these are our first and third Tuesday demos at afternoon shift change across the road from the Hancock main gate. We hope these will get the drone operators thinking about their role in the war machine. Lately, Reaper drones circle overhead.

Currently (Spring 2018), thanks to the initiative of WorldBeyondWar.org, we have several full-size billboards up around Syracuse: ARMED DRONES MAKE ORPHANS and DRONE WARS, LIKE ALL WARS, KILL INNOCENT CHILDREN, AND MAY MAKE US LESS SAFE.

In contrast to the impressive local coverage of the SOA Watch campaign—in which Central New Yorkers had long been active—local mainstream media mostly shun our Hancock campaign. No local journalist has ever been assigned on an ongoing basis to follow our actions, our trials, our incarcerations, or to report on drone terrorism. War crime has become so routine that most mainstream media ignored the March 7, 2016, U.S. drone massacre of *150* unknown Somalis.

A military base profits local enterprise and provides jobs. Hence, the local courts and the corporate media won't hear that that base perpetrates terrorism. Given that about half of our federal taxes feed the war machine, the taxpaying public shares complicity. But most are loath to hear it. Selective ignorance and cognitive dissonance rule. Further, Central New York reaps federal and state funds for drone industry research and development. Corporate investors and their friends in office envision Central New York becoming the Silicon Valley of drones. Military and commercial drone development cross-fertilize each other.

Serving capitalist hegemony and the vast weapons export industry, globally the Pentagon has some eight hundred military bases. Such ubiquity forestalls resistance and keeps brutal puppets in power. Curiously, even those aware of all these bases seem to overlook the *thousands* of military installations here in the United States. Such bases—few of them needed for national defense—assure that the citizenry and the mainstream media remain deeply vested in militarism. The redundancy also assures that every part of this huge, polarized, weaponized country remains under the gun. So comprehensive and so well-armed is the domestic military—along with the increasingly militarized police—that the homeland itself can seem militarily occupied.

∾

Like our adversaries, peace and justice activists are mixed bags. We are all shaped by our egos, our metabolisms, our circumstances, our opportunities . . . and our ideals. The trick, I think, is to fashion an ethic and a lifestyle that empowers us—one that frees us from distractions, co-optations, and addictions (especially consumerism). A lifestyle that provides right livelihood and frees us from debt—the great trap of our era.

Given the formidable forces arrayed against peace and social justice, there are no easy answers, no final victories. By its very nature our impact remains difficult to discern, impossible to assess. Fighting terror is about sowing seeds; the harvest may not be ours to see. We seldom know, though, when we're approaching a tipping point—whether for good or ill. What's called for, then, is what Latin American activists call *relentless persistence.* Also, like these activists *and like soldiers,* we need to prepare for risk and sacrifice.

As Dorothy Day, founder of the Catholic Worker movement, emphasized, it's not about "effectiveness," it's about faithfulness.

Chapter 12

Blind to Empire

NICK MOTTERN

I am among a group of about one hundred people in the United States who are actively involved on a regular basis in protesting against U.S. drone attacks. This is the only constant antiwar activity in the country that is regularly putting people in the street with vigils, protests, and risking arrest to block entrances to military bases; in this case, drone control centers.

This may seem an exaggeration, but note that I am talking about people consistently protesting in public as distinct from those attending occasional demonstrations, conferences, and engaging in internet communication.

There are a variety of reasons that the number of active, public protestors is so small. For one thing, tens of thousands of U.S. troops left harm's way when they were withdrawn from Iraq and Afghanistan in 2007 and 2008. With this withdrawal came a huge cutback in U.S. news staffs covering these wars, even though many thousands of U.S. troops continue to be involved in combat in Iraq, Afghanistan, Syria, and smaller wars. The total number of countries in which U.S. troops were in active fighting or training at the beginning of 2018 was seventy-six, according to The Costs of War Project.

The dramatic decline in the number of U.S. "boots on the ground" coincided with the dramatic increase in U.S. drone attacks since the first such attack in Afghanistan in 2001. Now drones have been integrated in the constant U.S. air war that is ranging over the Middle East, parts of Africa, Afghanistan, and Pakistan. Drone assassinations since 2001 number over ten thousand, based on information from the Bureau of Investigative Journalism, but in 2017 the U.S. government began cutting back on information on its air wars, and so we no longer know how many are killed by drones through assassination or in support of ground assaults.

However devastating to people and civil societies living under drones, U.S. drone attacks have meant nothing but relief to Americans, happy that their sons and daughters appear to be spared from death and injury because drones are being sent to do the killing. This way of thinking, induced by the government, and unchallenged by the press, means there is absolutely no conscious public recognition that killing always has consequences. Nor do people ask whether drone killing is reducing or increasing violence. Or, more fundamentally, there is no public curiosity about why the United States is really at war in so many places. In fact, I have found that relatively few people know where wars are happening, and most only have a vague sense that wars are happening. Perhaps most troubling, the U.S. Congress, obedient to war industrialists, raises no fundamental questions about U.S. wars, and votes faithfully to keep funding them.

So, who are the small number of people in the United States who are objecting to drone killing? In my experience they are, largely: (1) people who experienced the horror of the Viet Nam War and the exhilarating experience of bringing a deadly government to its knees in stopping that war; (2) people who are motivated by their spirituality, in many cases Catholics and non-Catholics who have been inspired to oppose war and violent repression by liberation theology and/or the Catholic Worker movement; (3) people who are repulsed by the savagery of a U.S. political economy that is comfortable with privilege based on war and other forms of violence directed largely at people of color, at home and overseas. They have experienced the oppression of empire, modeled on the plantation system, whether they know to call it that or not.

And, of course, there are also people who find drone assassination simply morally unacceptable and who foresee the possibility, indeed probability, of the institution of constant robotic surveillance and killing by a fascistic government.

Of the total group, I estimate that at least half of its leaders and rank and file are women. All have been encouraged in their protests by the fact that there are more than twenty drone control centers in the United States from which drone attacks are directed daily. This means American protesters can confront U.S. warmaking, appealing not only to the general public but to military people themselves, locally, not separated by thousands of miles from U.S. military operations.

My contribution to anti-drone war work has been to build replicas of the MQ-9 Reaper drone for use at protests; to provide information on drone war for the general public at Knowdrones.com; to publish a bulletin to counter drone war organizers; and, in cooperation with Veterans for Peace, to air fifteen-second counter–drone war ads on cable TV in areas near key drone control centers in the United States.

Like many in the small cadre who actively take on anti-drone war work as their primary peace work, I, at seventy-nine years old, came to antiwar resistance through the Viet Nam War.

Born in Viet Nam

In 1962, as a very inexperienced twenty-three-year-old lieutenant junior grade in the U.S. Navy, I walked through the door of a Boeing 707 that had carried me from the United States to Viet Nam's Tan Son Nhut airport into what was for me, a new world. I was overwhelmed by the warm, humid, gentle air, so rich with sweet and decaying smells. I was struck by the fantastically lush greenness of the place. I felt I was exiting a spaceship onto another planet.

I was entering a new life, but was not conscious enough to know it at that moment. Nor did I did know that I would never be able to fully reenter the world that I had left.

I had volunteered to go to South Viet Nam in part to escape the boring routine of being communications officer on the USS *Falgout* (DER-324). The *Falgout*, a World War II diesel-powered destroyer escort, based in Pearl Harbor, had been outfitted with powerful air search radar and was part of a squadron that had the mission of detecting Russian bombers should they attempt to cross the northern Pacific to attack the United States. This meant that the *Falgout* and the other "radar picket ships" went to sea for thirty days and were then in port for thirty days, for me a deadening rotation.

I also volunteered for Viet Nam because I was very much drawn by the excitement of war. I was born almost two years before the bombing of Pearl Harbor, and growing up during World War II I was fascinated by the pictures of warplanes, warships, and combat that appeared in *National Geographic* and *Life* magazines. The pictures did not, for the most part, show the abject horror of the war, and I was intrigued by the exotic characters created by the cartoonist Milton Caniff in the male-centric, military-oriented comic strips *Terry and the Pirates* and *Steve Canyon*. Notably, I found the Dragon Lady in the *Terry* stories extremely appealing.

While I was not conscious of it in my decision to go to Viet Nam, I see now that I was drawn to the cartoon world of Asia, which promised mystery, adventure, and romance, and in a place where the puritanical rules of the United States could be ignored. Looking at it now, I see that Milton Caniff's world was a fantastical world in which white males from the relatively rich and powerful U.S. empire could, and did, get away with virtually anything.

In Saigon, in my khaki summer Navy uniform, something as simple as climbing into a Jeep seemed exciting and even heroic because I was so identified with "heroes" like Steve Canyon and John Wayne, for whom Jeep riding was symbolic of power and prevailing.

I had been prepared by my culture to totally accept the U.S. government's argument for the reason for my being in Viet Nam, as expressed in a memo for new arrivals signed by Army Major General Charles J. Timmes, chief of the Military Assistance Advisory Group, Viet Nam:

> Many Americans are not aware of the important position of this country in the world struggle against communism. Since 1954, Vietnam has been fighting an implacable enemy whose sole aim is domination over this free republic. In assisting the Vietnamese to conquer this Communist enemy, you are undertaking an exceptionally challenging assignment.

It was great back then to be given a high-flown reason for entering on a male adventure.

Although I was a regular officer, not in the supply corps, I was assigned, like all Navy personnel in Viet Nam at that time, to the new logistics support command—Headquarters Support Activity Saigon (HSAS). This organization was responsible for providing all the supplies and services needed by the growing U.S. military force entering the country.

My assignment was assistant billeting officer, which meant I worked in the office that oversaw housing in Saigon for U.S. military personnel working there and for Army and Marine "advisors" heading to the countryside to coach South Vietnamese soldiers who were fighting their North Vietnamese brothers and sisters, in some cases literally.

Part of the work of the billeting office was monitoring maid and laundry contracts for the hotels used by U.S. military people. When I arrived, Wan

Wai Nam was the only maid and laundry contractor for the U.S. military in Saigon and the adjoining, largely Chinese, city of Cholon. Mr. Wan, as we called him, was an extremely thin, chain-smoking Chinese, who always seemed nervous and was always seeking additional contracts as new hotels for the Americans opened up. He so desperately feared losing his monopoly, which eventually happened, that he put himself completely at the service of the military personnel, officers and enlisted, working in the billeting office.

The central dynamic in Mr. Wan's quest for contracts, to which I was treated immediately upon my arrival and throughout my time in the billeting office, was partying. Occasions were constantly generated that merited fifteen-course Chinese dinners with shots of whiskey, usually Johnny Walker Red, between each course. Mr. Wan sometimes provided Vietnamese and Chinese women to accompany the male members of the billeting office's staff.

What War?

All this fit smoothly within a U.S. military culture in Saigon that was based on pleasure and taking advantage of anything money could buy. Some Americans rented apartments and created a domestic life that they could never have afforded in the United States.

The flood of materiel of all kinds coming into Viet Nam offered dishonest U.S. and Vietnamese military people the opportunity to make money.

Possibly the best example of this culture was Navy Captain Archie Kuntze, who became commander of HSAS at about the same time I left the billeting office and the Navy. Kuntze, a good-natured man who eventually was court martialed after a Navy corruption investigation, apparently became overwhelmed with the opportunities for power and notoriety provided by his control over the vast range of supplies entering Viet Nam as head of HSAS.

As reported by Larry Engelmann on the *Pushing On* blog, Kuntze, although married, fell in love with a Chinese woman who "had soft dark eyes and long black hair. She wore colorful dresses slit up the side to mid-thigh to reveal her long slim legs. She wore heels in public in Saigon and carried a parasol to protect her white skin from the bright sun."

Within two weeks of meeting her, Engelmann reports, Kuntze

> moved out of his plain officer's quarters and into a large and elegant villa at 74 Hong Tap Tu Street, a residence that was soon dubbed "The White House" by the Vietnamese press. Kuntze became

a social animal in Saigon, hosting parties at his residence that
were attended by high ranking political, military and diplomatic
personnel as well as American businessmen holding or seeking
supply and construction contracts.

The darkness of the hedonism of the American culture in Saigon was deepened by the opportunism of American officers who had volunteered for
duty in Viet Nam so that they could advance their careers by having seen
combat as an "advisor."

And there was also the experimentation with the technology of killing
carried out by representatives of DARPA, the Pentagon's Defense Advanced
Research Projects Agency, who were there testing a variety of "counterinsur-
gency" weapons that included: sensing devices to monitor travel of North
Vietnamese troops on the Ho Chi Minh trail; the M-16 assault rifle; and
eventually the herbicide Agent Orange.

It was obvious to me as I worked in the billeting office that we
Americans were living much richer and more privileged lives than most
Vietnamese military personnel. American officers ranking colonel or above
sometimes brought their wives and families, and they were usually provided
with completely renovated or brand new villas with full air conditioning, new
furniture, and servants. I remember one instance in which one of the wives
asked that new rattan furniture be painted white, and then, not liking that,
had the furniture repainted black.

The highest-ranking Vietnamese officers also lived rich lives, far, far
above those of their troops. For me this all was a huge contradiction to the
reality of the war that was spreading in the countryside where South Vietnamese soldiers were, understandably, showing a profound reluctance to fight.

What I Didn't Know

What I didn't know then was that the corruption I was witnessing was an
inevitable result of colonialism.

Viet Nam was invaded by France in 1858 at the port city of Da Nang,
later to become a major U.S. military base. By 1893, France would also control
Cambodia and Laos. The French created huge plantations for growing rice
and rubber and mined coal, tin, and zinc. Profits went primarily to French
businesses. The vast majority of Vietnamese were essentially slaves. France
was not driven from Viet Nam until 1954.

During this colonial period those Vietnamese who advanced in politics and the military were necessarily those who collaborated with the French; they enabled the colonial system to function. These people were deeply involved in the inevitable corruption generated in a poor country when a wealthy great power takes control and uses its money to keep control. The corrupt, repressive politico-military system left behind by the French was inherited by the United States. The United States then used its money and military power to create its own hierarchy of Vietnamese collaborators. Honest Vietnamese wanted no part of this system, and many joined the Viet Cong.

I, like the young American in Graham Greene's *The Quiet American*, was part of the old colonial adventure. Greene was speaking to the inevitable and profound personal and societal tragedy of empire. Pyle, the young American on a mission to manipulate Vietnamese politics through "terror" bombing is killed by Vietnamese. Fowler, the cynical, more experienced Englishman, seeks to capture the love of Phuong, a Vietnamese woman who eventually rejects him. His love for her and Viet Nam accounts for nothing in his futile struggle to bridge the unbridgeable chasm of empire between them, a chasm of disparity in wealth, experience, advantage, and racism, a chasm between the occupied and the occupier.

I had not taken time to read Vietnamese history, and when my active duty in the Navy was completed in early 1964 I continued to be in love with the beauty and drama of Viet Nam and wanted to stay longer. I did not at that time see myself as an imperial agent. My feelings are well expressed by Fowler:

> I can't say what made me fall in love with Vietnam—that a woman's voice can drug you; that everything is so intense. The colors, the taste, even the rain. Nothing like the filthy rain in London. They say whatever you're looking for, you will find here. They say you come to Vietnam and you understand a lot in a few minutes, but the rest has got to be lived. The smell: that's the first thing that hits you, promising everything in exchange for your soul. And the heat. Your shirt is straightaway a rag. You can hardly remember your name, or what you came to escape from. But at night, there's a breeze. The river is beautiful. You could be forgiven for thinking there was no war; that the gunshots were fireworks; that only pleasure matters. A pipe of opium, or the touch of a girl who might tell you she loves you. And then, something happens, as you knew it would. And nothing can ever be the same again.

I intended to be a reporter after leaving the Navy, and through Nick Turner, a reporter for Reuters with whom I had become acquainted, I found a job on the *Saigon Post*, a Vietnamese-owned, English-language newspaper aimed at Americans and the Vietnamese and Chinese who worked for them.

Although I was the *Post*'s sports editor, I also did general assignment reporting and came to learn more about the war than I could have from inside the Navy.

One Bullet Hole

Early in my work at the *Post*, an Australian colonel advising the Vietnamese army told me that the Viet Cong were winning the war, then a novel and, obviously, extremely troubling idea. At an airfield in the Mekong Delta, a U.S. Air Force officer told me that he thought an American pilot "advisor," a World War II hero who had been shot down over Viet Nam, might actually have been killed by a Vietnamese pilot whom he was training.

One of the most depressing experiences of my life was a visit to a U.S. Army helicopter medical evacuation unit from which, virtually every day, a pilot was killed as his chopper alighted, under fire, like a lumbering dragonfly, coming to a dead stop for that one, lethal, critical moment needed to pick up wounded. When we sat down to eat lunch there was no conversation, and the sadness was nearly unbearable.

The experience in Viet Nam that is most vivid and moving for me, and that comes back to me more often now, happened during a trip in November 1964 to Quang Nhai Province in the northern part of South Viet Nam to report on relief work in the aftermath of a series of typhoons that drove nearly a million people from their homes and brought flooding that killed seven thousand.

In the process of seeing whether relief supplies were actually reaching people, Dong Duc Khanh, a fellow *Saigon Post* reporter, and I boarded a Vietnamese Army truck loaded with food supplies and some refugees and began a bouncing ride inland from the South China Sea coast on a pot-holed, still-wet road, with flooded rice paddy fields on either side. We were standing next to the tailgate, and after a few kilometers, Khanh suggested that we exchange jackets because my military jacket might be making me, an American, a desirable target for the Viet Cong.

When the truck stopped perhaps twenty kilometers from where we exchanged jackets, Khanh thought that we were headed into danger and that we should catch a ride back to the coast on a returning relief truck, and we did.

Shortly, our new ride stopped, and we climbed down, looked ahead and saw the bodies of three Viet Cong, dressed in black, lying in a row like cordwood in the brilliantly green, soft grass, apparently just killed by Vietnamese soldiers. A temple gong was being struck in the distance, across the flooded fields.

One of the dead was a young woman, pale, almost white in death. The collar of her black shirt was pulled back slightly, revealing a single, bloodless bullet hole in her chest, right above her heart. I stood there for some minutes, looking.

I speculated that these three people may have come into contact with their killer(s) because they saw me in the back of the passing aid truck, but, of course, I will never know for sure. Who were they, individually? The whole thing left me terribly sad.

Reporter or Propagandist?

I did not report my feelings in the newspaper, and rereading my stories for the *Post* it is clear that I left out anything that might seem to be discouraging because I was very persuaded of the need to "win the war."

I had a concern that this was wrong, but that concern was not strong enough to pull me away from the sense of commitment that I had attached to "winning" the war.

After nearly a year working for the newspaper, I decided to return to the United States to attend Columbia University's Graduate School of Journalism.

Departing from Tan Son Nhut, I was relieved to be returning to a physically safer place, but at the same time I was very concerned that the war was being lost.

I did not see myself for what I was, a white young man of the U.S. empire who had the remarkable privilege of being able to be lifted up and away from growing mass suffering and death, a privilege of empire not shared by my Vietnamese and Chinese friends, who would suffer at the hands of that very empire.

So, in this blindness, I went to Washington, D.C., to visit congressional offices to urge that the United States send many more soldiers to Viet Nam, to essentially take over the fighting of the Viet Nam War. I believed that the war was going so badly because of corruption within the South Vietnamese

military, abetted by luxury-loving U.S. military leaders in Saigon. I was pro-
pelled in my thinking that the United States should take control of the war
by the notion that the U.S. was a land that had always generated superior
wisdom compared to poorer places like Viet Nam.

Entering journalism school in the fall of 1965 I also reentered white,
middle-class American life, with an ambition to become a prominent journalist. By graduation in 1966, I was engaged to be married, and that autumn
I headed with my new wife and three children by her first marriage to work
at the *Providence* (Rhode Island) *Journal and Evening Bulletin.* Three years
later we had twins.

My memory of the dead Viet Cong woman was effectively gone as my
new life of husband, father, and reporter began.

Of course, I was very much aware of the growing horror of the war.
But at the same time, I continued in my belief in the righteousness of the
American cause. I was also flattered and judgment-clouded because I was
friends with Bui Diem, a very decent person who was the publisher of the
Saigon Post and who would soon be Vietnamese ambassador to the United
States. I was also acquainted in a friendly way with Nguyen Cao Ky, the
Vietnamese Air Force commander who would become Viet Nam's vice
president in the last of a series of death-spiraling, made-in-America South
Vietnamese governments.

But, by 1968, challenged by friends and events, I came to oppose the
war because of the massive killing, not because I understood what was pro-
pelling it forward. I protested the war, but I viewed it as an aberration, a
bad decision by American politicians. I was ashamed of my ignorance that
had led me to go to Viet Nam in the first place and then, on top of that,
become an advocate for expanding the war.

Once the war was over, I thought, the United States will never make the
same mistake again. We will, I said to myself, finally have long-lasting peace.

What I did not see then was that, since the first Europeans arrived on
the North American continent, there has been an unwritten understanding
among white Americans that, regardless of political party, the U.S. military's
might will be used, sometimes in the U.S. and often overseas, to capture land
and resources, including human labor, for the advancement of U.S. business
interests. Simply put, this means an endless series of wars.

Indeed, one cannot fully understand what has happened in United
States history or to understand what will come, without understanding the
power and human destructiveness of the concept of empire.

For example, had I read carefully the Rev. Martin Luther King Jr.'s 1967 speech "Beyond Viet Nam" I would have seen that he traced the Viet Nam war to the drive for corporate profits.

> In 1957, a sensitive American official overseas said that it seemed to him that our nation was on the wrong side of a world revolution. During the past ten years we have seen emerge a pattern of suppression which has now justified the presence of U.S. military advisors in Venezuela. This need *to maintain social stability for our investments* accounts for the counterrevolutionary action of American forces in Guatemala. It tells why American helicopters are being used against guerrillas in Cambodia and why American napalm and Green Beret forces have already been active against rebels in Peru. (emphasis added)

I think that King did not use the term *empire* in his speech because he did not want to be called a communist for using the word often used by the Soviet Union and China in charges against the United States. Nonetheless, his challenge to the thinking that led to the Viet Nam war is a challenge to the mentality of empire, and I believe this was a prime factor leading to his assassination.

Avoiding the Meaning of Empire

I was not alone in not wanting to see the United States as a homicidal, imperial power. In the introduction to a remarkable book of essays on the subjugation of women overseas by the U.S. military, entitled *Over There: Living with the U.S. Military Empire from World War Two to the Present*, the editors and authors of several of the essays, Maria Hohn and Seungsook Moon, note that many scholars of United States economic and cultural imperialism have ignored the " 'hard power' that buttresses American influence across the globe—namely the worldwide web of American military bases."

> Given the unprecedented size and reach of the American military empire since 1945, it is surprising that the military dimension of America's global power has garnered strikingly limited attention from scholars working outside the narrow circle of strategic studies and military history.

I was also blind to the application of postcolonial analysis inside U.S. borders. I did not see Native and African American communities as colonies of the larger, white-dominated American society, and the civil rights struggle as a struggle to destroy a colonial system, a struggle that continues to this moment.

In looking at my working life over the last fifty years from this perspective, I thought it would be helpful to ask who were the real beneficiaries of my work from the perspective of people oppressed by U.S. imperial actions and thinking, overseas and at home. Here is a table that attempts to summarize this.

Table 12.1. Percent of Working Time and Probable Primary Beneficiaries

	White Middle-Class	African American/ Hispanic	Native American	Impoverished and/or under U.S. attack
Reporter *Providence Journal* 1966–69 General assignment and labor reporter	100%	0%	0%	0%
Antiwar Protest—part-time 1969–70 Protested the Viet Nam War while working full-time as a carpenter in the white community	0%	0%	0%	100%
Consumer News 1971–73 Consumer reporter	90%	10%	0%	0%
Senate Select Comm. On Nutrition and Human Needs 1974–77 Researcher and staff writer working on report on U.S. food aid program and on dietary goals for the United States	80%	10%	0%	10%

	White Middle-Class	African American/ Hispanic	Native American	Impoverished and/or under U.S. attack
General Accounting Office 1978 Researcher and writer of report on common policies among nations who had dealt effectively with hunger	90%	0%	0%	10%
Bread for the World 1979–80 1983–84 Researcher and lobbyist on behalf of domestic and international food aid legislation	0%	40%	5%	45%
Maryknoll Fathers and Brothers 1985–90 Researcher, writer and co-organizer with the American Friends Service Committee of the Africa Peace Tour, which brought Africans to U.S. communities to educate on U.S. policies, especially military and pro-apartheid policies that were affecting Africans. The tour visited a number of African American communities in the U.S. where commonalities in the struggles of Africans and African Americans were obvious	0%	20%	0%	80%

continued on next page

Table 12.1. Continued.

	White Middle-Class	African American/ Hispanic	Native American	Impoverished and/or under U.S. attack
Candidate for U.S. Congress 1990 Ran at the last moment opposing Congresswoman Nita Lowey (D) NY. Denied a position on the ballot due to a challenge from the Democratic Party. See flyer below for intended beneficiaries. **(ATTACHED)**	40%	40%	10%	10%
Co-manager of a performance space and political action center, later a natural food store/café cooperative 1991–2003 During the period also involved part-time in protests of both Iraq wars and the Afghanistan war.	0%	0%	0%	100%
and the successful protest of installation of police surveillance cameras along the main street of the small city in which I lived.	0%	100%	0%	0%
Consumers for Peace.com 2003–10 Created a website to promote a boycott of ExxonMobil, Shell and BP in opposition to the Iraq war.	0%	0%	0%	100%

	White Middle-Class	African American/ Hispanic	Native American	Impoverished and/or under U.S. attack
Knowdrones.com 2011–Present Created a website providing information on U.S. drone surveillance and attacks and promoting citizen action to ban weaponized drones and drone surveillance. As part of this campaign, also advocated a boycott of Honeywell consumer products because of the firm's manufacture of war drone engines, guidance and targeting equipment. See www.badhoneywell.org	0%	5%	0%	95%

It is apparent in studying this table that I came out of my experience in Viet Nam wanting to help relieve human suffering. But it is also true that as a person needing to support his family, I went to work for organizations that could pay me a living wage. As is obvious, none of the organizations I worked for had an agenda advocating for Native Americans, and I was not drawn to this work. In addition, none of the organizations that I worked for had a goal of advocacy in league with the African American community to decolonize that community within the United States.

The Senate Select Committee on Nutrition and Human Needs was beneficial to African Americans, Native Americans, and Hispanic people in forcing the expansion of the food stamp, school breakfast, and school lunch programs, but assistance did not extend to attempting to achieve liberation of these communities in a full sense. My work on the committee was directed toward nutritional policy, which possibly indirectly benefited African American, Native American, and Hispanic communities as part of larger society.

But the thing that is strikingly clear is that none of the organizations for which I worked had an explicit agenda of withdrawing U.S. military bases from around the world, or stopping all forms of U.S. military intervention.

When I look around and see how few Americans are involved in anti-war activity at this moment, I trace that in large measure to the comfort that many Americans have had in viewing the United States military venture as a huge, generally well-intended though sometimes tragically misguided enterprise that, overall, can do good. There are bad wars, bad weapons systems, and bad leaders, but the global U.S. military system itself is viewed as fundamentally good.

This thinking leads to the common liberal belief that good things can happen in an American society that has not addressed its colonial past and present, both internally and overseas.

Put another way, is it right, or practical, to think that it is possible to create an emotionally and physically healthy society while that society is an imperial society attempting to enrich itself by essentially stealing resources and lives at gunpoint, at home and abroad? Can climate change can be stopped without stopping the military interventions aimed at the resource rape of the planet?

I came of age loving the U.S. military for its apparent miracle of victory in World War II. I did not realize that even that war was a war between imperial powers for world domination, with the U.S. being one of those powers. To understand Viet Nam, it would have helped if I had known the real history of World War II as explained so clearly by Howard Zinn in *A People's History of the United States*: "Quietly, behind the headlines in battles and bombings, American diplomats and businessmen worked hard to make sure that when the war ended, American economic power would be second to none in the world."

The educator Bill Bigelow, writing on the website "Teaching a People's History—Zinn Education Project," spoke to the failure of institutionalized education to deal with the Viet Nam war and wars in general:

> Teaching students a deeper, more complete history of the American War—as it is known in Vietnam—is not just a matter of accuracy, it's about life and death. On the third anniversary of the U.S. invasion of Iraq, Howard Zinn . . . spoke bluntly about what it means when we fail to confront the facts of our past wars: "If we don't know history, then we are ready meat for carnivorous politicians and the intellectuals and journalists who supply the carving knives."

Ideally, at the end of the Viet Nam War, antiwar organizations would have undertaken the task of educating the American public on the imperial causes of the war and the prospect of future imperial wars. Instead, I think most Americans ended up believing that the Viet Nam War stopped because it was "unwinnable" and that the U.S. government would never again make the same intelligence, diplomatic, and military mistakes that led to defeat in Viet Nam.

The Plague of Empire and Men

But is it the evil in the U.S. empire, or are we faced with the evil of the perpetration of empire against humanity that is, in a sense, the history of human life on earth up to this point. A truth above others is that empires grow, flourish, and fall, like huge organisms, comprised of all the dreams, ambitions, energy, greed, racism, willingness to kill, and ignorance of their imperial citizenry. Another truth is that these empires have been conceived of and created by the brute force of men, tragic monuments to the male ego. And yet another truth is that these empires have been built on the forced servitude and suffering of women and the brutalization of children.

Now we see the U.S. empire, the Chinese empire, the Russian empire, and lesser empires, vying for power, controlled by men, doomed to violent competition. History offers no other than this certainty. As Percy Shelley wrote in his poem "Ozymandias":

> I met a traveler from an antique land
> Who said: Two vast trunkless legs of stone
> Stand in the desert . . . Near them, on the sand,
> Half sunk, a shattered visage lies, whose frown,
> And wrinkled lip, sneer of cold command,
> Tell that its sculptor well those passions read
> Which yet survive, stamped on these lifeless things,
> The hand that mocked them, and the heart that fed:
> And on the pedestal these words appear:
> "My name is Ozymandias, king of kings:
> Look on my works, ye Mighty, and despair!"
> Nothing beside remains. Round the decay
> Of that colossal wreck, boundless and bare
> The lone and level sands stretch far away.

With this inevitability in mind, and with the growing prospect of nuclear war, I am wondering now, as a man who went to enable war in Viet Nam: Is our next best step, for the sake of survival of life on earth as we know life, to ensure that women have their chance to take charge of governments, particularly those with nuclear weapons, and the negotiation of human affairs? This may be not just "a nice idea" but the only path that we humans might find on which to move from the violent competition of empire to the peaceful cooperation of survival.

The world, as we know it, is unlikely to survive male fantasies, as we know them.

Chapter 13

Initiation toward Spiritual Activism

Knowing, Calling, and Hope

REV. FELICIA PARAZAIDER

The Knowing

Only in the darkness can you see the stars.

—Martin Luther King Jr.

Have you ever felt like you just know something and you don't know how, but you do? This is how I felt at a very young age. I remember at four years old, praying in my candlelit closet to a picture of a glowing Jesus strategically balanced on a makeshift altar. At night before bedtime, I would try to explain to my mother, but to no avail. When I became old enough to read, I took the Bible I was given and moved my contemplative practice outside to the backyard. It was here, among the bird of paradise flowers and a gigantic evergreen tree which I had named Goliath, where I would sing the Psalms to my own improvisational melodies. I also played the typical childhood games children enjoy, such as hide and seek, as well as make believe I was the 1980s silver screen adventurer Indiana Jones, seeking treasures like the Ark of the Covenant in the family garden. In my seventh year, I wrote a prayer which read, *"Let us love everyone, not just the people who are easy to love, but everybody.*" This simple prayer was part of the knowing that has followed me no matter how occluded my sense of self has become in the coming years.

My family lived in a beautiful home in a then-sleepy San Fernando Valley neighborhood in Southern California. My mother and father had moved from Chicago with my older sister before I was born. My dad had a dream to start a rock band with horns, named after his hometown, and fortunately his vision was a successful one. Mostly a quiet, shy child, I took refuge in private ascetic moments, away from the fishbowl existence that came with being a daughter of a rock star. I also began to play the piano religiously and my piano teacher took a special interest in me, grooming me to be a famous concert pianist.

My family system, however, became progressively chaotic, riddled with alcoholism, mental illness, and perhaps the most troublesome (for my truth teller nature), denial. Sanctuary was found with prayers and contemplation, but also with my piano. It was my focus and my ticket out of a confusing, turbulent environment.

In my early teens, my father bought me the Jimi Hendrix album *Are You Experienced?* Sitting in my parent's living room, cross-legged on the floor, headphones in place, I listened to my father's collection of LPs, the Beatles White album, Frank Zappa and the Mothers of Invention, and Janis Joplin, among others. Unlike the overproduced '80s lost generation, this music brought me to a time where passion exploded and the world was changing. I could hear the charge for the "revolution of values" preached by Dr. Martin Luther King Jr. at Riverside Church in 1967. This music was full of passion, grit, and hope. It contained everything I was crying out for and would be the gateway to my evolution as a spiritual activist.

I began to appropriate the '60s generation, listening to its sound, taking drugs, musing at the art, even adopting the clothing. I also sought to learn as much as I could about the civil rights movement, the Free Speech Movement, Freedom Summer, the lunch counter sit-ins, and nonviolent figures such as Mohandas K. Gandhi and Dr. King. Here was a spiritual home at a time when I felt lost and scared by the violence in my own home and the world around me.

Extremely difficult times ensued, with unhealthy relationships; however, the dimly lit candle of knowing was not vanquished but waiting for me to kick up to the surface back to life. At twenty, it seemed as though I was coming back to the land of the living, but then the violence I had experienced and internalized, I began inflicting upon myself. I was diagnosed as manic depressive, suffering from anorexia, alcoholism, and drug addiction.

At twenty-five years of age, much like Andy Dufresne in the film *The Shawshank Redemption*, I had to either "get busy living or get busy dying." I checked myself into a recovery facility in North Hollywood, California. Outside my dorm window was a store called Circus Liquor with a maniacal-looking clown as its logo. Every night the sign's letters would go clockwise, some lit and some burnt out, much like my spirit. I wondered what would become of my life. One night I sat out on the patio of that rehabilitation center smoking a cigarette. I said no to the violence and yes to life, yes to God.

I had awakened from a sleeping victim state and realized I had much work to do on myself. I committed myself to honest inner work and continued to say yes to life, yes to God. I also revisited the greats of nonviolence from Dr. King to Bob Moses, Gandhi to Howard Thurman, as my life was presenting me with opportunities to serve and help others. Nonviolence was becoming a way of life for me, not only through study but action. I had come home to the child who knew there was a treasure in the family garden; a treasure containing the truth for us all. The child who knew there was good in this world no matter what the darkness said.

This is the first stage of spiritual initiation: *to connect with the knowing that at our core we are more than the fear, despair, violence, that in fact we are actually made in pure love.* This love sustains us, keeps us holy, and brings us back to the divine. No matter what has happened in our lives. No matter how the violence in the world may scream at our window at night. We are made in *and of* pure love. It is this knowing we must return to, no matter how painful, how frightening, how arduous of a journey back home, because this is our divine call. It is this knowing we must fight for with all the peace, courage, and radical love we can muster. The world is depending on us for we *are* better than this. We stand on the shoulders of great ones and now we are the great ones called to do the work as we pick up the staff.

The Calling

For some of us it takes years to hear our call. Still others may hear it and be too frightened to listen. I went looking for mine and found it.

—Rev. Felicia Parazaider

The second stage of initiation: *to recognize we are here to serve through the vehicles of healing and loving.* This basic truth is both simple and profoundly challenging. Buddhist meditation teacher and master Chogyam Trungpa once wrote, "We must try to think how we can help this world. If we don't help, nobody will."[1] We are called upon to serve in a way that is holy and unique. For some of us, it takes years to hear our call. Still others may hear it and be too frightened to listen. I went looking for mine and found it.

The calling came in an unlikely place: a fast food drive thru in Sun Valley, California. I was learning to take the broken pieces of my past and weave them into sacred wounds. It was (by the grace of God) in Alcoholics Anonymous that I became aware of my love for being of service. This particular summer was a difficult one because I was unclear about my next steps in life. Questions like, "What is my purpose and why am I here?" plagued me. One hot night, in the early morning hours of my twenty-eighth birthday, I drove to a nearby fast food restaurant, Carl's, Jr. I pulled up to the drive thru, ordered my food, spun round to the window, and there he was. He was probably in his forties, African American, and seemingly homeless. As soon as I rolled down my window, he asked me for a cigarette, and I said, "Sorry, man, I don't have another one." Then he asked me a question leaving me stunned in my tracks: "Do you want to get high?" Here it is my birthday, I'm clean and sober, getting my life together and someone comes from out of nowhere propositioning me back to my old life. I responded, "No, man, I'm clean, I don't do that anymore." The world stood still for a moment, and with tears welling in his eyes he said, "This shit is killing me."

My new friend and I talked for several minutes while I waited for my snack to come through the window. He talked of his family, a son and wife whom he hadn't seen in ten years. His voice broke into the night air, "I used to be somebody you know." I told him, "You still are, you still are." Right before I pulled away, I asked him his name and said the only thing I could think of, "Just don't give up hope."

I cried as I drove back home. Not long ago, *I* was this Carl's, Jr. man, so broken, so lost, barely living. Through choice, grace, and good old fashioned hard work, I came back. And then suddenly I knew, "Felicia, the pain you went through will be a service and inspiration to others. Felicia, you are here to speak and write." It was both a feeling of revelation and revolution. Now, almost twenty years later, I have been in relentless pursuit of bringing peace, love, and hope to all my relations ever since. This was the calling.

Overwhelmed with joy, my confusion had lifted and everything was fine . . . until I woke up the next morning. Quickly falling into self-doubt, I questioned what had happened only the night before. There was something else as well, I needed to radically heal before I could go out and do the good works. My inner work led me more deeply into Vipassana meditation, exploring Leonard Orr's rebirthing, Lectio Devina, Transcendental Meditation, and Vedanta philosophy. I earnestly asked God to remove this call from me if it was (1) based in ego and/or (2) not rooted in holy ambition. I returned to college and as my cleansing process continued my study was also directed to researching nonviolent movements. Gandhi became a guiding light. Learning about *satyagraha* (truth-force), as well as the historic salt marches through India, were some of the stepping stones to my first internship at the Anti-Defamation League (ADL). My main work was to crack down on hate groups and crimes in the Los Angeles area.

After leaving ADL, I became passionate about women's rights, interning for the Feminist Majority Foundation (FMF), forming a chapter on the college campus I was attending. I also began to travel outside of my figurative comfort zone, literally, including to the Blackfeet Indian Reservation in Montana. Upon my return however, I fell into a depression. What I had witnessed had left me in a disillusioned state. The opulence of my life in Sherman Oaks, California, now disoriented me. The most difficult part was that people seemed oblivious to the various shades and forms of violence all around them.

On December 19, 2002, at five in the morning, I drove to the beach. As the sun rose that morning, I recited the Third Step prayer of Alcoholics Anonymous, "God, I offer myself to Thee, to build with me, and to do with me as Thou wilt." I vowed to fully commit to the calling and devote my life to what Johan Galtung, a prominent founder of peace studies, described as positive peace—"not merely the absence of violence, but the restoration of relationships, the creation of social systems that serve the needs of the whole population, and the constructive resolution of conflict."[2] I also vowed to not let fear deter me from my purpose.

For several years I took panels of recovering alcoholics to visit other substance abusers in hospitals. Most of the people we visited would not recover from their addiction. I began to think of addiction as a form of self-inflicted violence. When we forget the *knowing that we are made in love,* we are lost to our *call to serve through the vehicles of healing and loving,* and become susceptible to soul sickness where a hollow space replaces love with (the potential for) a growing web of violence.

I left Los Angeles in 2006 and continued my studies at the University of California, Berkeley. I was double majoring in Religion and Peace &

Conflict Studies. I joined with Pace e Bene nonviolent service (PeB). We had weekly spiritual practice together, facilitated nonviolent training workshops at churches and schools, and attended vigils and protests such as the annual march at the School of the Americas.

I began thinking of becoming a human rights lawyer. Bill Moyer, social change activist and author, laid out four types of political activists: the citizen, the change agent, the reformer, and the rebel. Moyer believed that each type worked together for good bringing about change in an integral way. The citizen gives a movement legitimacy, making it harder for authorities to discredit it. Dr. King is an example of the *citizen*. The *change agent* is a powerful role because they create paradigm shifts, support developing coalitions, and work with groups of people. Pace e Bene inhabited the realm of "change agent" through its training workshops. The *reformer* is the person who goes within the system to create social change and transformation. They work to create and expand new laws and policies. Human rights lawyers can be considered "reformers."[3] This I thought was my direction, until I learned about the fourth role: *the rebel*.

My first trip to the Nevada National Security Site (NNSS; also called the Nevada Test Site or NTS) was in 2009. I traveled with the Nevada Desert Experience (NDE), an anti–nuclear weapons organization. The United States has detonated more than one thousand nuclear weapons at the Nevada Test Site since 1951. This beautiful desert is now the most bombed out place on the planet.[4] Arriving at the NTS, the cries emanating from Mother Earth were almost too much to bear and contrasted greatly with the striking desert beauty. The night before, we had been briefed by NDE staff about possible consequences if we risked arrest by crossing the line onto the NTS property. All night I prayed. I wondered what it would feel like to break the law, and the situation was dripping with irony. At one time, I was as wild as anything, yet managed to avoid getting arrested. Now years later, stable, sober, and spiritually fit, I was going to get arrested.

The next morning, our group drove back out to the test site. Was I going to get arrested? What would this mean for my future? A big "who cares?" bellowed from my depths and the answer was loud and clear, "This *is* what counts, so stand up for what you believe in. Cross today!"

Dr. Vincent Harding, a prominent civil rights activist, gave us a blessing before the nonviolent action and together about sixty of us held hands, singing "Peace is Flowing like a River" and made our way to the line. Suddenly it was time. I stepped across affirming what I had said to myself at the rehab center, "No to violence and yes to life, yes to God, yes to remembering the knowing!" This time it wasn't about me, it was about the world, the children, and our children's children. My calling had taken me here and I was astounded. Although we were told this is a low-risk arrest, when you feel your legs move across that white painted line, something shakes and it isn't the earth. After crossing we were placed in a holding pen until, one by one, issued a ticket with a hefty fee (that you need not pay), we walked back down the road.

A higher-risk arrest soon followed at Creech Airforce Base while protesting drones. As Bill Moyer illustrated so fully, all the activist types are needed to make our new paradigm work in the most efficacious way possible. Some of us are citizens, others change agents or reformers. Rebels often dramatize social problems through nonviolent action. We shine a light on violence and help society wake up through direct action. It may seem scary, pointless, or even silly to some, but here are some reasons why it still matters: Getting arrested means getting in the way of an unholy machine. It means truth telling. It means not slipping into denial. It means knowing we are all made in love, that everything is made in pure love, and therefore we cannot stand by and watch violence happen. It means recognizing the divine honor and responsibility we have by moving into action when we see degradation happening. It creates opening for dialogue, paradigm shifts, and curiosity where there was none. Even if people do not agree with our worldview or methodology, they are typically struck by the nonviolent action, and the impact is often far reaching. Getting arrested is one of the ways I have responded to the calling. With each arrest, I come away with a new piece of truth about myself, about others, and about the world we live in.

In 2012, I joined the annual NDE Sacred Peace Walk. I had decided I would risk arrest protesting drone warfare at Creech Airforce Base in Indian Springs, Nevada. Unlike at the NTS, an arrest at Creech had higher risks. We would likely be driven back to Las Vegas, booked, and spend some time in jail. Early Wednesday morning arrived and we assembled near the entrance to the base. It was business as usual, the new shift of base workers arriving in a steady stream. My sign said, "When the power of love overcomes the love of power, the world will know peace" (Jimi Hendrix). I stood, very nervous, breathing rapidly and unconsciously clenching my jaw. Erik, a pastor from Boston, came over to speak with me. Initially I had difficulty listening to him. I was so nervous that I could not focus on anything but what was exactly in front of me. Then he said, in a thick Boston accent, "Felicia, when you are an old lady, and your grandchildren say, 'Grandma, did you ever do anything to make this world a better place?' You can tell them about this moment. This time."

With that, four of us suddenly were moving onto the roadway to stop traffic, and for a few minutes successfully obstructed the vehicles from being able to go into the base. We were immediately arrested after presenting indictments to the police for the commanding officers at Creech then driven to Las Vegas and held at Clark County jail for almost a day. I met other women inside who shared their stories with me. We prayed, laughed, and cried together. There is the arrest, and then there is what happens after the arrest. It is one of the most sacred times I have ever experienced in my life.

The truth is, we never know where or when our lives are going to change, like lightning bolts spackling the life path, filling in the crevices of question marks with the solidity of purpose and meaning making. We never know when we might experience a Carl's, Jr. moment. We may not know how we will be used as conduits of change and peace or what our specific role is in this life, but we must go looking. This second stage of spiritual initiation calls upon us to be abandoned to God and everything in between. We must be desperate to hear the calling. We take the steps to free ourselves of any distractions, hindrances, or blockages that come in the form of doubt, anger, fear, grief, or, most of all, violence. Once we commit ourselves to the call, our lives will never be the same. It may get hard. It may feel like too much sometimes seeing the suffering in the world, but we need to keep doing the good work. We need to only rest and begin again. Here is truth: if we stop the killing for even a minute, we've won. If we stop it for two minutes, we've succeeded. If we stop it for three, we've something to say to our children who look to us in earnest asking, "What did you do?" And in that moment, with the setting sun facing our lives, we can say in grace, "This is what we did and here is how. We do it together, with our knowing, with our love, and with our calling to service laid closely upon our hearts."

The Hope 1857

We, the undersigned scholars from around the world and from relevant sciences, have met and arrived at the following Statement on Violence. In it, we challenge a number of alleged biological findings that have been used, even by some in our disciplines, to justify violence and war.

—The Seville Statement

Violence. It's everywhere. We have all experienced it. No one is exempt. Moreover, if we are truly honest with ourselves, we have all been violent.

Some individuals have a propensity to be more violent toward themselves (imploding), whereas others have an inclination to be violent toward people, places, and things (exploding). The fact is we have been witness to, experiencers of, and participants in various forms, and shades of violence. When we say no to denial, we can extricate ourselves from the cycle of violence. Let us first define and name the injury before we research the solution. Violence is any physical, emotional, verbal, institutional, structural, or spiritual behavior, attitude, policy, or condition that diminishes, dominates, or destroys ourselves or others.[5] From this definition we recognize the great expanse that violence inhabits. Violence is not only physical force with intent to hurt, harm, or kill someone. There are other forms of violence: racial slurs, bullying, poverty, addiction, homelessness, homophobia, prejudice, bigotry or hatred toward religious groups, sexism, classism, speciesism, environmental degradation, and more.

Johan Galtung identified three types of violence: direct, structural, and cultural. Direct violence refers to physical acts of violence. Structural violence is built into the fabric of our social, political, and economic systems. It is the unequal allocation of goods, resources, and opportunities, between different groups, classes, genders, and nationalities. This type of violence—poverty, racism, homelessness—is often overlooked. Cultural violence is the way a culture legitimizes violence, making it seem acceptable. It is also a way by which a community or individuals see themselves as superior, thereby dehumanizing the other. China's occupation of Tibet is a form of cultural violence (as well as direct and structural).[6]

Defining and naming violence can feel daunting. When we first start to investigate and awaken to the suffering in the world it can leave us cold and paralyzed. However, by recognizing the violence within and without, we can now go deeper and notice the ways we react or respond to it. Therefore, it is essential, as we move through the initiation process, to not focus only on the outer work through spiritual activism, while never forgetting the primary importance of one's own inner work. This way we become keenly aware of the violence in our personal lives, whether present or past, in order to see it in the world at large. This takes willingness, bravery, and courage.

If we are committed to our *knowing and* accepting the *calling*, then we must delve deeply into the darkness to come into the light, to hug the demons. For by first embracing the demons, we will then embrace *hope: the third stage of initiation toward spiritual activism*.

The Rev. James Lawson, activist, leading theoretician and tactician of the civil rights movement, claims, "Violence has a clear objective: I hurt, you hurt." Hence, whatever form it takes, be it structural, direct, cultural, the intention is the same. However, the ways we respond or react to violence vary. According to Pace e Bene's "Engage: Exploring Nonviolent Living" curriculum, there are three ways we commonly meet violence: through avoidance, accommodation, or counterviolence.[7] The first way, that of avoidance, means we steer clear of any involvement. We look the other way. For example, if we see a person on the street who is homeless, we may feel uncomfortable, avoiding eye contact; or we might say, "It's not my problem. It's not up to me to save anybody."

The second way is by accommodating the violence. We think, "It's not so bad." We enter into *positive* thinking—the way it *is*—versus normative thinking—the way it *ought* to be. Interestingly enough, many spiritual activists tend to confuse accommodation and nonviolence. They use an inordinate supply of compassion, which bleeds into codependency, toward unjust situations or violent people. Third, the most obvious way people react to violence is through violence itself, or counterviolence. This is the "eye for an eye" trope.

This process of deconstruction has included defining violence, naming the different types, and analyzing ways we react to it. This may seem pointless if one believes we are hardwired for violence. The Seville Statement of 1986 from UNESCO elucidates five propositions about war. "It is scientifically incorrect to say: 1) that war is inherited from our animal ancestors, 2) that war is genetically programmed, 3) that in the course of human evolution there has been a selection for aggressive behavior more than for other kinds of behavior, 4) that humans have a violent brain, and 5) that war is caused by instinct."[8] If this is true, then why violence?

We have a soul sickness, which makes us susceptible to violence. If gone untreated for too long, and without a spiritual intervention, we slip into violence. Like the alcoholic who thinks it will be different upon taking the first drink, we believe that the violence we see, indirectly perpetuate, or directly engage in, will be different this time. It won't.

The third stage toward spiritual activism requires us to first admit we have a problem. This is our path to hope. However, if we do not admit that we have a disease that renders us powerless over violence, we stay in its ugly cycle. With all our might we must seek a spiritual experience that will restore us whole. Let us start at the beginning, like the alcoholic who realizes they can no longer continue on like this, taking the first step together: "My name is _____, and I am addicted to violence. I am powerless over violence and my life is unmanageable" (adapted from *The Big Book of Alcoholics Anonymous*).

We find the answer is in the initiation itself. When we forget the *knowing* that we are made in pure love, we develop this soul sickness. This does not mean there is something intrinsically wrong with us, it means our souls need healing. Remember the child in the yard who sang the Psalms to God, who prayed in her closet, who tried to express what she knew to her mother? This is the child who just knew she was made in love by love Itself. There was no doubt, no question, no fear.

At some point in our lives we were connected to our *knowing*. In a deep existential way, we knew we were made in love. Whether we were conscious or unconscious to this fact does not matter. It may have been a long time ago, *but it was there*. Every single person on this planet—from the serial killers, the Hitlers, the babies born with HIV, to the seemingly unscathed by any disappointment in life—have known this truth. Conversely, at some point we stopped believing. We stopped *knowing*. We stopped hearing our *calling*, and then the candle of *hope* began to dim. However, the higher truth of who we are never changed. The complexity of our biology, physiology, psychology, socialization, and yes, our wounding story, can change us. The choices we make from this place of wounding can change us. But our true self, our Higher Self, can never be broken, stolen, or stopped. Moreover, the changes can lead us down the road to perpetuate addictive cycles of violence—direct, structural, and cultural—or they can allow us, as individuals and as a planet, to bottom out in our addiction, crying out, "Please God, I/ We can't do this anymore. Help us." It is then we become more susceptible to the Holy, and begin to start the process of reigniting the sacred flame.

The enormous grief to bear is that some of us will continue to have a soul sickness. Some of us will not bottom out but will stay lost to their knowing. This does not mean we should give up hope, just the opposite. It means we embrace our demons and keep moving forward. This third stage charges us to fiercely look the soul sickness in ourselves in the eye and reckon with it, making no apologies. It invites us to become awake to all the kinds of violence that we are asleep to. It encourages us to be honest and examine the ways we react to violence. It wants us to be so uncomfortable, so pained, that we say enough is enough, exclaiming, "My life, our life, is worth more than the violence! We are better than this!" We have a huge opportunity as well as great capacity to create extraordinary change. It is time we accept the truth that if we are truly made in pure unadulterated love, if everyone is also made in this love, and if we all began this way, then no one, nothing, can ever take that away. Our light can be dimmed, and we may not leave the earthly realm in alignment with this knowing reclaimed, but the potential for transformation always exists. This is the radical hope for us and this planet.

Notes

1. Chogyam Trungpa, *The Sacred Path of the Warrior* (Boston: Shambhala, 1984), 5.

2. Temesgen Tilahun, "Johan Galtung's Concept of Positive and Negative Peace in Contemporary Ethiopia: An Appraisal," *International Journal of Political Science and Development* 3, no. 6 (June 2015): 251.

3. Bill Moyer, ed., *Doing Democracy: The MAP Model for Organizing Social Movements* (Gabriola Island, BC: New Society Publishers, 2001).

4. Andreas Knudsen, "Native Americans Bear the Nuclear Burden," *Republic of Lakotah,* April 20, 2010; http://www.republicoflakotah.com/tag/newe-sogobia/.

5. Laura Slattery, Ken Butigan, Veronica Pelicaric, and Ken Preston, *Engage: Exploring Nonviolent Living* (Oakland: Pace e Bene Press, 2005), 33.

6. Ibid., 34.

7. Ibid., 54–57.

8. Ibid., 44–45.

Chapter 14

No Justice, No Peace

BILL QUIGLEY

"No justice, no peace," is not just a chant for protests. Fighting for justice and peace are inseparable. As one pope said, "If you want peace, work for justice." I am a lawyer who works with people and organizations struggling for peace and struggling for justice.

These nonviolent fights have taken me to death row, to prisons in Port au Prince, to public housing developments, to Baghdad, to homeless shelters, to Gaza, and to protests and courtrooms across the country. I have represented hundreds of people who have voluntarily gone to jail for reasons of conscience. I have also represented thousands of people who have been in jail and want to be treated with dignity and respect. To me, this is all peace work. And to me, this is all justice work.

My Background

I grew up as one of nine kids in an Irish Catholic family in the Midwest. Early on, I was interested in social justice. I was inspired by the witness of Catholic activist priests such as Dan and Phil Berrigan, as well as nuns and the Catholic Worker movement who opposed the Vietnam War, helped the poor, and marched for civil rights. Though I studied for many years to become a priest, it did not happen. It turns out I was much more interested in social justice than I was in the mass and sacraments, so I turned to social work.

Through my theology studies I met and later worked with a group of Catholic sisters living in the giant St. Thomas housing development in New Orleans. I went there to help the families in public housing. But a funny thing happened. It turns out that though I was in fact helping them, they were in fact also helping me. Most of them were raising their children and sometimes their children's children on shoestring budgets despite tremendous challenges of crime, racial discrimination, violence, and government neglect. The mothers and grandmothers had their own individual struggles but they also gathered together to make their living conditions better. They showed me courage and determination and inspiration in their daily lives in ways I had never seen before. They accepted me into their community and many of us became lifelong friends. In retrospect, I think they may have been the best teachers I ever had.

During this time, I was part of a small faith community of social justice people who met, studied, prayed, and ate together. We studied Jesus, the prophets, Dorothy Day, Gandhi, Martin Luther King Jr., and many others whose lives blended faith and action for justice and peace. One of the great women I met through this community, who had also studied for religious life and who was also dedicated to social justice, was kind enough to marry me and become my life partner for the last forty plus years.

The families I was working with had many legal problems. And the lawyers they met did not really seem all that committed to working with them in a respectful relationship. So, my wife and I decided she would earn money as a teacher and put me through law school. Our community thought it was a good idea, so I did it. Loyola Law classes were demanding and instructive but I learned the most by working as a law clerk for two longtime civil rights lawyers.

After law school I worked for several years with Legal Aid on issues such as civil rights, housing, and police brutality. During that time, I was fortunate enough to be partnered with an experienced community organizer named Ron Chisom. Ron taught me about the importance of people organizing and working together to reclaim their dignity and power. And he also taught me how pervasive white privilege and institutional racism is. Not only in those systems we were challenging, but also in the well-intentioned and goodhearted people and institutions, including ourselves, that were dedicated to fighting for justice. These issues and injustices have troubled me and kept me learning and relearning from Ron and others ever since.

Campaigns

I was helping individual people, but I was finding that more progress seemed to come about when people got together to push for change. I read about the people who challenged slavery in the early 1800s, about the women who agitated for the right to vote, about the labor movement which fought for the right to bargain collectively, about the antiwar movement, the civil rights movement, the environmental movement and the anti-nuclear movement. I want to make it clear at this point that justice is a team sport. I have never done anything alone. I always work with teams of great people.

In the 1980s, I was part of local campaigns for voting rights for the African American community, for decent housing, against the death penalty and against police brutality. I became a part of Pax Christi, the Catholic peace organization, after my wife's work with the organization showed me the way. Our family continued to be a part of a small faith community that gathered twice a month to discuss social justice and peace issues and to pray together. We petitioned and marched for civil rights and public housing and against police brutality, against U.S. intervention in Latin America, and against the first Gulf War.

Our family joined with many others protesting the death penalty in Louisiana. At a time when lawyers were not appointed to represent people facing execution, I joined in representing several men who had been condemned to death, most unsuccessfully, and accompanied one to his tragic execution. With Sr. Helen Prejean, part of our prayer group, we walked eighty miles to our state capital to pray to stop the killings. We held candlelight vigils outside the penitentiary when executions could not be stopped, and we advocated in articles and press conferences to stop the killings. The violent response to violence was beyond belief. Defending those on their way to executions exposed myself and my family to intense hatred and threats. But with our strong faith and our community we continued to push for life.

In 1989, Salvadoran troops trained by the U.S. military murdered six Jesuits, their housekeeper, and her daughter at the University of Central America. I was part of a team of lawyers who represented Daniel Berrigan and a number of others who were arrested on federal charges for blocking entrances to our federal building to protest the murders and U.S. military involvement in Latin America.

This marked the beginning of a new legal specialty, representing people whose beliefs have compelled them to break the law. I have had the honor of being a part of teams of lawyers representing well over a hundred people arrested over the years at Fort Benning protesting the infamous training site for Latin American human rights violators, the School of the Americas. I have stood alongside activists protesting against nuclear weapons as part of the Plowshares Movement. I appeared with them in courts in Arizona, Georgia, New York, Nebraska, South Dakota, Tennessee, Washington State, and Washington, D.C. I have been fortunate enough to represent activists arrested protesting for peace, economic justice, human rights, decent housing, immigrant rights, and sustainable energy.

These folks, people whose beliefs are so strong that they are willing to risk going to jail, constantly inspire me. Standing beside them in court is an honor. I am so proud of their willingness to challenge the unjust status quo and their refusal to wait for things to get better. They teach me and re-energize me again and again.

Participating in the School of Americas Watch (SOAW) movement since the 1990s helped me meet thousands of deeply committed peace and justice activists across the United States and to connect with the many social justice movements they represent.

I have spent a quarter-century working at a Jesuit law school, Loyola New Orleans. Though the physical presence of Jesuits has diminished in that time because there are fewer and fewer of them, their commitment to justice has liberated me and many others to engage in actions for peace that would be highly problematic at other institutions. They generously allowed me to spend two years working on human rights campaigns across the globe with the Center for Constitutional Rights in New York.

SOAW connections also led me to a series of visits to Haiti, where I worked alongside Pere Gerard Jean-Juste, a charismatic grassroots priest/prophet of the poor. A friend from SOAW asked me to join a human rights delegation to Port au Prince after that country's most recent coup. While there I met Pere Jean-Juste who, upon finding out I was a lawyer, explained he might need a lawyer someday because the government was trying to silence him. I was so taken with him I told him of course I would come and help him if he ever got in trouble with the law. Within two weeks he was arrested and jailed and got word to me through members of his church that he was taking me up on my promise. That led to many trips to the prisons and courts of Port au Prince as he was in and out of jail on totally bogus charges designed to silence him and his critiques of the unelected government.

Pere Jean-Juste said his office and mass every day and led the parish in the rosary every night. He slept on the floor. He would give his last penny to the poor who surrounded him. He spoke out about injustice whenever he had the chance. He gave thunderous homilies that brought crowds to their feet. He ran a feeding program that fed hundreds of children every day. He wore a rosary around his neck and his computer screen saver was the Blessed Virgin Mary. He was absolutely unafraid despite constant death threats. And he laughed more than any person I have ever met. Through him I met hundreds of Haitian people who allowed me to join in their campaigns for human rights and human dignity.

Another campaign that impacted me grew out of the prophetic work of Kathy Kelly and the organizations she has quarterbacked—Voices in the Wilderness and Voices for Creative Nonviolence. Kathy Kelly and a team of other great people organized dozens of human rights trips to Iraq when the U.S. government was beating the war drums against Saddam Hussein and imposed crippling sanctions on the country. The United States declared such trips illegal and threatened to prosecute people who went. Kathy and others openly went again and again and took doctors and physicians and teachers and nurses and all kinds of people who risked arrest to engage in people-to-people diplomacy with the people of Iraq. A few weeks before the second Gulf War was launched by our government I joined a delegation that went to Iraq and I brought bags and bags of medical supplies donated by people in our New Orleans community. My contact with the people of Iraq made it clear that the people of both Iraq and the United States appreciated each other's individual citizens but were seriously afraid of each other's countries because of the propaganda of our governments. Kathy also invited me to accompany her to Gaza to stand witness to the bombardment of Palestinian settlements by Israeli bombs. I felt the same way I did when my client and friend was executed on death row. How can people do this to other people? Where do violence and war come from?

To me, the same dynamics are at work in the death penalty in Louisiana, the shock and awe of our military bombardment of Baghdad, our evil system of mass incarceration, the death squads in Latin America, the gun violence that plagues our country, and police brutality in our poor and African American communities. All are based on disregard of human rights.

To me, our nuclear arsenal, which can destroy the world many times over, comes from the same place as the blatant and shocking poverty, which our economic systems and governments at best allow and at worst create in our country and around the world.

To me, as Martin Luther King Jr. preached, our racism, our militarism, and our materialism are all interconnected. Our governments, our military, our police, our educational systems, our economic systems, and sadly even our churches, have racism, militarism, and materialism built into their DNA.

War and violence are nourished by fear, fanned by politicians, maintained by profit-seeking corporations, and enabled by our inability to sense our own powers to stop them.

Hope for the Journey

Yet I am filled with hope for our future. The people I have met inspire me. In my experience, it is at the sharpest point of violence and oppression that I discover people who exhibit a spirit of courage, generosity, and determination that shames my fears. Issues can be overwhelming but the people can energize us.

Yes, we must have our eyes open to the violence and war and hatred that are too often paraded in front of us by ratings-hungry media. Too many just change the channel and avoid looking at the tragedies and injustices of our sisters and brothers. We peace and justice people cannot look away from the horrors visited upon our sisters and brothers. But we cannot look only on the horrors. We cannot only see the injustices.

We must also be open to the joy and inspiration and courage and love that our sisters and brothers can share with us. We must walk toward injustice with open hearts and open minds and join with the people at the center of these wrongs.

When our hearts and eyes are open we can join with those who are suffering and help lift up and amplify their voices. Not voices for the voiceless, because all can communicate. But not all who communicate are allowed to be heard. No, instead of voices for the voiceless, we stand in solidarity with those whose voices are rarely heard and with our voices join with theirs so their cries for justice and peace can be heard. And once heard, can be addressed.

It is in this work for justice with others that we can establish peace based on respect and human rights. Peace as not just the absence of conflict but the presence of justice. If we want peace, we must work for justice.

Chapter 15

How I Became a Peace Activist

DAVID SWANSON

When I was teaching myself how to write, when I was about twenty to twenty-five, I churned out (and threw out) all kinds of autobiographies. I wrote glorified diaries. I fictionalized my friends and acquaintances. I still write columns all the time in the first person. I did write a children's book in recent years that was fiction but included my oldest son and my niece and nephew as characters. But I haven't touched autobiography in more years than I'd been alive when I used to engage in it.

I've been asked a number of times to write chapters for books on "how I became a peace activist." In some cases, I've just apologized and said I couldn't. For one book called *Why Peace*, edited by Marc Guttman, I wrote a very short chapter called "Why Am I a Peace Activist? Why Aren't You?" My point was basically to express my outrage that one would have to explain working to end the worst thing in the world, while millions of people not working to end it need offer no explanation for their reprehensible behavior.

I often speak at peace groups and colleges and conferences about working for peace, and I'm often asked how I became a peace activist, and I always politely dodge the question, not because the answer is too long but because it is too short. I'm a peace activist because mass murder is horrible. What the hell do you mean, why am I a peace activist?

This position of mine is odd for a number of reasons. For one thing, I'm a strong believer in the need for many more peace activists. If we can learn anything about how people have become peace activists, we damn well ought to learn it and apply those lessons. My nightmare for how the peace movement ends, other than the nuclear apocalypse ending, is that the peace movement ends when the last peace activist acquires Alzheimer's. And of course I fear being that peace activist. And of course that's crazy, as there are peace activists much younger than I am, especially activists against Israeli wars who haven't necessarily focused on U.S. wars yet. But I still not infrequently find myself among the youngest in the room. The U.S. peace movement is still dominated by people who became active during the U.S. war on Vietnam. I became a peace activist for some other reason, even if influenced by those slightly older than myself. If the peace movement of the 1960s seemed admirable to me, how do we make today's peace movement seem admirable to those yet to be born? This sort of useful question arises in large numbers once I'm willing to investigate this topic.

For another thing, I'm a strong believer in the power of environment to shape people. I wasn't born speaking English or thinking anything that I now think. I got it all from the culture around me. Yet somehow I've always assumed that whatever made me a peace activist was in me at birth and holds little interest for others. I was never pro-war. I have no Saul on the road to Damascus conversion story. I had a typical suburban U.S. childhood pretty much like those of my friends and neighbors, and none of them ended up as peace activists—just me. I took seriously the stuff they tell every child about trying to make the world a better place. I found the ethics of the Carnegie Endowment for Peace inevitable, although I'd never heard of that institution, an institution which in no way acts on its mandate. But it was set up to abolish war, and then to identify the second-worst thing in the world and work to abolish that. How is any other course even thinkable?

But most people who agree with me on that are environmental activists. And most of them pay no attention to war and militarism as the primary cause of environmental destruction. Why is that? How did I not become an environmental activist? How did an environmental movement grow to its current strength dedicated to ending all but the very worst environmental disaster?

If becoming a peace activist seems so obvious to me, what in my early childhood could have helped make me this person? And if it seems so obvious to me, why did it take me until I was thirty-three to do it? And what of the fact that I meet people all the time who would work as professional peace activists if someone would only give them that job? Heck, I hire people now to work as peace activists, but there are one hundred applicants for each one hired. Isn't part of the answer to why the peace movement is old that retired people have time to work for free? And isn't part of the question of how I became a peace activist actually a question of how I found out one could get paid for it, and how I managed to become one of the small number of people who does?

My interaction with the 1960s was a month in length, as I was born on December 1, 1969, along with my twin sister, in New York City, to parents who were a United Church of Christ preacher and an organist at a church in Ridgefield, New Jersey, and who had met at Union Theological Seminary. They'd left Right-leaning families in Wisconsin and Delaware, each the only child of three to move very far from home. They'd supported civil rights and social work. My Dad had chosen to live in Harlem, despite the need to periodically buy back his possessions from people who stole them. They left the church theologically and physically, moving out of the house that went with the job, when my sister and I were two. We moved to a new town in suburban Washington, D.C., that was just being built as a planned, pedestrian, mixed-income utopia called Reston, Virginia. My parents joined the Christian Science church. They voted for Jesse Jackson. They volunteered. They worked at being the best parents possible, with some success I think. And they worked hard at making a living, with my Dad having set up a business building additions on houses, and my Mom doing the paperwork. Later, my Dad would be an inspector and my mom write up the reports for prospective buyers of new houses. They forced the builders to fix so many mistakes that the companies started writing into their contracts that people could get inspections by anyone other than my Dad. Now my parents work as coaches for people with attention deficit disorder, which my Dad has diagnosed himself as having had his whole life.

I'm well aware that most people think Christian Science is crazy. I was never a fan of it, and my parents dropped it decades ago. The first time I heard of the concept of atheism, I thought, "Well, yeah, of course." But if you're going to try to make sense of an omnipotent benevolent god and the existence of evil, you do have to either (1) give up and just let it not make sense, as most people do who identify with some religion, often denying death, celebrating virgin births, and believing all sorts of things no less crazy than Christian Science including that a benevolent omnipotent being creates war and famine and disease, or (2) conclude that evil does not really exist, and that your eyes must be deceiving you, as Christian Scientists try to do, with all kinds of contradictions, very little success, and disastrous results, or (3) outgrow millennia-old worldviews based on anthropomorphizing a universe that really could not care less.

These were the lessons from my parents' example, I think: be courageous but generous, try to make the world a better place, pack up and start over as needed, try to make sense of the most important matters, pack up ideologically and try again as needed, stay cheerful, and put love for your children ahead of other things (including ahead of Christian Science: use medical care if truly needed, and rationalize it as required).

My family and close friends and extended family were neither military nor peace activists, nor any other sort of activists. But militarism was all around in the D.C. area and on the news. Friends' parents worked for the military and the Veterans Administration and an agency that was not to be named. Oliver North's daughter was in my high school class at Herndon, and he came into class to warn us about the Commie threat in Nicaragua. Later we watched him testify about his misdeeds before Congress. My understanding of those misdeeds was highly limited. His worst offense seemed to be having misspent money on a security system for his house over in Great Falls, where my friends who had the coolest parties lived.

When I was in the third grade, my sister and I tested into the "gifted and talented" or GT program, which was essentially a question of having had good parents and not being too dumb. In fact, when the school gave us the tests, my sister passed and I didn't. So my parents got someone to give me the test again, and I passed it. For the fourth grade, we rode on a bus for an hour along with all the GT kids from Reston. For fifth and sixth, we attended a GT program at a new school on the other side of Reston. I got used to having school friends and home friends. For seventh grade we went to the new intermediate school in Reston, while my home friends went to Herndon. That year was, I think, both a letdown from the better teaching of grades 4–6 and a disturbing social scene for an immature little kid. For eighth grade I tried a private school, even though it was Christian and I was not. That was no good. So for high school I reunited with my home friends at Herndon.

Throughout this education, our textbooks were as nationalistic and pro-war as is the norm. I think it was in fifth or sixth grade that some kids performed in a talent show a song made notorious many years later by Senator John McCain: "Bomb bomb bomb, bomb bomb Iran!" In the case of my classmates, there was no criticism or disapproval, not that I heard. There were, however, yellow ribbons on trees for the poor hostages. I still have in my possession a lot of my schoolwork, including reports that glorify people such as George Rogers Clark. But it was a war victims' story I wrote, with the British Redcoats as the evildoers and details including the killing of the family dog, that I recall elicited the comment from my fifth grade teacher that I should be a writer.

What I wanted to be was perhaps an architect or a town planner, the designer of a better Reston, the creator of a house who wouldn't have to actually build it. But I gave very little thought to what I should be. I had very little notion that kids and adults were of the same species and that one day I would become the other. Despite attending school in one of the top-ranked counties in the country, I thought most of it was a load of manure. My perfect grades dropped steadily as I went through high school. The easy classes bored me. The AP (advanced placement) classes both bored me and required more work than I would do. I loved sports, but I was too small to compete at a lot of them, except back home in pickup games where I could get picked based on reputation rather than appearance. I did not finish growing until well after high school, which I finished at seventeen, in 1987.

My awareness during these years of U.S. warmaking and facilitating and coup-instigating in Latin America was negligible. I understood there to be a Cold War, and the Soviet Union to be a horrible place to live, but Russians I understood to be just like you and me, and the Cold War itself to be lunacy (that was what Sting said in his song *Russians*). I'd seen the Gandhi movie. I think I knew that Henry Thoreau had refused to pay war taxes. And I certainly understood that in the sixties the cool people had opposed war and had been right. I knew *The Red Badge of Courage*. I knew that war was horrible. But I had no notion of what prevented the making of more wars.

I did have, for whatever reasons—good early parenting or screwy genetics—a couple of key things in my skull. One was the understanding taught to most children the world over that violence is bad. Another was a fierce demand for consistency and a total disrespect for authority. So, if violence was bad for kids, it was also bad for governments. And, related to this, I had a nearly complete arrogance or confidence in my own ability to figure things out, at least moral things. At the top of my list of virtues was honesty. It's still pretty high up there.

War didn't come up much. On television it showed up in *M*A*S*H*. We once had a guest visit us from out of town who wanted to visit the Naval Academy at Annapolis. So, we took him, and he loved it. The day was sunny. The sailboats were out. The mast of the *U.S.S. Maine* stood proudly as a monument to war propaganda, though I had no idea what it was. I just knew that I was visiting a beautiful, happy place where great resources were put into training people to engage in mass murder. I became physically ill and had to lie down.

What had the biggest impact, I think, on my view of foreign policy, was going somewhere foreign. I had a Latin teacher named Mrs. Sleeper who was about 180 years old and could teach Latin to a horse. Her class was full of shouting and laughing, signals from her like kicking the trashcan if we forgot the accusative case, and warnings that "tempus is fugitting!" She took a group of us to Italy for some weeks junior year. We each stayed with an Italian student and their family and attended Italian high school. Living briefly in another place and another language, and looking back on your own place from the outside ought to be part of every education. Nothing is more valuable, I think. Student exchange programs merit all the support we can find them.

My wife and I have two sons, one almost twelve, one almost four. The little one has invented an imaginary machine that he calls a nexter. You pick it up, push some buttons, and it tells you what you should do next. It's seriously helpful throughout the day. Perhaps I should have had a nexter to use when I graduated from high school. I really had no idea what to do next. So, I went back to Italy for a full school year as an exchange student through the Rotary Club. Again, the experience was invaluable. I made Italian friends I still have, and I've been back a number of times. I also made friends with an American stationed there in the military at a base whose expansion I've been back to protest years later. I'd skip school, and he'd skip whatever soldiers do in a peaceful Renaissance city, and we'd go skiing in the Alps. One Italian friend, whom I've not seen since, was at that time studying architecture in Venice, and I'd tag along for that too. When I got back to the United States, I applied to and began attending architecture school.

By that time (1988) most of my friends were off at second-rate colleges studying the effects of high consumption of alcohol. Some had already bailed out on college. Some who'd gotten great grades through high school were seriously studying. One was hoping to get into the military. None had been attracted by the peace movement's billion-dollar recruitment campaign, which didn't exist.

I did a year of architecture school in Charlotte, North Carolina, and a year-and-a-half, I think, at Pratt Institute in Brooklyn, New York. The former was by far the better school. The latter was in by far the more interesting location. But my interest went to reading, as it never had before. I read literature, philosophy, poetry, history. I neglected engineering in favor of ethics, which was unlikely to make any buildings stand up for long. I dropped out, moved to Manhattan, and taught myself what I took to be a liberal arts education *sans* tuition, supported by my parents. The first Gulf War happened at this time, and I joined in protests outside the United Nations without giving the matter much thought. That just seemed the decent, civilized thing to do. I had no notion of what one might do beyond that. After a while I moved to Alexandria, Virginia. And when I'd run out of ideas, I did again what I'd done before: I went to Italy.

First I went back to New York City and took a month-long course on teaching English as a second language to adults. I got a certificate in that from Cambridge University, which I've never been to in my life. It was a very enjoyable month spent with would-be teachers and English students from around the world. Before long, I was in Rome knocking on the doors of English language schools. This was before the EU. To get a job, I didn't have to be able to do anything a European couldn't do. I didn't have to have a visa to legally be there, not with white skin and a pre-war-on-terror U.S. passport. I just had to do an interview without seeming too shy or nervous. That took me a few tries.

Eventually, I found that I could share an apartment with roommates, work half-time or less, and devote myself to reading in and writing in English and Italian. What eventually sent me back home, back to Reston, was not, I think, a need to get onto something serious so much as a need to not be a foreigner. Much as I loved and still love Europe, much as I loved and love Italians, as long a list as I could make of things I believe are done better there than here, as much progress as I made toward speaking without an accent, and as huge an advantage as I had over my friends from Ethiopia and Eritrea who were randomly harassed by police, I was forever at a disadvantage in Italy.

This gave me some insight into the lives of immigrants and refugees, just as exchange students at my high school (and my being an exchange student abroad) had done. Being treated like a thirteen-year-old when I was eighteen, and a fifteen-year-old when I was twenty, just because I looked like that, gave me some slight notion of discrimination. Being resented by some African Americans in Brooklyn whom I believed I'd never done anything cruel to helped as well. The piles of novels and plays I read, however, were the primary means of opening my eyes to many things, including the vast majority of people on earth who'd gotten a worse deal than I had.

It must have been at least late 1993 when I was back in Virginia. My parents wanted a place in the country to build a house and move to. Utopia had turned to sprawl. Reston had become a mass of weapons makers, computer companies, and high-end condominiums, with the Metro train set to be built out to there any moment, just as they'd been saying for two decades. I proposed the area of Charlottesville. I wanted to study philosophy with Richard Rorty, who was teaching at the University of Virginia. My parents bought land near there. I rented a house nearby. They paid me to cut down trees, build fences, move dirt, etc., and I signed up for a class at UVA through the school of continuing education.

I had no Bachelor's degree, but I got professors' approval to take graduate school classes in philosophy. Once I'd taken enough, I got their approval to write a thesis and pick up a Master's degree in philosophy. I found much of the course work quite stimulating. It was the first school experience, at least in many years, that I'd found to be so stimulating, and non-insulting. I simply adored the UVA Honor Code, which trusted you not to cheat. But I also found a lot of the stuff we studied to be sheer metaphysical bunk. Even ethics courses that sought to be useful did not always seem aimed at determining the best thing to do so much as determining the best way to talk about, or even to rationalize, what people were already doing. I wrote my thesis on ethical theories of criminal punishment, rejecting most of them as unethical.

Once I'd done the Master's degree, and Rorty had transferred elsewhere, and nothing interested me more, I proposed to move to the building next door and do a PhD in the English Department. Sadly, that department let me know that first I'd need a Master's in English, which there was no way to get without picking up a Bachelor's first.

Goodbye, formal education. It was nice knowing you.

While I'd studied at UVA I'd worked in the library and at local stores and restaurants. Now I looked for more full-time work and settled on newspaper reporting. It paid terribly, and I discovered that I was allergic to editors, but it was a way into some kind of career in putting words on paper. Before I recount that career, I should mention two other developments in this period: activism and love.

At UVA I took part in a debating club, which made me comfortable with public speaking. I also took part in a campaign to get the people who worked at UVA cooking food and emptying trashcans paid a living wage. This got me involved with living wage activists around the country, including those working for a national group called ACORN, the Association of Community Organizations for Reform Now. I didn't start the living wage campaign at UVA. I just heard about it, and immediately joined in. Had there been some sort of campaign to end war, I would no doubt have jumped into that as well, but there wasn't.

Also during this time, I was falsely accused of a crime. Because I had my parents' help in finding lawyers and experts and other resources, I was able to minimize the damage. The primary result, I think, for me was a greater awareness of the incredible injustices experienced by a great many people as a result of deeply flawed systems of criminal punishment. Certainly the experience influenced my choice of articles to pursue as a newspaper reporter, where I came to focus on miscarriages of justice. Another possible result may have been some contribution to my turn away from autobiography. You cannot mention a false accusation of a crime without people believing you really did it. The most painful experiences in my life have always been the experience of not being believed. You also cannot mention a false accusation of a crime without people believing that you're taking some sort of cartoonishly simple position that all such accusations are always false against everyone. Why get into such stupidity? And if you cannot mention something important to your story, you certainly cannot write an autobiography.

I said something about love, didn't I? While I'd always been shy with girls, I'd managed to have some short-term and long-term girlfriends during and since high school. While I was at UVA I learned about the internet, as research tool, as discussion forum, as publishing platform, as activism tool, and as dating site. I met several women online and then offline. One of them, Anna, lived in North Carolina. She was great to talk to online and on the phone. She was reluctant to meet in person, until the day in 1997 that she phoned me late at night to say she'd driven to Charlottesville and had been calling me all evening. We stayed up all night and drove up to the mountains in the morning. We then started driving four hours, one of us or the other, each weekend. She eventually moved in. In 1999 we got married. Best thing I've done so far.

We moved to Orange, Virginia, for a job in Culpeper. Then I picked up a job in D.C. at a place called the Bureau of National Affairs and began a crazy daily commute. I'd accepted a job there writing for two newsletters, one for labor unions and the other for "human resource managers." I'd been promised I would not have to write against workers or unions. In reality, I was required to take the same piece of news, such as a ruling by the National Labor Relations Board, and report on it in terms of how to build up a union and then in terms of how to screw your employees. I refused to do it. I quit. I had a wife now with her own job. I had a mortgage. I had no job prospects.

I took a temporary job knocking on doors to raise money to save the Chesapeake Bay. The first day I set some kind of record. The second day I sucked. It was work I believed should be done. But it sure was a drag doing it.

I clearly could not do a job with a supervisor editing me, or a job I opposed morally, or a job that didn't challenge me. What in the world could I do? Here's where ACORN came in, and the model I've followed ever since of working for people based at least five hundred miles away from me.

ACORN had gone for decades without ever having a public relations person, someone at the national level to write press releases and schmooze with journalists, to train activists in speaking to TV cameras, to place op-eds, ghostwrite speeches, or go on C-Span to explain why restaurant lobbyists don't actually know better what's good for workers than workers do. I took the job. Anna took a D.C. job. We moved to Cheverly, Maryland. And I became a workaholic. ACORN was a mission, not a career. It was all-in and I was all into it.

But it did sometimes seem like we were taking one step forward and two back. We'd pass local minimum wage or fair lending laws, and lobbyists would preempt them at the state level. We'd pass state laws, and they'd move on Congress. When 9/11 happened, my immaturity and naiveté were staggering. When everybody working on domestic issues immediately understood that nothing could be done anymore, that the minimum wage would not be having any value restored to it as had been planned, etc., I'll be damned if I could see any logic or connection. Why should people earn less money because some lunatics flew planes into buildings? Apparently this was the logic of war. And when war drums began beating I was flabbergasted. What in the world? Hadn't 9/11 just proved the uselessness of weapons of war to protect anybody from anything?

When the Bush-Cheney wars started, I went to every protest, but my job was domestic issues at ACORN. Or it was until I picked up a second job working for Dennis Kucinich for President 2004. A presidential campaign is a 24/7 job, just like ACORN. I worked them both for months before switching over to Kucinich alone. At that point, my colleagues in the communications department of the campaign let me know that (1) the campaign was a disastrous pile of infighting and incompetence, and (2) I was now going to be in charge of it as "press secretary." Yet I was and remain grateful for having been brought on, I grew ever more to admire, and still do, our candidate, whom I found generally terrific to work with, and I simply proceeded to take few bathroom breaks, eat at my desk, and bathe infrequently, until I could do no more for the hopeless cause.

Years later, ACORN was destroyed, in large part by a right-wing fraud. I wished I was still there, not because I had a plan to save ACORN, but just to be there to try.

Kucinich for President was my first peace job. We talked about peace, war, peace, trade, peace, healthcare, war, and peace. And then it was over. I got a job for the AFL-CIO overseeing their organization of labor media outlets, mostly labor union newsletters. And then I got a job for a group called Democrats.com trying to stop a disastrous bill in Congress on bankruptcies. I'd never been a fan of most Democrats or Republicans, but I'd supported Dennis, and I thought I could support a group aimed at making the Democrats better. I still have many friends I fully respect who believe in that agenda to this day, while I find independent activism and education more strategic.

In May 2005, I proposed to Democrats.com that I work on trying to end the wars, in response to which I was told I should work on something easier, like trying to impeach George W. Bush. We began by creating a group called After Downing Street and forcing news of what was called the Downing Street Memo or the Downing Street Minutes into U.S. media as evidence of the obvious, that Bush and gang had lied about the war on Iraq. We worked with Democrats in Congress who were pretending that they'd end the wars and impeach the president and the vice president if they were given majorities in 2006. I worked with many peace groups during this time, including United for Peace and Justice, and tried to nudge the peace movement toward impeachment and vice versa.

In 2006, the exit polls said the Democrats won the majorities in Congress with a mandate to end the war on Iraq. Come January, Rahm Emanuel told the *Washington Post* they'd keep the war going in order to run "against" it again in 2008. By 2007, Democrats had lost much of their interest in peace and moved on to what seemed to me like the agenda of electing more Democrats as an end in itself. My own focus had become ending each and every war and the idea of ever starting another one.

On Armistice Day 2005, and expecting our first kid, and with me able to work by internet from anywhere, we moved back to Charlottesville. We made more money by selling the house we'd bought in Maryland than I've made from any job. We used it to pay for half of the house in Charlottesville that we're still struggling to pay for the other half of.

I became a full-time peace activist. I joined the board of the local peace center here. I joined all kinds of coalitions and groups nationally. I traveled to speak and protest. I sat in on Capitol Hill. I camped out at Bush's ranch in Texas. I drafted articles of impeachment. I wrote books. I went to jail. I built websites for peace organizations. I went on book tours. I spoke on panels. I debated war advocates. I did interviews. I occupied squares. I visited war zones. I studied peace activism, past and present. And I began getting that question everywhere I went: How did you become a peace activist?

How did I? Are there patterns to be found in my story and others'? Does something in the above help explain it? I now work for RootsAction. org, which was created to serve as an online activist center that would back all things progressive including peace. And I work as the director of World Beyond War, which I co-founded as an organization to push globally for better education and activism aimed at abolition of the systems that sustain war. I now write books arguing against all justifications for war, critiquing nationalism, and promoting nonviolent tools. I've gone from writing for publishers to self-publishing, to publishing with publishers after I've published a book myself, to just now pursuing a major publisher despite knowing that it will require editing as the tradeoff to reach a larger audience.

Am I here because I like to write and speak and argue and work for a better world, and because a series of accidents planted me in a growing peace movement in 2003, and because I discovered a way to never leave it, and because the internet grew and has been—at least thus far—kept neutral? Am I here because of my genes? My twin sister is a great person but isn't a peace activist. Her daughter is an environmental activist though. Am I here because of my childhood, because I had lots of love and support? Well, many people have had that, and many of them are doing great things, but usually not peace activism.

If you ask me today why I choose to do this going forward, my answer is the case for war abolition as presented on the website of World Beyond War and in my books. But if you're asking how I got into this gig rather than something else, I can only hope that some of the preceding paragraphs shed some light. The fact is that I cannot work under a supervisor, I cannot sell widgets, I cannot be edited, I cannot work on anything that seems overshadowed by anything else, I cannot seem to write books that pay as well as writing emails, and the job of resisting wars and weapons dealing never seems to have enough people—and sometimes, in certain corners of it, seems to have nobody at all—working on it.

People ask me how I keep going, how I stay cheerful, why I don't quit. That one is pretty easy, and I don't usually dodge it. I work for peace because we sometimes win and sometimes lose but have a responsibility to try, try, try, and because trying is far more enjoyable and fulfilling than anything else.

Chapter 16

Cultivating Peace

Ann Wright

I am writing this chapter while at Standing Rock, North Dakota, in solidarity with Native Americans in our challenge against the Dakota Access Pipeline. Big Oil and war go together and stopping pipelines that feed our addiction to oil will help stop our addiction to war.

In late September 2016, I returned from an Israeli prison where I was taken after the Israeli military stopped our Women's Boat to Gaza in international waters thirty-four miles off the coast of Gaza. The Israeli government charged the thirteen women on the boat for entering Israeli illegally. We protested that we never wanted to be in Israel, but were kidnapped in international waters, arrested, brought to Israel against our will, imprisoned, and ultimately given a ten year deportation. The Israeli government stole our boat, and we have sued in Israeli court for the return of the vessel.

Unlike most of the peace activists whose stories you will read in this anthology, most of my life I worked for the United States government. Despite the actions of the political leadership of the various administrations of our government, most who join the government in either the military or the civilian part of the government hope they will be contributing to a more peaceful and just country and world. I recognize that the history of our country of invading and occupying other countries and its racism toward African Americans and Latinos provide little evidence of that hope coming to fruition, but it still was a part of my belief, naive as it may seem, and, I suspect, in the beliefs of many who work for the U.S. government.

I served twenty-nine years in the U.S. Army/Army Reserves and retired as a colonel. I also was a U.S. diplomat for sixteen years and worked in U.S. embassies in Nicaragua, Grenada, Somalia, Uzbekistan, Kyrgyzstan, Sierra Leone, Micronesia, Afghanistan, and Mongolia. I also had one short assignment in arms control and was sent on a U.S. delegation to Geneva for talks with the Russian Federation on the Comprehensive Test Ban Treaty.

However, in March 2003, I resigned from the U.S. government in opposition to President Bush's war on Iraq. In my letter of resignation, I wrote that there was no evidence of weapons of mass destruction and that the blowback of young men and women in the Middle East for the invasion and occupation of another oil-rich, Arab, Muslim nation could jeopardize U.S. national security. I was one of three federal government employees who resigned in opposition to the Iraq war.

I was living in Mongolia when I resigned. I was the deputy chief of mission, or deputy ambassador of the U.S. embassy. In late 2002 and early 2003, I became increasingly concerned about the George W. Bush administration's march to war in Iraq. I had just returned from Afghanistan, having been on the small team that had reopened the U.S. embassy in Kabul in December 2001, and had remained there until the first permanent embassy staff arrived in April 2002, when I proceeded to my scheduled assignment as deputy chief of mission in the U.S. embassy in Ulan Bataar, Mongolia.

The war rhetoric from President George Bush, Vice President Dick Cheney, Secretary of Defense Donald Rumsfeld, National Security Adviser Condoleezza Rice and my boss, Secretary of State Colin Powell, increased weekly, as did my unease. I was unable to figure out how Iraq could still have had weapons of mass destruction after Gulf War I and intense UN inspections, sanctions, quarantines, and blockades for ten years, the imposition of two no-fly zones and regular U.S. air attacks on military and civilian installations in Iraq.

On February 5, 2003, I watched in Mongolia the live TV broadcast from the United Nations as Secretary of State Powell pitched the "evidence" that Iraq had weapons of mass destruction. His presentation did not convince me, nor the hundreds of Foreign Service colleagues who got in touch with me later when I resigned. Nor did it deter the millions of U.S. citizens who marched in the streets, much less the vast majority of UN member states. They quickly voted against authorizing any military operations against Iraq.

After Secretary Powell's briefing to the United Nations, I used the State Department's Dissent Channel to express my ever-growing concerns in a letter to Secretary Powell in early March 2003, just weeks before the war began. My concerns were dismissed in the response from the department, signed by Policy Planning Director Richard Haass, who subsequently was the president of the Council on Foreign Relations. His response paralleled the daily press guidance from the department, which rehashed the administration's rationale for why Saddam Hussein's regime was dangerous to the international community and should be eliminated.

My decision to resign came after several months of my internal and external debate. I had been very upset about the rhetoric of the Bush administration about regime change in Iraq. I woke up in the middle of the night for many nights to write of my concerns about a U.S.-sponsored overthrow of Saddam Hussein.

During this time, as a part of my cultural appreciation of Mongolian history, I had been attending classes for the international community on Buddhism. As I read the various Buddhist tracts that had been provided, many of the writings spoke to the situation the world faced.

One Buddhist commentary reminded me that all actions have consequences, that nations, like individuals, ultimately are held accountable for their actions. I felt that waging war in Iraq would have the consequences of harming America rather than making it safer, both in the short and long term.

In particular, the Dalai Lama's September 2002 remarks in his "Commemoration of the First Anniversary of September 11, 2001" were important in my deliberations on Iraq and even more relevant in our approach to the real war on terrorism. The Dalai Lama said:

> Conflicts do not arise out of the blue. They occur as a result of causes and conditions, many of which are within the antagonists' control. This is where leadership is important. Terrorism cannot be overcome by the use of force because it does not address the complex underlying problems. In fact, the use of force may not only fail to solve the problems, it may exacerbate them, and frequently leaves destruction and suffering in its wake.

After revising many drafts, on March 18, 2003 (Washington time), but already March 19 in Mongolia, I cabled through State Department communications channels my letter of resignation to Secretary of State Colin Powell. I became one of only three U.S. government employees, all Foreign Service Officers (FSOs), to resign over the issue.

Several other FSOs apparently resigned later for the same reason, but did not make their resignations public. In addition, a large number of FSOs retired from the service much earlier than they had planned because of their opposition to the war.

However, neither dissent within nor without the government affected the Bush administration's decision to wage war on Iraq and on March 19, 2003 (Washington time), the horrific U.S. attack on Iraq named "Shock and Awe" began. The aftereffects of this decision continue to this day: hundreds of thousands of Iraqis dead, more than one million living as refugees, and many of the tens of thousands the United States put in prison forming ISIS and waging a brutal campaign in western Iraq and northern Syria.

In my letter of resignation, I stated:

I believe we should not use US military force without United Nations Security Council (UNSC) agreement to ensure compliance. In our press for military action now, we have created deep chasms in the international community and in important international organizations. Our policies have alienated many of our allies and created ill will in much of the world.

Countries of the world supported America's action in Afghanistan as a response to the September 11 Al Qaida attacks on America. Since then, America has lost the incredible sympathy of most of the world because of our policy toward Iraq. Much of the world considers our statements about Iraq as arrogant, untruthful and masking a hidden agenda. Leaders of moderate Moslem/Arab countries warn us about predicable outrage and anger of the youth of their countries if America enters an Arab country with the purpose of attacking Moslems/Arabs, not defending them. Attacking the Saddam regime in Iraq now is very different than expelling the same regime from Kuwait, as we did ten years ago.

I strongly believe the probable response of many Arabs of the region and Moslems of the world if the US enters Iraq without UNSC agreement will result in actions extraordinarily dangerous to America and Americans. Military action now without UNSC agreement is much more dangerous for America and the world than allowing the UN weapons inspections to proceed and subsequently taking UNSC authorized action if warranted.

I firmly believe the probability of Saddam using weapons of mass destruction is low, as he knows that using those weapons will trigger an immediate, strong and justified international response. There will be no question of action against Saddam in that case. I strongly disagree with the use of a "preemptive attack" against Iraq and believe that this preemptive attack policy will be used against us and provide justification for individuals and groups to "preemptively attack" America and American citizens. (http://www.govexec.com/defense/2003/03/mary-a-wrights-resignation-letter/13704/)

Early Years

I grew up in a typical Midwestern/Upper Southern small town of 2,500. My family went to the local Methodist Church. As a part of the Methodist Youth Fellowship, the youth leader, who was also the local Arkansas National Guard non-commissioned officer (NCO) responsible for the day-to-day operation of the unit, filled Sunday evening youth meetings with teaching on the dangers of communism and the Soviet Union—gulags, state surveillance, and state regulation of all aspects of life. No mention was made of the ever-growing U.S. prison system or of civil rights abuses for African Americans, even though the largest high school in the state of Arkansas had been closed rather than agree to integration.

When President Eisenhower sent in the U.S. Army's 82nd Airborne troops to ensure that the Little Rock Nine were able to go to high school in Little Rock, Arkansas, many schools around the state remained closed rather than open to integration. However, no one in Little Rock seemed to know that our small school in Northwest Arkansas was already integrated by the only African American family in our town, who had lived there for several decades. After school, several of us would walk home together and my mother told us, "If anyone stops and tries to harm Carl, you grab him and you all run to the nearest house for help." We knew everyone and every house on the way home.

I joined the U.S. military after college, not because I wanted to kill anyone, but because I wanted get out of the state of Arkansas where I grew up—and travel. The Army's motto was "Join the Army and See the World." As a woman, and not trained as a nurse, I was assured by the recruiter that I would not be sent to Vietnam, where many of my male high school friends had been sent after they were drafted. In college, I had been trained as a teacher and after doing student teaching for several months, I decided I didn't want to spend the rest of my life teaching high schoolers so I was looking for different job after graduation from college—and I wanted to travel and see the world.

We did not have a "military family," although my father had served in the South Pacific in World War II, so it was quite a surprise to my parents when I announced that they didn't have to worry about my job after I graduated from college—I had joined the Army! At that time in the late 1960s, less than 1 percent of the U.S. military were women. Women were not allowed into college ROTC (Reserve Officer Training) nor into the military academies. The attraction of the military to me was that for a two-year commitment, one was eligible for a four-year G.I. Bill educational program. I figured I could wear a uniform and march for two years, if the Army would help me travel—and would provide funding for a graduate degree.

Like so many young people today, I used the military for my own purposes. As we know, for many young people the military is their first employment and an opportunity to learn discipline, skills, and perhaps land a job afterward. However, it comes with a heavy price. Those who were sent to the war on Vietnam fifty years ago have post-traumatic stress and an extraordinarily high suicide rate. Many suffer from exposure to Agent Orange. Likewise, many of those who have served in the U.S. military over the past fifteen years since the invasions and occupations of Afghanistan and Iraq are suffering from post-traumatic stress, emotional injuries, and horrific physical injuries. More than twenty veterans a day are dying from self-inflicted wounds because they cannot cope with what they have seen or done.

I joined the U.S. Army as the war on Vietnam raged. Remarkably, the Army followed through with its assignment promises to me. I did not go to Vietnam, but instead to the Presidio of San Francisco for my first assignment. I met many people who did not agree with the war, as San Francisco was one of the cities most opposed to the war. Many in the military who were being sent to Vietnam went AWOL (absent without leave) instead and were living underground in the San Francisco area. When they were tracked down by the U.S. government, those who had refused to go to Vietnam were court-martialed and put in military prison. One of those prisons was the stockade at the Presidio of San Francisco. The stockade was notorious for human rights abuses—some of the guards were brutal toward the prisoners who refused to go to Vietnam. Over time, the parents of some of the prisoners wrote their congresspersons about the conditions in the stockade and the treatment of their sons. The congressperson would forward the letter to the military command with a request for an investigation. The military had to have an interim written response to the congressional inquiry within forty-eight hours. As a second lieutenant, I was given the responsibility of keeping track of the congressional inquiries and ensuring that the units responded in a timely manner to the inquiries.

The leadership at the stockade was lax about responding to the numerous questions about what was happening in the prison. My job was difficult, as those responsible for the abuses certainly were not going to blow the whistle on themselves. I talked with as many people as I could, then sent reports on the lack of effort by the prison warden to investigate allegations of misconduct among prison guards. Eventually, after extensive documentation of the cover-up of the systemic bad treatment of prisoners, the Army prosecuted some of those who committed criminal acts on the prisoners.

Years later, as a major in the U.S. Army, a senior rank for women at that time, while assigned at Fort Bragg, North Carolina, the home of the macho 82nd Airborne Division and the U.S. Army Special Forces, I heard from many enlisted women at Fort Bragg about harassment, discriminatory treatment, and being taken out of positions which were key jobs for promotion in favor of men. I decided to host a meeting for women to discuss these issues and advertised a "Women in the Army" meeting at Fort Bragg. More than one hundred women came to the first meeting and I learned of a new program called "Direct Combat Probability Coding" being implemented at Fort Bragg that eliminated women from jobs they had been serving in for years.

I took this information to a conference in Washington, D.C., in which the senior leadership of the Department of Defense would be speaking and during Q & A asked why women in the Army were being denied opportunities for advancement. The documentation I provided of women being taken out of key jobs was used by the Department of Defense to challenge the rationale for the change in policy and forced the U.S. Army to reinstate women into these positions.

Throughout my career in the U.S. military, I continued to openly challenge policies on the utilization of women in the military in public confrontations with senior leadership of the U.S. Army through an organization called the Defense Advisory Committee on Women in the Services (DACOWITS).

During the early 1980s we formed Women in the Military groups on several major U.S. Army bases to provide a voice for women.

Peace Work after Resignation

After I resigned from the U.S. diplomatic corps in 2003, I was asked by peace groups and universities to speak about my decision to resign. As a U.S. diplomat, I had met many people in other countries who challenged the policies of their governments, but I did not know personally anyone in my own country who was challenging the U.S. government, except those I had read about in books. These speaking opportunities were important to me as they put me in touch with Americans who had spent their entire lives protesting U.S. wars and other government policies.

From speaking about my decision to resign, I was asked to participate in marches and events organized by antiwar organizations. The first group that I encountered was Veterans for Peace. In 2004, I was walking along the beach in Santa Barbara, California, and saw a cemetery of crosses in the sand. I asked the man at the information tent what the crosses were about. He said they represented both Americans and Iraqis who had been killed because of the U.S. invasion of Iraq. He added that he was a veteran and that the organization sponsoring the crosses was called Veterans for Peace. I responded that I was a veteran of twenty-nine years in the military and that I had resigned from the U.S. diplomatic corps a year earlier in opposition to the war on Iraq. Lane Anderson said, "Then you are one of us! Why don't you join us at our annual convention in Boston in the summer—we have some great speakers."

So I went to the 2004 Veterans for Peace Convention and met Pentagon Papers whistleblower Daniel Ellsberg and historian Howard Zinn. Over time, Ellsberg introduced me to a family of dissenters and whistleblowers that continue to be some of my best friends. Veterans for Peace has provided me a voice within the veteran's community.

The following year, in 2005, at the Veterans for Peace convention in Dallas, Cindy Sheehan, whose son Casey had been killed in Iraq in 2004, decided to travel two hours from Dallas to Crawford, Texas, where President Bush was spending his August vacation on his ranch. Her decision to go to Bush's ranch to attempt to ask him what "noble cause" her son had died for, brought fifteen thousand people from all over the world to Crawford to echo's Cindy's question, "What is noble about the Iraq war?" For the entire month of August 2005, the world's media covered the incredible outpouring of protest against the Iraq war. I helped organize Camp Casey and met thousands of activists from all over the country during those long, hot days in Texas.

As President Bush returned to Washington, D.C., in late August 2005, Hurricane Katrina hit the Gulf Coast. From Camp Casey we sent food and materials to New Orleans. A Veterans for Peace bus provided a base for extensive assistance to the Ninth Ward of flooded New Orleans.

After Bush left Crawford, we organized three groups of speakers from military families and veterans who made more than two hundred presentations in towns and cities around the eastern United States in the next three weeks as the groups slowly headed to Washington, D.C., for the big antiwar march in late September 2005. As one of the organizers of Camp Casey, I spent the next year traveling around the United States speaking to groups about the war on Iraq, illegal detention, and torture.

Thus began my fifteen-year mission to use my voice as a retired U.S. Army Reserve colonel and a former U.S. diplomat to express my concerns about various aspects of U.S. foreign policy and military operations. I was an outspoken critic of the Bush administration's policies on war, invasion and occupation, kidnapping, extraordinary rendition, torture, indefinite detention, curtailment of civil liberties, extrajudicial killings, targeted assassinations, and eavesdropping. As an equal opportunity critic, I also have challenged the Obama and Trump administrations on assassin drones, persecution of whistleblowers, increased NSA surveillance, indefinite detention of migrants, solitary confinement, and the death penalty.

During these fifteen years, I have participated on fact-finding trips to Afghanistan in 2007, 2011, and 2012, to Pakistan in 2012 and to Yemen in 2013 to learn more about the blowback from the U.S. military's assassin drone program.

My interest in the Middle East came to a sharp point in early 2009 with the twenty-seven-day Israeli attack on Gaza and the continued U.S. protection of the State of Israel no matter what it does to Palestinians. I assisted CODEPINK: Women for Peace in organizing trips to Gaza after the attack ended and helped organize the December 2009 Gaza Freedom March that brought 1,350 activists from thirty-five countries to Cairo. My work on Gaza continued in 2010 as a passenger on the Gaza Freedom Flotilla and an organizer for the 2011 U.S. Boat to Gaza, the Audacity of Hope. I was on the international coalition organizing the 2012–13 Gaza's Ark project, and was an organizer and participant for the 2015 Gaza Freedom Flotilla, the 2016 Women's Boat to Gaza, and am an organizer for the 2018 Boats to Gaza.

In 2005, I began writing articles about sexual assault of women in the U.S. military by fellow military members. About the same time, activists in Okinawa asked me to speak on the issue of U.S. military violence against women in countries where the United States has military bases. While in Okinawa I learned of a U.S. military plan to build a runway into a pristine marine area—and the large citizen protest against the runway. Over the next seven years I have made numerous trips to Okinawa in solidarity with activists there, and to Jeju Island in solidarity with activists there, where the South Korean government was building a new naval base in another pristine marine area on behalf of the U.S. Aegis missile defense system.

In 2014, with the possible opening of U.S. diplomatic relations with Cuba, I assisted CODEPINK with two trips, including leading the U.S. delegation to the Symposium on the Abolition of Foreign Military Bases held in the city of Guantanamo in November 2014. And then in 2017, after the opening of relations, Veterans for Peace and CODEPINK participated in another symposium on ending the U.S. military base in Guantanamo.

In 2015, I was honored to be asked to participate in a unique fact-finding trip through the Women Cross the DMZ initiative which brought thirty international women, including two women Nobel Peace laureates to both North Korea and South Korea for a "Peace on the Korean Peninsula" symposium in both Pyongyang and Seoul. In February 2016, our group met separately with a delegation of women from North Korea and one from South Korea in Indonesia to continue our efforts at providing a forum for women's voices for peace. In January 2018, we successfully pressed the Canadian government for an NGO Forum "Maximum Engagement Not Maximum Pressure" as a part of the meeting of the foreign ministers of the UN Command Korea countries.

Dynamics of War and Violence

The dynamics that give rise to war and violence that become obstacles to peace and justice have been on full display for the past seventeen years. Retaliation and retribution for Osama Bin Laden's and al Qaeda's September 11 actions situated Afghanistan and many countries in the world as perpetual targets in the U.S. proclaimed "Global War on Terror." The power elites of our political system implement strategies of violence to meet goals for resource domination such as President Bush's war on Iraq as a part of the notorious neo-con Project for the New American Century to control oil resources across the Middle East.

Following Russian action to secure its strategic naval port in the Black Sea after the U.S.-sponsored coup in Ukraine overthrew the elected, pro-Russian president, the United States and NATO placed sanctions on Russia and special sanctions on Crimea and dramatically increased the number of U.S. military and NATO exercises in former Warsaw Pact countries, all of which border Russia. Because of the increasing U.S. vilification of Russia, I joined a small group to visit four cities in Russia in the summer of 2016 to gauge how ordinary Russians felt about increasing tensions with the United States. As we suspected, Russians do not desire a military confrontation with the West, just as American citizens do not want a new Cold War. The challenge now is getting the politicians of both countries to dialogue about their concerns rather than planning military responses.

Military overthrow of regimes that are disliked by the United States and the West have left the Middle East in chaos. Hundreds of thousands of innocent civilians killed and millions of persons fleeing the uncontrollable violence within the region as well as a large number who attempt to flee the entire region. The U.S. attempt to overthrow the Syrian government has been thwarted by Russia and Iran. Seventeen years later, the Taliban now control more territory in Afghanistan than at any time since their overthrow by the United States in late 2001.

The overthrow of other governments, no matter how despicable the policies of the leaders of those governments are, does not ensure peace for the citizens who have been the victims of these policies. Instead, the overthrow provides the opportunity for wholesale looting of resources by the major powers and their local allies, which is usually the goal of the overthrow.

Vision for Peace

My vision for peace sees a world in which national leaders use dialogue rather than military operations. It understands that no one form of government fits all countries in the world. Strong citizen involvement to challenge aggressive governmental responses to situations that should be resolved with words instead of bullets is key to maintaining peace.

Chapter 17

Peacemakers

Apostates of the U.S. National Religion

Chris J. Antal

The war that ultimately landed me in a Muslim country, clad in U.S. Army fatigues, with an American flag patch on my right shoulder and a Christian cross on my chest, began in 1980, just a month short of my eighth birthday. That year President Jimmy Carter delivered his State of the Union address and inaugurated America's War for the Greater Middle East—pledging U.S. military forces would repel "any outside force" seeking to gain control of the Persian Gulf.[1] The first time America's War for the Greater Middle East entered my consciousness I was a college freshman. Then, President George H. W. Bush launched Operation Desert Storm and the U.S. military became a permanent occupying force in Saudi Arabia. But America's War for the Greater Middle East only became my war when President George W. Bush sent U.S. forces into Afghanistan and Iraq. I was teaching and doing research in South Korea with my wife and our first child at the time. Even so, a decade would pass before I would volunteer to serve under President Barack Obama as a chaplain in the U.S. Army. What follows is an account of this journey, and some reflections about what I have learned along the way. While I have written this for an American audience, some of what follows may be of use to others striving for peace and justice.

As a white male raised by educated and affluent parents in a relatively safe New England community I enjoyed a privileged and peaceful childhood.

I was born in New York, near Niagara Falls, in 1972—one of the final years of the American war in Vietnam. My father was a medical officer in that war and has always remained enormously proud of his military service. My parents divorced soon after America withdrew from Vietnam. I was raised in a large home with my mother and sister on the coast of Maine that we operated as a guest house while my father worked as a physician in private practice in a nearby town. My parents provided no formal religious education and encouraged me to explore diverse ideas and cultures. I found inspiration in frequent visits to the ocean, where I encountered beauty and wonder. I attended public schools and traveled with my father to Central America, where encounters with poverty awakened me to the world's pain, my own privilege, and an abiding sense that life is unfair unless we make it otherwise. My parents taught me the values of hospitality, compassion, and responsible citizenship. I read *Civil Disobedience* by Henry David Thoreau, visited his hermitage at Walden Pond, and learned the sacrament of resistance. At eighteen, inspired by Thoreau (and rebelling against my father's guidance) I refused to register for Selective Service. When I left Maine in 1990 to attend Rhode Island School of Design, I was a determined pacifist resolved to live a life creating and not destroying. All these formative experiences have shaped my path in life.

In my early twenties, I witnessed racial violence in the streets of America, blowback from America's War for the Greater Middle East, and homegrown terrorism—experiences that motivated me to abandon the creative path of an artist and seek resources in religious communities for creating peace. My first experience of this blowback was in February 1993, after I had moved from Rhode Island to New York City. Just eight days after my twenty-first birthday, a van in the parking garage beneath the World Trade Center exploded, killing six, injuring a thousand, and causing more than $500 million in damages. In April 1995, I was traveling in Oklahoma when a massive homemade bomb concealed in a rental truck destroyed the Alfred P. Murrah Federal Building. I saw ground zero just days after the explosion, while rescue workers were still trying to exhume what was left of the bodies of the 168 people killed. On July 27, 1996, I was operating a vendor table at Centennial Olympic Park in Atlanta when Eric Rudolph detonated three pipe bombs. I heard screams. I saw bloodied people fall to the ground. I learned two important lessons from that horrible night. First, I have the capacity to remain calm amid chaos and function well under extreme stress. Second, terrorism is not a tactic monopolized by Middle Eastern Muslims—anyone can be a terrorist, even white American men like me. These insights have helped me develop the capacity to be peaceful even when violence rages around me, to keep situations in perspective, and to avoid the trap of moral dualism that results in polarized thinking. Peace work, I have learned, is best accomplished in the gray-zone.

The first peace movement I ever joined was the Unification Church. A month after the first World Trade Center attack in 1993, I met several bright young people on a New York City sidewalk who invited me to a workshop to learn more about their path to world peace. I was intrigued by the multiracial and international community I found there, and drawn to a vision, which responded to racism, violence, and war with explanations of underlying causes and concrete initiatives that fostered forgiveness and reconciliation. I was also inspired by the life of the church founder, Reverend Sun Myung Moon, who experienced the horror and destruction of war on the Korean peninsula, was rescued by a United Nations–backed military intervention, and then launched a movement from the ruins of his homeland that grew to impact people around the world. Over the next decade I invested myself in various Unification Church campaigns and affiliated movements and cultivated spiritual disciplines such as prayer, fasting, study, worship, and service. The Unification Church is perhaps best known for the large public wedding ceremonies in which men and women commit themselves in marriages arranged by Rev. Moon. A unique and often underappreciated aspect of these marriages is their intention to unite partners from countries that had once been at war or who are from races or ethnic groups that have a history of conflict, in order to facilitate reconciliation and produce children who can serve as bridge builders and peacemakers. I participated in one of these ceremonies in 1997 and married Mitsuko Ishikawa, a Japanese citizen. Our marriage and the five children we are raising at the time of this writing continue to be my primary school of love and source of peace education.

Early in our marriage, I traveled to Japan and visited Hiroshima and Nagasaki, and began a long process of moral reckoning with the savagery of World War II and the human and moral cost of the United States' decision to drop atomic bombs on two cities. In my first visit, I felt numb and was most disturbed by my own inability to feel the pain of what happened there. Fifteen years later, on the seventieth anniversary of the bombings, now a father of five biracial children, I was able to return to Hiroshima and Nagasaki with my oldest son. Certainly my interracial marriage and family helped me humanize and find solidarity with the people Americans just like me had once regarded as enemies and dehumanized as "dirty yellow monkeys." On the morning of August 6, 2015, I entered sacred time and sacred space in a ceremonial ritual that aroused my moral imagination and helped me traverse the empathy gap, touch upon catastrophic pain, and fall to my knees weeping before a place called "The Mound"—said to contain the remains of the seventy thousand people incinerated in the atomic blast. Throughout this pilgrimage I apologized personally to the *hibakusha* I met with a letter in English and Japanese, with mixed response. Some survivors embraced me in tears. One presented me with the gift of a Hiroshima Peace Shawl. Another gave me a cold look that conveyed unshakable resentment and told me the bombing was "unforgivable." Ayako Okamura, one of the *hibakusha* I met in Nagasaki, taught me that "the foundation for peace is having the kind of heart that can understand another's pain."

After the U.S. Congress passed the International Religious Freedom Act in 1998 I entered the Unification Theological Seminary and began work as a research associate for the Unification Church–affiliated International Coalition for Religious Freedom. Life in the Unification Church catapulted me to the margins and for the first time I experienced, together with my new spouse, discrimination and persecution from people who perceived us as intolerable others. I found value in this experience because I was sensitized to the plight of persecuted minorities and motivated to work as a religious freedom advocate. I met then Ambassador-at-Large for International Religious Freedom Robert Seiple at the U.S. State Department Office of International Religious Freedom and members of the U.S. Commission on International Religious Freedom. I attended public hearings where I heard testimonies of abuse from victims who had come from around the world, having endured terrible suffering intentionally inflicted by people who often belonged to different religious faiths or sects. I was astonished to learn the perpetrators spanned the ranks of all the world's major religions. After one such hearing I was so revolted that I vomited on the steps of the State Department. I did two years of this advocacy in Washington, while commuting for coursework in New York, then withdrew from seminary and moved in January 2001 with my family to South Korea where I enrolled in the graduate program at Yonsei University and took up a part-time job as the English editor at the National Human Rights Commission in Seoul. For the next two years I researched the persecution of Unification Church members and Jehovah's Witnesses and helped document violations. My job at the Human Rights Commission also exposed me to the gulags in North Korea through refugee testimonies. I remember one starving man had carried a poster across the border and I was asked to translate it for Amnesty International. It read, "WARNING. THOSE CAUGHT STEALING RICE WILL BE SHOT." During these years

I contributed to the first five editions of the annual International Religious Freedom Report to Congress and was further awakened to the privileges I enjoy as an American and the responsibilities I have as a citizen to mobilize American power for the good of the world.

When the World Trade Center was destroyed and the Pentagon was attacked, killing 2,996 people and injuring thousands more, I had been living in South Korea for nine months and would stay there for seventeen more. While America grieved and media outlets bombarded the public with the horrific images of collapsing towers, I was physically and emotionally removed from the scene. This distance allowed me to maintain perspective and watch from afar while American leaders reacted violently, launching wars of aggression, first in Iraq and then Afghanistan. Although the geographic distance shielded me from the nationalistic hysteria and self-righteous hubris that swept America in that period, I witnessed a different kind of fallout in Seoul. Four months after the tragedies of September 11, President George W. Bush delivered his State of the Union Address. He labeled Iran, Iraq, and North Korea—a country less than a hundred miles from the apartment where I lived with my wife and family—as an "axis of evil" that he claimed threatened U.S. security. The Bush administration justified an aggressive military response by introducing a new concept into the National Security Strategy—"preemption," defined as "preemptive and preventive action."[2] After the United States invaded Iraq, I became the projection screen for outrage against America, by Koreans understandably anxious their home would be the next target of "preventive war" and North Koreans would act on their threat to retaliate against U.S. aggression and "turn Seoul into a sea of fire."

I returned to the United States in the spring of 2003 and learned that Robert Seiple had resigned, citing American hubris as the reason he could no longer serve as Ambassador-at-Large for International Religious Freedom. What I learned from his abrupt departure is best expressed in a proverb from the book of Luke: *Physician, heal thyself.* In my five years as a religious freedom advocate I had assumed America was blameless. Yet I had failed to consider the religious dynamics of America's War for the Greater Middle East. I had failed to consider how American evangelicals had influenced U.S. foreign policy, ascended to the highest offices of American power, and saturated the ranks of the U.S. military, filling most slots in all branches of the military chaplain corps. I had failed to consider the phenomenon T. Jeremy Gunn has called American National Religion—the unholy trinity of governmental theism, military supremacy, and capitalism as freedom—that has operated as unexamined bedrock values in American society for the past seventy years.[3] I was terrified at the thought of Americans evangelicals, clad in military uniforms, occupying Muslim lands, under the orders of a crusading commander-in-chief. I had failed to recognize the relationship between a certain strain of American Christians and what Andrew Bacevich calls *The New American Militarism*. "Were it not for the support offered by several tens of millions of evangelicals," he writes, "militarism in this deeply and genuinely religious country becomes inconceivable."[4]

I decided to shift the focus of my work to the United States, where I intended to advance the cause of religious freedom as a uniformed member of the Armed Forces. Three days after I returned from Korea, I walked into an Army recruiting office. I did not yet have the necessary credentials for direct commission as a chaplain, and I had little understanding of Islam and no experience in Muslim cultures, but I thought with my Korean language skills and graduate degree in Korea studies I might contribute as a cultural interpreter to a military that seemed to be gearing up for a "preemptive and preventive" attack on the Korean peninsula. However, I still had not registered for the Selective Service, which I learned was a prerequisite for any federal employment. I was thirty-one years old and the window of opportunity for me to register had closed at twenty-five. The Army recruiter recommended I submit a request for a "moral waiver," so I did, but the possibility I would ever serve in the military seemed remote.

That spring I returned to the Unification Theological Seminary in New York to finish my degree, and met Isidore Munyakazi, a new classmate, who was a Tutsi from Rwanda and survivor of the 1994 genocide. My relationship with Isidore sparked another moral reckoning, this time not with something America *had done* with our military might, as was the case in Japan, but rather something America *had failed to do*. Romeo Dallaire, the commander of the UN Assistance Mission for Rwanda at the time of the genocide, wrote, "At its heart, the Rwandan story is the story of the failure of humanity to heed a call for help from an endangered people."[5] General Dallaire claims he could have stopped the killing with a brigade—about 5,500 troops—and thus saved as many as 500,000 lives. These words leave me haunted and ashamed. In 1994, I was deeply immersed in the activities of the Unification Church in America, ostensibly doing peace work, yet the plight of Tutsis like Isidore had never crossed my mind. What if Americans had heard Dallaire's urgent request and provided those troops? I realized I had failed a moral responsibility and civic duty to respond to the world's pain by speaking out and appealing to President Bill Clinton and other elected officials, imploring them to intervene in Rwanda and protect the innocent from certain harm.

After I graduated from seminary, I left the Unification Church. It had become too focused on life after death and no longer seemed aligned with my commitment to create a just and peaceful world. Moreover, I observed with chagrin a core group of Koreans in power who clung to dangerous ideas of racial purity and racial superiority that had a frightening resemblance to Adolf Hitler's belief in a master race. These leaders showed little tolerance for diversity or commitment to authentic interfaith dialogue, and were blatantly homophobic. My experience advocating for religious freedom and encounters with victims of religious persecution had emboldened my commitment to pluralism and dialogue. Moreover, my encounter with people from Japan, North Korea, and Rwanda who suffered from intentional human acts of violence—from atom bombs to political torture to genocide—instilled in me a cynical view of human nature, doubt about the existence of a benevolent God, and a sense of urgency to work for peace and justice in this world rather than wait for a savior or something better after death. These encounters also impacted me in another way. I rejected pacifism, accepting that darkness lurks in every human heart and lethal force may sometimes be necessary to restrain it. I also discovered a new respect for the U.S. military. I believe the only moral justification for lethal force is to protect the innocent from certain harm. Still, I'm a nuclear pacifist. There can be no moral use of such weapons and no moral grounds to possess them. They should be completely abolished.

Although I left the Unification Church, I found new community in a Unitarian Universalist congregation. Unitarian Universalists are a motley crew of humanists, atheists, theists (and just about everything else) who covenant to affirm and promote, among other things, respect for the inherent worth and dignity of every person, justice, equity, and compassion in human relations, and a free and responsible search for truth. Unitarian Universalists celebrate religious pluralism grounded in authentic dialogue. They take stands on issues that matter, work for social justice, and maintain sufficient humility to reexamine positions and beliefs, adjusting them in light of new insight and knowledge. Unitarian Universalists in the United States have a distinguished history laboring for peace and justice, a history that includes the influential pacifist Adin Ballou, social reformer Susan B. Anthony, political leader John Adams, the great humanitarian Clara Barton, military leader Sylvanus Thayer, regarded as the father of the U.S. Military Academy at West Point, and the activist minister Homer Jack, who labored for decades to abolish nuclear weapons. Unitarian Universalists have recently produced a statement of conscience called *Creating Peace* which summarizes this heritage and serves as important grounding for public witness. *Creating Peace* acknowledges "the complex task of creating peace" and approaches it with essential nuance.

> We bear witness to the right of individuals and nations to defend themselves, and acknowledge our responsibility to be in solidarity with others in countering aggression. Many of us believe force is sometimes necessary as a last resort, while others of us believe in the consistent practice of nonviolence. We repudiate aggressive and preventive wars, the disproportionate use of force, covert wars, and targeting that includes a high risk to civilians.[6]

By my fortieth birthday I had been ordained into the Unitarian Universalist ministry, granted a moral waiver from the Army, sworn in as a reserve commissioned officer, accessioned as a military chaplain, and assigned to a battalion mobilizing for a deployment to Afghanistan. Could I bear witness to *Creating Peace* in uniform? Could I be a prophetic voice? Or would I renege on my covenant and be the military house priest, preaching the gospel of redemptive violence and offering uncritical devotion to the gods of American National Religion?

A critical incident occurred on Armistice Day, which fell on a Sunday in 2012, about six weeks after I arrived in Afghanistan. That morning I decided to speak out in the context of a religious sermon I called "A Veteran's Day Confession for America." In that sermon I addressed a small gathering of Unitarian Universalists at Kandahar Airfield about events I had witnessed or learned about, including the use of armed drones to kill people who present no continuing imminent threat to U.S. persons. To continue to remain silent, when confronted with acts that violate my core moral commitments, felt like betrayal. I spoke up even though I anticipated reactive sabotage (it came in just two days). Several officers read the text of the sermon online and notified the commander, a colonel, who summoned me to his office. "Your message doesn't support the mission," the colonel said. "You make us look like the bad guys." He ordered a formal investigation which resulted in an official memorandum signed by General Scottie D. Carpenter reprimanding me for "politically inflammatory" remarks. The colonel used that reprimand as grounds to release me from active duty and send me back to the United States with a "do not promote" evaluation. I had supporters, and with their help I decided to push back with legal assistance from the Government Accountability Project and a congressional inquiry. Eventually, I won. The Pentagon Office of the Chief of Chaplains intervened and, although the reprimand was never rescinded, the Army issued long-overdue orders promoting me to captain and assigning me to a new position in the reserve component. Still, I continued to struggle with the role conflict of serving both as a religious leader and military officer. When the Obama administration failed to respond to calls for greater transparency and accountability in the secret drone assassination program, and then authorized $30 billion to miniaturize and modernize the U.S. nuclear arsenal, I resigned in protest, deciding for myself to end my brief military career.

I have tried to awaken Americans to the pain of war and violence. First through a public confession and then through a public resignation, I spoke up with brutal honesty in order to challenge Americans to face real problems and confront the dynamics of American National Religion that enable war and violence and impede justice and peace. Among the faithful, we see the conflation of God and Country—the core of governmental theism; we see unprecedented devotion to military supremacy—a military force that drains the federal budget in order to garrison the globe and project enough destructive power to end all life on earth; we see a new form of empire—dominating global markets ostensibly in the name of freedom. These structures and systems escalate income inequality, normalize self-deception and lying, and set the United States on a trajectory of permanent war on a global battlefield. I have tried to expose these dynamics by bearing witness to the experiences and moral pain carried by veterans and conveying them to American audiences as a speaker and writer. I have tried to correct false views, nurture empathy, build capacity, and produce apostates of American National Religion. Sadly, most Americans seem entirely comfortable with these conditions, continue to worship the false gods of the national faith, and wonder with bewilderment in the face of terrorism, "Why do they hate us?"

While there is no justification for terrorism, Americans who humble themselves to honest self-examination and listen deeply to voices beyond our borders may understand why much of the world hates the United States. The operative theology of American National Religion is what Walter Wink calls the myth of redemptive violence—the belief that good violence will save us from bad violence.[7] The belief that violence can save us goes unchallenged in the American imagination because so few Americans have direct experience of violence. Moreover, Hollywood, video games, politicians, and the media have a strong hold on the popular imagination and reinforce the myth. Sheldon Wolin notes, "[F]or the vast majority of Americans modern warfare [has been] largely imagined rather than actually felt or observed firsthand."⁸ "Americans of the twentieth century," he adds, "had no direct experience of [war] and hence were receptive to having warfare imagined for them—and Hollywood happily obliged with war movies."⁹ Meanwhile, the 1 percent of the population who serve in the U.S. military today—the ones who may actually experience the human cost of war—are disproportionately less educated, lower income, and from ethnic minorities. Whereas Selective Service maintains the possibility for an all military-age male draft, America already has an economic draft, where "those who choose to enlist may be conscripted, in effect, by economic necessity."¹⁰ "Domestic poverty produces non-white soldiers for wars directed against poor non-white populations abroad," Wolin writes. Thus, we arrive at the present situation of "superpower warfare" where "the less well-off fight wars instigated by the well-off, well-educated and well-represented."¹¹ Such an unjust system shields the wealthiest and most powerful Americans from experiencing the pain wrought by the American National Religion they so readily embrace.

Although I suffered retaliation from those intent on defending and protecting these vital lies and unexamined bedrock values, I have my supporters as well. Larry Shook, a veteran of the American war in Vietnam, responded to my sermon with a beautiful letter appealing to General Carpenter. "The terror of facing the enemy is nothing compared to carrying the knowledge that you have helped cause innocent suffering brought by a nation unwilling to look itself in the mirror," Shook wrote. "As I see it, the solution to this crisis of our national soul, and the private soul crisis faced by every veteran like me, is precisely what Rev. Antal expressed in his sermon: confession." I also received an outpouring of support in response to my public resignation. These Americans of conscience can kindle a new great awakening and an honest moral reckoning out of which will arise a different future that promises greater liberty and justice for all.

What we need in response to American National Religion and global terrorism is what psychiatrist, author, and teacher Ronald Heifetz calls *adaptive leadership*.¹² Adaptive leaders approach complex conditions not as technical problems easily resolved with quick-fix solutions—such as the assassination of so-called high value targets with drone strikes—but rather as *adaptive challenges* that call the whole American society and beyond into a process of change. "Instead of looking for saviors," Heifetz writes, "we should be calling for leadership that will challenge us to face problems for which there are no simple, painless solutions—problems that require we learn in new ways."¹³ American National Religion and global terrorism are both adaptive challenges. They give rise to war and violence and present significant obstacles to peace and justice. America the superpower is, ironically, powerless to stop global terrorism. The so-called War on Terrorism is a war that can never be won. Yet Americans are the only ones with the power to challenge the consensus ideology and unexamined bedrock values that form the basis of American National Religion. And when we are able to do that, I believe we will see a decline in global terrorism. Adaptive work begins with acknowledging our special privilege as citizens of the lone superpower nation. This privilege gives all Americans the power of choice. Americans can choose to live with the world's pain, carry it, and seek to relieve it. Or choose to avoid the pain, insulate from it, and even deny that it exists at all. Privilege can stimulate great compassion and heroic altruism; it can also enable deep slumber, historical amnesia, and the tragic coldness of heart that results in apathetic resignation.

Creating peace requires compassion, which is both empathy for another's pain and action to relieve that pain. What, then, is the right thing to do? Taking appropriate action in an age of superpower and terror requires that Americans resist the escape that privilege provides, avoid quick-fix solutions, and face adaptive challenges with the necessary humility to change lifestyles in order to advance a more just and peaceful world. Perhaps the first change is to cultivate empathy, "the kind of heart that can understand another's pain," including empathy for the kind of pain that drives many people to terrorism. Doing so requires Americans to resist the traps of self-absorption and self-deception and embrace painful truths about who we are, what kind of people we are becoming, and the challenges we face together as human beings on this beautiful and fragile planet. Living with and bearing our fair share of moral pain is a critical step. But remaining with pain is not enough. We need to act. The particular course of action largely depends upon the context. Sometimes the compassionate action is nonviolent resistance to systems and structures of hate and violence, or mediation and negotiation between parties in conflict. Sometimes it is the practice of spiritual disciplines such as deep listening and remembering, or prayer, confession, and lamentation. And sometimes, the compassionate action may be managed violence, such as a military intervention in a distant land using armed drones, to either protect a persecuted minority from a marauding band of ethnic cleansers, or to kill terrorists who possess a backpack nuclear bomb before they detonate it outside a U.S. embassy. Such is the complex task facing citizens of the lone superpower nation striving for peace and justice in an age of endless war.

Notes

1. Andrew Bacevich, *America's War for the Greater Middle East: A Military History* (New York: Random House, 2016), 28.

2. Jon Rosenwasser, "The Bush Administration's Doctrine of Preemption (and Prevention): When, How, Where?" CFR.org, Council on Foreign Relations, Feb. 1, 2004, Web, May 10, 2016; www.cfr.org/world/bush-administrations-doctrine-preemption-prevention-/p6799.

3. Jeremy Gunn, *Spiritual Weapons: The Cold War and the Forging of an American National Religion* (Westport, CT: Praeger, 2009).

4. Andrew Bacevich, *The New American Militarism: How Americans Are Seduced by War* (New York: Oxford University Press, 2005), 146.

5. Romeo Dallaire, blog post; www.romeodallaire.com/index.php/rwanda-genocide/; visited July 30, 2016.

6. Unitarian Universalist Association Creating Peace 2010 Statement of Conscience.

7. Walter Wink, "The Myth of Redemptive Violence," *The Bible in Transmission* (Spring 1999), 7–9; www.biblesociety.org.uk/uploads/content/bible_in_transmission/files/1999_spring/Bit_Spring_1999_Wink.pdf; visited February 5, 2016.

8. Sheldon S. Wolin, *Democracy Incorporated: Managed Democracy and the Specter of Inverted Totalitarianism* (Princeton: Princeton University Press, 2008), 21.

9. Ibid., 21, 32.

10. Michael J. Sandel, *Justice: What's the Right Thing to Do?* (New York: Farrar, Straus and Giroux, 2009), 82.

11. Wolin, 147.

12. See generally Ronald A. Heifetz, *Leadership Without Easy Answers* (Cambridge: Belknap Press of Harvard University Press, 1994).

13. Ibid., 2.

Conclusion

STEVE BREYMAN, JOHN W. AMIDON, AND
MAUREEN BAILLARGEON AUMAND

> But they lived those extraordinary lives that can never be lived again.
> And in the living of them, they gave me a history that is more profound,
> more beautiful, more powerful, more passionate, and ultimately more
> useful, than the best damn history book I ever read.
>
> —Utah Phillips

We hope this book and the voices within will inspire American society to
strive for its most deeply held values. We're optimistic that the United States
can emerge from the current age of war and terrorism, toward a future of
love, peace, and the realization of a fully democratic society. Our authors
continue to work, as they have for decades, to move Americans from denial
and dangerous fantasy to honesty and a commitment to resist injustice and
warmongering.

Bending the Arc is thus, among its other features, a book about journeys.
Chapter by chapter, each author explored the contours of a life committed
to peace and justice. Certain themes and commonalities emerged, even as
each "traveler's tale" is marked by unique voice and experience. Wisdom and
humility underlay these accounts with an implicit understanding of human
interdependence and community of those who hunger and thirst for peace.
It is central to understanding the worldview that permeates their work.

Our authors force us to confront some uncomfortable questions. What
does it mean to be an American patriot? What is best about our culture?

Is it the vast and overwhelming military strength, including the power to incinerate the planet and all its inhabitants many times over? Are we justified in feeling superior to other countries? How are we to understand the opioid epidemic, underfunded schools, child poverty, racial policing, sexual assaults, and insatiable consumerism? Or unaffordable housing, climate change death wish, low-paying tax-dodging trillion dollar corporations, abuse of immigrants and refugees, and total disregard for the future?

The lives of our activist authors are testimony to their continuing opposition to a collapsing U.S. culture, which they seek to replace with sustainable, humane, just, and peaceful alternatives. And in this deeply felt desire, our authors are no different than the vast majority of their fellow citizens. Poll after poll show that most Americans don't want napalm, torture, and drone killings any more than do peace activists.

What to make of this long-lived policy disconnect? Some political scientists question whether the United States can still be considered a democracy when the ruling elite so frequently disregard the will of the people. Americans tell pollsters what they want from their federal governments, and those governments often produce programs directly opposite to the popular will. Voters don't want endless war. They don't want bloated Pentagon budgets. They do not prefer ever more lethal weapons systems over renewed national infrastructure. They don't want reduced pollution controls over clean air and water. They don't want tax cuts for the 0.1 percent over quality health care. They don't want their elected officials in thrall to corporate interests. Our contributors do their best to expose the gulf between what people want—peace and justice—versus what they end up with—war and terror.

Why work for peace and justice in a society hell bent on its own destruction, so lacking in vision and empathy, so lost in the meaningless pursuit of excessive materialism and militarism that it is willing to embrace planetary suicide through catastrophic climate change? Or, for that matter, spend twenty years running a small annual peace conference (even if it did bring the authors and editors of this volume together)? One intriguing answer is provided by Leo Tolstoy: "Love is life. All, everything that I understand, I understand only because I love. Everything is, everything exists, only because I love." Love is the most radical of answers and one of the most easily brushed off. Who among us understands love as a methodology for learning, for shaping our logic and reason, giving us direction for a creative and life-affirming society, brimming with kindness and generosity, and filled with joy. With love there is no accountant's ledger for money earned, degrees held, books published, or houses owned. There is, however, a consciousness that slowly comes to terms with mortality and fear, that holds truth and beauty to be sacred.

Dr. King also gave expression to this notion:

> In speaking of love we are not referring to some sentimental emotion. . . . we speak of a love which is expressed in the Greek word *Agape*. *Agape* means nothing sentimental or basically affectionate; it means understanding, redeeming goodwill for all men [*sic*], an overflowing love which seeks nothing in return.

Our activists share in these values of compassion and kindness which steer the dynamic of their lives. Each, in his or her own way, believes in the malleability of history, the transformative revolutionary power of the moral imperative to love.

Each author's biography demonstrates a profound caring for others, a willingness to work for the good of humanity even at the cost of personal hardship, a great and wondrous curiosity about life and about the way others live it, and a willingness to be open, tolerant, and respectful. Our contributors work to resist oppression, attempting to do what is right regardless of what's currently "popular." There is the knowledge too, that one's actions, no matter how worthy, are never fully conceived in isolation. Work for peace and justice is judged not by immediate results but rather by the persistent necessity to act for the common good within a fragile and often misled world community. The work must also be connected to a long-term vision developed and nurtured by both the immediate and the extended community.

Faith traditions, whether deeply embraced or consciously rejected, figure frequently in our activists' accounts. These faiths range from the Liberation Theology and Catholic Worker movements within Roman Catholicism, to Buddhism, Judaism, and mainline Protestantism. They also include the Unitarian Universalist vision, the Unification Church, and Quakerism. Perhaps unsurprisingly, these varied traditions led our writer activists to the same basic belief: war is an avoidable evil that must be prevented or stopped.

Our contributors also share an important understanding regarding the central place of fear in working for peace and justice. Our government—the G. W. Bush administration stands out here—controls us with fear, keeping us docile and complacent if not willing accomplices. Without overcoming fear, we will be unable to address what Dr. King called "The Fierce Urgency of Now."

> We are now faced with the fact that tomorrow is today. We are confronted with the fierce urgency of now. In this unfolding conundrum of life and history, there "is" such a thing as being too late. This is no time for apathy or complacency. This is a time for vigorous and positive action.

How did this group of peacemakers, mostly unknown and unheralded, move past their fears and work for peace in a society that worships brute force and savagery beyond comprehension? How did our contributors learn to love enough to cast out fear? Or conversely, how did they get past fear to move forward with varying degrees of love and understanding?

For most there were a number of successive steps in gradually moving forward, learning that while fear might paralyze or inhibit action, it may also be both motivator and teacher. None of our group waits for perfection. Each step forward requires understanding that mistakes will be made, knowledge is incomplete, and that the consequences of action are sometimes unexpected and even unwanted. There is no guarantee of success, only the willingness to make a good effort. They do share the unshakable belief that we cannot solve our problems by killing one other.

Some of the peacemakers within these pages had their commitments forged in the cauldron of military service and war or by working for the military-industrial complex; one of a fierce battle with addiction; others, solidified by the experience of prison.

A striking commonality among these accounts is how world travel shaped the worldview of many of these writers. Their paths led them far and wide, their peacemaking peripatetic and global. They have wandered on almost every continent, embracing the world's cultures and peoples in a quest to witness for peace. These activists had their vision and focus shaped by living in the homes of, teaching the children of, looking into the eyes of, breaking bread with, and singing and dancing in solidarity with so many for whom the horrors of war and the crushing burdens of human injustice and inequality have been all too real.

Our contributors sat under the searing cacophony of bombardment in Baghdad, Lebanon, and Gaza. They saw the dead and mutilated of war. They held dying children poisoned by depleted uranium. They sat in prison mess halls and heard the sobs of prisoners caught in the maw of the prison-industrial complex primarily incarcerated for the crime of being born poor in America. They sat in sorrow with those who ran from death squads. They sat up night after night with sleeping babes by their side to write an outline for a Department of Peace. They walked, marched, and fasted before the United Nations. They blocked roads leading to military bases. They sailed with medical supplies under threat of death to break the blockade of Gaza. They preached in Afghanistan, and climbed over the rubble of air attack to witness for victims. They write, speak, and travel tirelessly to resist war and celebrate peace.

Our authors, looking for inspiration and grounding, reflected on the impact of books and formal and informal education on their lives. There's activism fueled by the ancient Greeks, nineteenth-century American transcendentalists, and twentieth-century theorists and visionaries. Interactions with centers of mid-twentieth-century dissent, along with radical and transformative concepts, as well as iconic activist heroes also formed choice and direction: Berkeley in the '60s, the School of the America's Watch, the Catholic Worker Movement, Ploughshares, the Peace Corps, and the Vietnam antiwar movement. Important personalities included Caesar Chavez, Dan and Phil Berrigan, Dorothy Day, Karl Meyer, Fr. Roy Bourgeois, Archbishop Oscar Romero, Sister Megan Rice, Dennis Kucinich, and our own Kathy Kelly and Medea Benjamin. Our writers built lives centered on voluntary poverty, prison witness, and war tax resistance. They studied liberation theology, and took part in nonviolent direct action.

Our peacemakers continue to plant the seeds of peace, even in the face of new threats to a just and sustainable future. The creeping authoritarianism of the "Imperial Presidency"—taken to new heights by Donald Trump—along with the warmongering and fiscal force-feeding of the Pentagon clearly threaten the nation and the world. The declining incomes, inadequate health care, and failing quality of life for many American families cause deep divisions, anguish, and despair. The early warning signs of fascism are abundant and worrisome: hypernationalism, disdain for human rights, identification of enemies (including asylum seekers and the critical news media) as a unifying cause, rampant sexism, efforts to intimidate and control the news media, obsession with national security, bolstering corporate power while suppressing labor power, and more. Is it not time to consider the life-affirming alternatives?

Nonviolent resistance is as urgent today as ever. Yet we have a president who openly calls for violence against protestors. Antiwar activists are routinely bullied and pilloried. They're called names and shamed. Recently passed legal restrictions on peoples' right to protest in nearly two dozen American states are hard proof that protesters pose a threat to business as usual.

This disrespect is ironic, as major parts of the U.S. peace movement of recent decades turned out to be right, correct in its complaints and predictions about the likely outcomes of U.S. foreign policy, and the stupidity of armed intervention in the Middle East and elsewhere. But instead of thanking and praising the anti-warrior, popular culture and political leaders frequently demonize and ridicule them as weak, traitorous, un-American. Stereotypes about "hippies" and "peaceniks" live on to this very day. How many statues can be found in American city centers to honor antiwar campaigners? How many holidays do we celebrate for those who opposed war? Exactly one: Rev. Dr. Martin Luther King Jr. Day. And, of course, Dr. King was widely condemned at the time for his opposition to the Vietnam War. We grudgingly, long after the fact, valorized Abolitionists, Suffragettes, Civil Rights campaigners. We have yet—again with the single and partial exception of Dr. King—to celebrate the struggles of antiwar activists. Try to imagine a celebration of peace activism during the halftime of an NFL game. Players simply kneeling to protest police killings of unarmed black men has been enough to—with a great assist from the president—roil and divide the country.

Think of the shame and horrors of the Vietnam era—My Lai, carpet bombing, free fire zones, torture, rape. Recall the overt and covert support for bloodthirsty killers less than a decade later—the Contras, Salvadoran death squads, School of the Americas trainees, the anti-Soviet mujahedeen who would become al Qaeda and the Taliban. Remember Abu Ghraib, Guantanamo, extraordinary rendition, the children of Yemen and Palestine. These atrocities and more could've been avoided had we heeded the advice of peace advocates.

The 2003 U.S. invasion of Iraq is clearly among the greatest foreign policy blunders in U.S. history. Many of our Kateri Conference presenters were leaders of the opposition, the tens of millions of people who did not fall for the poisoned sales campaign of the Bush-Cheney gang for the invasion. But for our contributors, the invasion and years-long insurgency that followed were more than merely a mistake: they were a crime, intentionally committed. Yet during the bloody, desperate years of suicide bombings, widespread destruction, and repulsive contractor scandals our authors kept plugging along, day after day, year after year, decade after decade.

The many peace workers who have taken part in the Kateri Peace Conference and contributed to this anthology understand that fundamental system change is necessary. The new system they envision will be based on the values of nonviolence, feminism, ecology, and grassroots democracy. They're united in their rejection of materialism and consumerism. They share a clear understanding of what matters in life. These activists yearn for the day when the seeds of peace take root and blossom. That day may come but not before more years of nonviolent resistance, active citizenship, and deeply engaged political participation—the tools with which to bend the arc.

Acknowledgments

We offer heartfelt thanks to the following, whose labors of love have truly enabled the Kateri Peace Conference to proceed for so long; our gratitude is deep and constant. Thank you, Father Kevin Kenny, for seeing what this was about and saying "yes," PRESENTE! For access, year after year, to such a lovely, resonant Mohawk Valley site on the edge of the forest, thank you to the Saint Kateri Tekakwitha National Shrine and Historic Site and its clergy and staff. Early on, Cathy Callan, you helped plant the seeds deeper and look how they flourish! For meals that, year after year, nourish with delight, for humor that lightens spirit, and for activism that kindles fires, Linda LeTendre, there are not enough thank you's. Year after year, so many pitch in to make the days run smoothly, to sing songs to delight our hearts, to schlep and move and monitor: to the intrepid among you, Harry and Joan Thornhill, Terri Roben and Pete Looker and all who give and give and give, thank you. To our man behind the scenes, Steve Wickham, your patience and skill which have built and maintained the conference website (kateripeaceconference.org) is appreciated, more than words can ever say. Finally, to all who continue to attend, support and leave the conference to act with even deeper commitments, thank you for the continuing inspiration

Appendix A

Kateri Peace Conference Titles and Presenters

1998 **Prisoners of Conscience Interfaith Pilgrimage—To Close the US Army School of the Americas.** March from the National Kateri Tekakwitha Shrine, Fonda, N.Y., to the Leo O'Brien Federal Building, Albany, N.Y. September 19–22, with John W. Amidon.

1999 **The Kateri Tekakwitha Interfaith Pilgrimage—To Close the US Army School of the Americas and End the Oppression of Indigenous People.** March from the National Kateri Tekakwitha Shrine, Fonda, N.Y., to the New York State Capitol, Albany, N.Y. September 18–21. Featuring: Bishop Howard J. Hubbard, Rabbi Paul Silton, Charlie Liteky, Imam Djafer Sebkhaoui, Wolf Clan Chief Jake Teharonianeken Swamp.

2000 **Preparing Fertile Fields—An Indigenous Rights Conference and Concert.** Featuring: Ed Kinane, Ann Tiffany, Luis Yat, and Francie Traschen.

2001 **Indigenous People Under Siege** Featuring: Ed Kinane, Luis Yat, and John W. Amidon.

2002 **Indigenous People Under Siege** Featuring: Rae Kramer and Frank Houde.

2003 **Ethics, Truth, and Terrorism—A Closer Look at America's Role.** Featuring: Laura MacDonald, Cynthia Banas, and Connie Frisbee Houde.

2004 **Creating Peace in a World at War.** Featuring: Bishop Thomas Gumbleton and Kathy Kelly.

2005   **A Call to Conscience.** Featuring: Blase Bonpane, Colleen Kelly, and Bill Quigley.

2006   **The Convergence of Hope and History—Sustainable Solutions for a Peaceful World.** Featuring: Jim Merkel and Jim Jennings.

2007   **Hope and Resistance: Transforming the Course of History.** Featuring: Stephen Eric Bronner and Father Louis Vitale.

2008   **Nurturing Peace.** Friday and Saturday, August 15 &16, 2008. Featuring: Bishop Thomas Gumbleton, Father Roy Bourgeois, and Colonel (ret.) Ann Wright.

2009   **Harnessing the Winds of Change.** Featuring: Bruce R. Hare, Lawrence Davidson, Janet Amighi, and Joanne Sheehan.

2010   **A Question of Balance?** Featuring: Ed Kinane, Father Jerry Zawada, Daine Reiner, Joyce Reeves, and Rich Goodhart.

2011   **Awakening to the Circle of Life.** Featuring Johnnie Bobb, Bonnie Bobb, Randy Kehler, Kelly Branigan, Julie Huntsman, and Eric Marczak.

2012   **Crossing the Line: A Call to Revolutionary Love.** Featuring: Kathy Kelly, John Horgan, Clare Grady, David Swanson, Matt Southworth, Walt Chura, and James Ricks.

2013   **The Moral Imperatives for Activism: What you need to know! What you need to do!** Featuring: Ray McGovern, Stephen F. Downs, Cathy Breen, Martha Henessey, Ellen Barfield, Brian Terrell, and Rev. Chris J. Antal.

2014   **Rise Up! Resist! Transform Now! Rocking the Boat for Peace.** Featuring: Jill Stein, David Swanson, Steve Breyman, Kristin Christman, and Bishop Gumbleton.

2015   **Truth Tellers: Radical Honesty in the Age of Deception.** Featuring: Medea Benjamin, Sister Megan Rice, Robert Shetterly, Nick Mottern, Michael Walli, Kay Olan, and Rev. Felicia Parazaider.

2016   **Confronting the Politics of Fear.** Featuring: Amani Olugbala, Mary Anne Grady Flores, Rev. Chris Antal, Dr. Ed Landing, Paul K. Chappel, Linda LeTendre, Imam Djafer Sebkhaoui, and Father Mark Steed.

2017   **Prophets, Rabble Rousers, and Agitators: A Call to Creative Action.**
Featuring: Dave Lippman, Bill Jacobs, Rev. Emily McNeill, Barbara
Smith, Jonathan Wallace, Mark Emanatian, and Rev. Chris J. Antal.

2018   **The Fierce Urgency of Now.** Featuring: Ann Wright, Kathy Kelly,
Ray McGovern, and Rosemary Armao.

Appendix B

Some Groups Striving for Peace and Justice

350.org	https://350.org
9/11 Families for Peaceful Tomorrows	www.peacefultomorrows.org
An Act of Conscience	www.der.org/films/act-of-conscience.html
The Action Network	www.actionnetwork.org
The Afghan Youth Volunteers	http://ayva.course.af
American Friends Service Committee	https://afsc.org
Americans Who Tell the Truth	https://www.americanswhotellthetruth.org
The Audacity of Hope Flotilla	www.freegaza.org
Bethlehem Neighbor's for Peace	www.bethlehemforpeace.org
The Catholic Worker Movement	https://www.catholicworker.org
Christian Peace Maker teams	www.cpt.org
Code Pink	https://www.codepink.org
Conscience International	www.conscienceinternational.org
Costs of War Project	costsofwar@brown.edu
The Fellowship of Reconciliation	https://www.forusa.org
Foreign Policy in Focus	www.fpif.org
Gaza Freedom March	https://www.facebook.com/GazaFreedomMarch/

Global Action for Children Coalition	www.globalactionforchildren.org
Grafton Peace Pagoda	www.graftonpeacepagoda.org
The Green Shadow Cabinet	https://www.facebook.com/ GreenShadowCabinet/
The Interfaith Alliance	www.interfaith alliance.org
The Inter Help Council	https://interhelpnetwork.org
The Institute for Policy Studies	www.ips-dc.org
Iraq Veterans Against the War	www.ivaw.org
The Islamic Center of the Capital Region	https://www.iccdny.org
Jewish Voices for Peace	https://jewishvoiceforpeace.org
Kanatsionhareke Traditional Native Community	www.mohawkcommunity.com
Know Drones	https://www.knowdrones.com
The Labor Religion Coalition	https://laborreligion.org
The National Priorities Project	www.nationalpriorities.org
The Nevada Desert Experience	www.Nevadadesertexperience.org
Nuclear Age Peace Foundation	https://www.wagingpeace.org
The Office of the Americas	www.officeoftheamericas.org
The Omega Institute	www.eomega.org
The Revolution of Love	www.feliciaparazaider.com
Pace e Bene	www.paceebene.org
Palestine Solidarity Campaign	www.palestineinformation.org
Peace Action	www.peaceaction.org
The Plowshares Disarmament Movement (see Catholic Worker Movement)	
Poor People's Campaign	https://.www.poorpeplescampaign. org
Project Salam	www.projectsalam.org

The Sanctuary for Independent Media	www.mediasanctuary.org
The School of the America's Watch	www.soa.org
Shoshone Walk on the Sacred Land	https://sacredpeacewalk.wordpress.com
Soldier's Heart	www.soldiersheart.net
The Solidarity Committee of the Capital Region	https://www.facebook.com/Solidarity-Committee-of-the-Capital-District-and-New-York-Solidarity-300962384369/
The Syracuse Peace Council	www.peacecouncil.net
Talk Nation Radio	www.davidswanson.org/talk-nation-radio
The Thomas Merton Society	www.merton.org
The Traprock Peace Center	traprock.org
United for Peace and Justice	www.unitedforpeace.org
United National Antiwar Coalition	https://www.unacpeace.org
Upstate Drone Action	https://upstatedroneaction.org
Veterans for Peace	www.veteransforpeace.org
Veteran Intelligence Professionals for Sanity	www.warisacrime.org/VIPS
Voices for Creative Non-Violence	www.vcnv.org
War Is a Crime	www.warisacrime.org
War Resisters League	https://www.warresisters.org
Witness for Peace	http://www.solidaritycollective.org
Women Against War	www.womenagainstwar.org
World Beyond War	www.worldbeyondwar.org

Contributors

John W. Amidon, BA, is founder and co-facilitator of the Kateri Tekakwitha Interfaith Peace Conference. He served as president of Veterans for Peace, Chapter 10, Albany, New York.

Rev. Chris J. Antal served five years as a military chaplain. He resigned his commission on April 12, 2016, in a letter to President Obama, an act of protest against U.S. policies regarding killer drones, nuclear weapons, and preventive war.

Maureen Baillargeon Aumand, MA; MLS, State University of New York at Albany, is a retired public school English teacher and librarian. She is a member of Women Against War, and co-facilitator of the annual Kateri Tekakwitha Peace Conference.

Medea Benjamin co-founded the fair trade group Global Exchange and the feminist peace organization CODEPINK. She is author of several books, including *Drone Warfare*, *Kingdom of the Unjust*, and *Inside Iran*. She was Green Party candidate for U.S. Senate in California in 2000.

Blase Bonpane† was director of the Office of the Americas. He worked on human rights issues and identification of illegal and immoral aspects of United States government policy. Bonpane served as a Maryknoll priest in Guatemala until he was expelled in 1967 in the midst of a revolution.

Steve Breyman recently retired as associate professor of science and technology studies at Rensselaer Polytechnic Institute. He is a U.S. Army veteran, former New York State climate change official, and former U.S. State Department Fellow. He is author of *Movement Genesis* and *Why Movements Matter*.

Kristin Y. Christman has been writing for peace since 9/11/01, when she began her multivolume work, *Taxonomy of Peace: A Comprehensive Analysis of the Roots and Escalators of Violence and 650 Solutions for Peace*, which she is currently preparing for publication. She has a bachelor's degree in Russian from Dartmouth, and master's degrees in Slavic languages from Brown and in public administration from the University at Albany.

Lawrence Davidson is a retired professor of history at West Chester University. His research focuses on American foreign relations with the Middle East, and he is the author of *Islamic Fundamentalism* and *Cultural Genocide*.

Stephen F. Downs was the chief attorney for the New York State Commission on Judicial Conduct until he retired in 2003, shortly after he was arrested for wearing a peace T-shirt at Crossgates Mall in Albany, New York. He was a member of the defense team for Yassin Aref in 2006, a founding member of the Muslim Solidarity Committee, and a founding member of Project SALAM, which documents and advocates against preemptive prosecution and prisoner abuse.

James E. Jennings, PhD, is founder and president of Conscience International and executive director of US Academics for Peace.

Kathy Kelly co-coordinates Voices for Creative Nonviolence, a campaign to end U.S. military and economic warfare. She has led many delegations to conflict zones, and spent time in federal prison for direct actions against nuclear missile and drone sites.

Ed Kinane is an anti-militarist and anti-imperialist based in Syracuse, New York. He works with the Upstate (New York) Drone Action coalition and his local Beyond War and Militarism committee.

Jim Merkel is the author of *Radical Simplicity* and founder of the Global Living Project. He lives in Maine, volunteers, writes, lectures, and consults with campuses and municipalities on sustainability initiatives. www.radical simplicity.org.

Nick Mottern is the founder and coordinator of Knowdrones.com. While in the U.S. Navy, he was part of the U.S. occupation of Viet Nam in 1962–63. A graduate of the Columbia School of Journalism, Nick has worked as a reporter, researcher, writer, and political organizer over the last thirty years.

Rev. Felicia Parazaider attended the Chaplaincy Institute for Arts and Interfaith Ministry, and was ordained in March 2012. She holds degrees from University of California, Berkeley, in Religious Studies and Peace and Conflict Studies. She has ministered extensively to drug addicts and alcoholics on the streets of Los Angeles and in the Bay Area. She is founder of the Revolution of Love ministry, which focuses on both the inner work of the self and the outer work of the world.

Bill Quigley is professor of law and director of the law clinic and the Gillis Long Poverty Law Center at Loyola University New Orleans. He served as counsel to public interest organizations on issues ranging from Hurricane Katrina recovery, voting rights, public housing, death penalty, living wage, constitutional rights, and civil disobedience.

David Swanson is an author, activist, journalist, and radio host. He is the director of World Beyond War, a global nonviolent movement to end war and establish a just and sustainable peace. David is campaign coordinator for RootsAction.org.

Ann Wright is a retired Army Reserve colonel and a twenty-nine-year veteran of the Army and Army Reserve. She was a diplomat for many years, and resigned from the Department of State on March 19, 2003, in opposition to the Iraq war. She is the co-author of *Dissent: Voices of Conscience*.

Index

www.ingramcontent.com/pod-product-compliance
Lightning Source LLC
Chambersburg PA
CBHW030731280326
41926CB00086B/1152